D0120015

Issue

N.N.

THE HISTORY OF

GLOUCESTERSHIRE
COUNTY
CRICKET CLUB
David Green

THE CHRISTOPHER HELM COUNTY CRICKET HISTORIES

Series Editors:
Peter Arnold and Peter Wynne-Thomas

DERBYSHIRE
John Shawcroft, with a personal view by Bob Taylor

GLAMORGAN
Andrew Hignell, with a personal view by Tony Lewis

HAMPSHIRE
Peter Wynne-Thomas, with a personal view by John Arlott

KENT
Dudley Moore, with a personal view by Derek Underwood

LANCASHIRE
Peter Wynne-Thomas, with a personal view by Brian Statham

MIDDLESEX
David Lemmon, with a personal view by Denis Compton

SURREY
David Lemmon, with a personal view by Peter May

WARWICKSHIRE
Jack Bannister, with a personal view by M. J. K. Smith

WORCESTERSHIRE
David Lemmon, with a personal view by Basil D'Oliveira

YORKSHIRE
Anthony Woodhouse, with a personal view by Sir Leonard Hutton

THE HISTORY OF

GLOUCESTERSHIRE
COUNTY
CRICKET CLUB

David Green

With a personal view by
B.D. WELLS

CHRISTOPHER HELM

London

© 1990 David Green and B. D. Wells
Christopher Helm (Publishers) Ltd, Imperial House,
21–25 North Street, Bromley, Kent BR11SD

ISBN 0-7470-1229-6

A CIP catalogue record for this book is available from the British Library

Typeset by Cotswold Typesetting Ltd, Gloucester
Printed and bound by Biddles Ltd, Guildford, Surrey

CONTENTS

A PERSONAL VIEW
Bomber Wells

I DEFY ANYONE TO NAME a more glorious place to play the summer game than Gloucestershire. In the north of the county the glorious Cotswolds dominate the horizon, whilst the west cradles the jewel of the crown—the Forest of Dean—and visiting sides to the county are quite often awestruck by the beauty of the grounds they play on.

It was in such an environment as this that I learned my apprenticeship with regard to slow bowling and what a joy it was. Yet, as a young boy, I never thought for one moment that my life would eventually be taken over by the game of cricket. I suppose having a dad and five uncles (all his brothers) who spent hours around my parents' home talking of nothing else but rugby and cricket would be bound to have some effect on me. The fact that all the brothers had been very good local rugby players always made the oval ball game the number one topic. This was followed by cricket, and finally the local regiment, 'The Glorious Gloucesters'. I can actually remember the time when Hitler was beginning to throw his weight about in Europe and one of my uncles saying: 'I don't know why they don't send the regiment over and sort the bugger out!'.

If I might dare to suggest it, I would say that Gloucestershire folk are among the proudest people around. One has only to visit Kingsholm, the headquarters of the mighty Gloucester RFC, to realise that. They are tremendously proud of the fact that 90 to 95 per cent of their players are county bred and born. No matter if they have a weakness in their side—to mention getting an outsider is taboo. I first took notice of the Rugby Club when they were referred to as the 'Elver Eaters' by my dad and his brothers (in those days elvers were spring luxury of the working classes when the tides brought up the young eels from their spawning ground in the Sargasso Sea, across the Atlantic to the Bristol Channel and up the River Severn by their billions). Today they are more expensive than fresh salmon and the City fifteen are now simply called 'Glos'.

Inevitably, the conversations at home always concerned 'Gloshire' cricket—the exploits of W. G. Grace, 'Wally' Hammond, Gilbert Jessop ('The Croucher' as he was nicknamed, because of his extraordinary stance at the wicket), Tom Goddard, Charlie Parker, Charlie Barnett, 'Old Dip', as Charlie Dipper was affectionately known, and Bev Lyon. All mighty characters of Gloucestershire cricket, loved and admired by one and all. In those days I had no idea that destiny, or fate or whatever one might call it, would lead me into that lion's den. Thus, in an atmosphere of cricket, rugby and the regiment, I began my sporting life, still never dreaming that one day I would briefly rub shoulders with the likes of Hammond, Goddard, Parker, Barnett and Sinfield, to name but a few.

Yet why I and not either of my two more athletic brothers should be born with the ability to play cricket at a professional level, I shall never know. The only type of cricket I had ever played as a young lad was in the street, the top half versus the bottom half. One day, however, I was amongst 25 to 30 ten-year-olds who at school were selected by a Master for a trial to select a team to play another local junior school. This particular teacher bowled at a military medium pace and had enjoyed a huge success against a motley crew of youngsters. Unfortunately for the pair of us, when he bowled at me I did not realise I had such a wonderful eye for the ball—I deposited the first ball I received out of the playground, over the top of the school itself into the street outside. For my pains, I received a clip around the ear and was called a stupid idiot by the teacher. Needless to say, I did not make the side and it was to be a further two years before I played the summer game again and that was at a local, secondary modern school.

Yet, at that school, there was no organised cricket at all—the sports ground had been turned into allotments to help the war effort. The only reason we played at all was because of our own determination. To begin with, I bowled quickly, but as soon as our little gang played on the local park, I soon took to slow bowling because what we played on was a minefield. Out little gang consisted of five boys and five girls, the only difference between us being that the girls were not allowed to bat. I insisted it was because I was fearful for their legs, they insisted it was because I was a chauvinist pig! Anyway the die had been cast and from the playing fields of Gloucester I made my debut for the County side and then, to my delight, met many of the players who ten or eleven years earlier had been just names to me—revered ones, of course—but players I never, ever dreamed I would one day meet and talk to.

One of the first personalities I had the pleasure to meet and speak with was Bev Lyon, the incredible pre-war Gloucestershire captain. Bev was a man who made the MCC governing body tear their hair out more than once because of his astonishing interpretation of the laws. He manipulated them in quite extraordinary ways to make a game of cricket interesting, not only for the players but for the spectators as well, which is what it's all about, isn't it? I was told that Bev had made and lost a million pounds by the time he was 21 and, if that's true, it must have been a piece of cake for him to twist the opposing captains and umpires around his little finger. So, one of my father's 'names' I had rubbed shoulders with—not for long admittedly, but in his company you could feel the charisma of the man and realise why everyone respected him and would fight to the bitter end for him.

Sadly, the great Tom Goddard was not the same sort of chap. He was not a communicator and I don't think John Mortimore, David Allen and myself (three off-spinners) really benefited from his experience and undoubted tremendous ability. Yet Tom's famous lbw appeal, 'how was er', will forever remain with me and many other people. One thing which amazed me at first was the size of his enormous hands (something like $11\frac{1}{2}$ inches from the heel to the finger tips)—his fingers were like a bunch of bananas. He would, for a laugh, pick a cricket ball up off the table with his fingers outspread pointing downwards and it rested between his forefinger and its next door neighbour quite easily, like the average person might well be able to manage with a ping pong ball.

One of my greatest thrills was to meet C. W. Parker, 'Charlie' to Gloucestershire men. To every club supporter he was the greatest left-arm bowler of his day and they believed that even Wilfred Rhodes, the marvellous Yorkshire all-rounder, was not in his class as a bowler. He was, I discovered, a man of few words but many, many deeds.

He was once selected in a twelve for England but to the amazement of 99.9 per cent of the population he was made twelfth man. To add insult to injury, he was then told to take the drinks out to the players and, according to legend, he told the England Captain of the day: 'if you wanted someone to do that you should have selected a waiter instead'. Needless to say the great man was never selected again, which was a tragedy really because the great Don Bradman had always struggled against him whenever they played against each other. I loved seeking his counsel and when I asked him one day what he thought about my run up (it was one pace on a hot day and two on a cold one!) he replied: 'remember son it's not what happens this end what matters, 'tis what happens at t'other end that counts'. Looking back now, one realises that the great man was absolutely right, because too many bowlers take a run which is completely ludicrous; in fact they have so little control over what they're doing that they often spray the ball all over the place. Charlie once told us at Bristol: 'you can do hand-springs on the way to the wicket, but at the other end—well, that's serious business'.

Charlie Parker knew more about the summer game than anyone else I have ever known and what my father and my uncles had told me about him was absolutely right. On the subject of spin, Charlie advised us all that when it turned, we should bowl at the batsman. 'There's no need to give it air,' he said. 'In fact, try to stop them using their feet against you. On a good pitch, however, it's the opposite: keep it in the air as long as possible and in doing so you'll keep it above the batsman's eye level, and if he can't see above the flight he'll have great difficulty in judging line and length. So quite often when they advance down the pitch to you they are taking a gamble and that, son, gives you a fifty-fifty chance against them.'

It was, however, just sheer luck that I had the great honour to play in the same side as W. R. Hammond, 'Wally' to everyone throughout the world of cricket. I was in the army doing my National Service in the RAOC and didn't know that the County had been able to get him to play in this particular game, which was the Bank Holiday one against Somerset. Needless to say, the ground was packed to the gunnels—in fact at 10.30am when I arrived, the queues to get into the ground stretched from the main road to the Grace Gates—some quarter of a mile, I would say. When I was introduced to him in the dressing room, I almost bowed, for this was the man who, when batting in Gloucestershire—and elsewhere no doubt—shops and offices closed so that the staff could see him. A man who made catching a cricket ball a thing of immense beauty, a man with the reflexes of a striking cobra, a batsman rated by all and sundry of his day as the greatest cricketer of all time.

Gloucestershire people all know that Bradman scored more runs than Hammond, but they'll tell you as well that the Don was a cross-batted slogger whereas their idol, Wally, was a classical batsman; 'the greatest ever', the old boys will still tell you. As well as that, he was a first-class bowler, as fast as Larwood if he wanted to be, or as cunning as Clarrie Grimmett with his legbreaks and googlies. The ovation he received when he eventually went in to bat that day was fantastic; when he was out and making his way back to the pavilion many Somerset and Gloucestershire supporters, knowing full well they would never see him again, unashamedly wept. The vast crowd stood as one as the ageing giant, making his last appearance for the County which he had graced so magnificently for so many years, slowly made his way up the steps of the pavilion. I can tell you now there was a lump in my throat and I remember thinking that if only my dad had been alive what stories I could have told him and his brothers about the very men they had told me about when I was so very young.

Much later in my career I had the pleasure to meet the legendary Charlie Barnett, as dashing a batsman as one could ever wish to see. When I first met him, he was umpiring at a benefit game and Charlie, I discovered, was and still is a very forthright person. During the course of the match, I had an occasion to speak to him and I asked what he thought was wrong with the England team. His answer was short and to the point. He replied succinctly: 'There's not enough good players around'. 'Why is that?' I asked, and he replied: 'They've forgotten about the "V". If they played through that they wouldn't go far wrong.' That was the end of our conversation, short and to the point, for he had been brought up in a very hard school—Gloucestershire was always that. Now I suppose what he said is true. Today many batsmen do play across the line of the ball far too much, especially when the ball is fairly straight, and in doing so they pay the penalty.

My love for the game of cricket is as much about its past as its present and future and two great Gloucestershire players from a more distant past come to mind. Messrs Gilbert Jessop (The Croucher) and W. G. Grace, without argument the creator of the modern game. There is no doubt the 'Doc' was not only a very great cricketer, probably the greatest ever, but a man with both tremendous personality and charisma. My father and his brothers told me some incredible stories about him. All, of course, handed down through the ages from father to son, and like a good wine the older they became the better they ended.

A story generations have heard was the one when W.G. hit a six which carried for 36 miles. This was achieved by landing the ball in a railway wagon on its way to Bristol from Gloucester. There's also the one about the umpire who tried to give the Doc out lbw almost as soon as he came in. W.G., as the story goes, refused to go telling the umpire that the crowd had come to see him bat, not to see the umpire make a fool of himself.

All this for a lad was very heady stuff—for me, he was a player I would have loved to have seen play and to have spoken with. For not only was he a great cricketer, he was also a great athlete, who won gold medals, and later a superb bowls player, captaining England. Furthermore, he was a Gloucestershire man.

Little did I know one day I would meet a man on the Gloucestershire committee by the name of Spry, a man who had actually played with W.G. Discovering this, I spent many happy hours with him discussing the great man. When I enquired about the authenticity of some of the stories about Grace, he laughed and told me: 'They're like the angler's fish that got away—they began two inches long and ended up a whale.' What he did say which was interesting was that many folk didn't take into consideration that W.G., as well as playing, also tried to raise the standard of umpiring and everything else, and much of what is accepted as normal in the game now was probably instigated by the 'Doc'.

Thus, in the course of a few seasons, nay a few months, I had met and spoken to everyone other than W.G. and Jessop—could anyone ask for more. Playing at the same time as W.G. was possibly the most underrated of players Gloucestershire and England have ever had. This was 'The Croucher'—the immortal Gilbert Jessop. A phenomenal hitter of the ball, he played in an era when a six had to be hit right out of the ground—yet he achieved this with ease. Can you imagine what might have happened if he had been playing today with the much smaller boundaries and the improved bats? He would probably set up records for the fastest century every other week. My father told me that 'The Croucher' once hit a ball so hard, straight back along the pitch, that it hit middle stump out of the ground breaking it in half, with one of the halves being deposited over the boundary some 70 yards away.

Another tremendous hit of Jessop's lifted the ball out the ground at The Oval and landed it on top of a hansom cab passing the ground on the road outside. Not only was he such a brilliant batsman but he was equally as good at cover-point where it is estimated he ran out 30 or 40 batsmen per season, and he was no slouch with the ball. Unfortunately, I never met or have ever met anyone who ever played with him or saw him play, but I did speak to his son, who I believe is or was a vicar in Bath. He told me he was too young to remember his father's exploits; he did, however, recall that his father did nothing out of the ordinary to help his phenomenal reflex actions and his immense timing and power. 'He was simply a great natural athlete and sadly a player who was overshadowed by W.G. himself' his son told me, yet not once did he ever hear of his father complaining about this.

Thus, in one way or another, all the great names and characters of Gloucestershire cricket with which my father and uncles had filled my young mind as a child, I had met, or had met some who had done so.

It's now time to take interest in my contemporaries, for some are just as interesting as players of yesteryear and in some cases as good, which makes life very rich and entertaining for me.

There was, however, one other player I was longing to meet—my own special hero, Denis Compton, or 'Compo', as he was and still is affectionately known. Although the great Len Hutton is still around, I'm afraid there weren't many Gloucestershire supporters who held him in too much esteem; for they will always blame Len, rightly or wrongly, for not letting Charlie Barnett have the strike in the last over before lunch in the 1938 Test match at Trent Bridge, where Charlie wanted three or four runs for a century, which would have been a remarkable achievement. However, Len kept the bowling and perhaps, who knows, robbed Charlie of his hour of glory. On the other hand, Compton may well have, had he been in with Charlie, encouraged him to have got his century. 'Compo' was the 'Brylcreem boy'—scoffed at maybe by the ignorant at times, but loved and adored by the cricketing public the world over. He was probably one of the game's greatest improvisers, a magnificent batsman, a more than useful slow left-hand bowler, with a very safe pair of hands. He became my hero, for like him I too loved doing my own thing—I quite easily got fed up when things proved to be too easy. To me, 'Compo' was the gentlest of giants—I like to think that he and Gary Sobers have been the most outstanding pair of natural cricketers in my lifetime. Thus, when I met him for the first time my cup floweth over, for although not a Gloucestershire man he had the right qualifications to be so.

I shall always be very grateful to my native county for giving me the chance to play the professional game. In my years there no one ever tried to alter the raw local cricketer who was thrust upon them one day. I actually entered the game completely uncoached in July 1951 and left it altogether in 1966 still uncoached. This enabled me to do things my own way; to begin with I hated batting but would have bowled all day long on any type of wicket—good, bad or indifferent. My fielding was a cross between the ungainly and the unkindly—all I could do was to catch reasonably well and throw a long distance. My running between the wickets was once described as very risky and problematical—the problem was the other player's survival.

Another snag was that I was born a natural conversationalist and, for the sake of a sweet or something of that like, I would often stray from the position laid down by the captain just to partake in a natter with the spectators, and on several occasions to enjoy a cup of tea with them whilst the game was going on. Yet for all my misdemeanours, I was rarely ever hauled over the coals. I suppose I was lucky that I had a natural rapport with cricket spectators all over the country which made life a great deal easier for me.

I was also not a player who worried over what I did or didn't do. My greatest enjoyment was watching others play very well—it still is—even though at times it might have been a member of the opposite side.

In my career very few players have excited me as much as George Emmett who, when he was playing well, probably played more shots in an over than some players do in a season. Speaking to me one day about what I called his extraordinary ability to improvise so beautifully, he amazed me by saying that Wally Hammond never even rated him a player. In fact, he went on to say: 'On one occasion when batting with Hammond, who had come in after me against Glamorgan at Newport, I already had 30 runs to my name but Wally scored his first 50 of a treble hundred and I had only advanced a further five to 35. So, I rather naively asked the great man if I could have a bit more of the strike, to which he replied "if you did, you wouldn't know what to do with it".'

This was rather a shock to me, because I always rated George as one of the best little players I have ever had the pleasure to watch—and so did many others. George was also a very strict disciplinarian and a stickler for fair play and everything else which goes with it. An instance of this was the day I was captaining the Club and Ground side against an unbeaten Australian Club who were touring the country—we had made a fairly respectable score and on a wicket turning and lifting we had eight of the side out for next to nothing with about an hour left to get the remaining two wickets. I thought 'an earlier train to Gloucester and home'. From the Pavilion, however, appeared one of the Bristol Rovers football players, who the county employed on the ground, with a note in his hand which he presented to me—it was signed by Emmett and read: 'Don't you dare win this game'. Thus, Graham Wiltshire and myself had to bowl for a good hour not to get anyone out and, my word, it was a difficult experience but we achieved it. After the game George thanked me for doing what he had asked. His motive was simple—he didn't believe that the pitch we had supplied for this game was in the best interests of cricket and it would be a shame if this side returned to Australia having lost their unbeaten record on such a minefield. Whether they ever knew what we had done, I doubt, but this was the type of man George was.

The Gloucestershire dressing room was quite different to that at Trent Bridge. At 'The Bridge' conditions were like those of a first-class hotel, while those at the County

Ground in Bristol were somewhat lacking—yet to offset that the one at Bristol was a hive of industry and knowledge. It was the place where you learned from your senior professionals all about the strengths and weaknesses of opposition players. You were advised on the different balls to bowl at the batsmen, for example half volleys if need be to the back-foot players and short of a length to the front-foot ones. To the off-side players you were told to concentrate on ther legs, and *vice versa* to the on-side players. From the wicket-keeper, Andy Wilson, came this sound advice 'throw it at the keeper's head when you return it to him. He'll be sure to stop it then, son, for remember we do enough bending all day long.'

I loved the practice month of April when I could bowl for hour after hour each day. Then while having a cup of tea and sandwiches at lunch time, I would take a look at the fixture list to see where we were playing and hope to God that we were not away to Derbyshire at Buxton, where that most under-rated bowler (by the media), Les Jackson, would be waiting to get to grips with us on the green pitch there. And maybe not at Bradford against Yorkshire, where like some mad bull F. S. Trueman would be waiting to launch himself at us seemingly from the back of the stand. However, there was always Cheltenham to look forward to, where if we won the toss we normally won the match, and Stroud and Gloucester, where the ball usually turned for our spinners.

The captains I played under were all completely different. George Emmett was a 'bossy boots' of a skipper but he knew what he was talking about. Jack Crapp was quiet and not really captain material I would say. One of the most interesting characters of Gloucestershire cricket was Sir Derrick Bailey, Bart. Quite often he would do the exact opposite to what the senior pros had advised him to do—and after he had asked them for their advice in the first place. We clashed often, not in a nasty way but in a hilarious manner. For instance, he was a great theorist and he told me quite firmly in one game it was impossible for me to bowl leg-breaks and off-breaks in the same over to the same field placings. Yet, in that same game, he himself bowled an over of three left-hand and three right-hand deliveries! On another occasion he informed me that I was making the game look stupid by not taking a run and he insisted I did. I began by stepping out a couple of paces, then it went to three and finished up at six yards. With a smile of satisfaction on his face he told me to bowl it from there, so I did! He was not amused. However, to his credit, or our credit, the game was never dull with him as a captain—he was a true amateur and that can only be very good for the game. His sort of man brought a sense of sanity, where far too often now we see how professionalism can go to the extremes at times. With the likes of Sir Derrick Bailey around it would have never done that.

Back to the dressing room—there were our two fast bowlers, Lambert and Scott, both of whom were so unfortunate at the start of their careers when the war intervened and they lost those valuable five years. Whoever I spoke to about them rated the pair as potential England material, and if ever a fast bowler had a better action than George Lambert, I have yet to see him. Our keepers were Andy Wilson, who I have already mentioned (by the way he was probably the shortest ever keeper in the game) followed by Peter Rochfort—and a better keeper I've yet to see. Unfortunately, circumstances didn't allow Peter to carry on for very long, which was sad. John Mortimore and David

7

Allen were two dedicated England off-spinners, and Ron Nicholls and Tony Brown two young batsmen who both attempted to copy the elegant style of Tom Graveney, which was no mean goal.

In Arthur Milton we had the fastest man I have ever seen on two legs on the cricket field—and he took catches with the ease of Wally Hammond—a man with so much talent it was an embarrassment, yet most of his contemporaries would say he never used half of it. Nevertheless, the half he did was marvellous. David Smith was a lovely fast-medium bowler, but sadly bowled into the ground. Then there was Tom Graveney—personally I haven't seen a more elegant player in my time, but I think he never really did himself justice when he played for England.

Of course there were others, like Graham Wiltshire—still with the club after almost 40 years—Dennis A'Court, Derek Hawkins and the late Bobby Etheridge, all in their own way Gloucestershire characters to the bone, all of whom helped me to enjoy my career with the Club.

Yet along with ability one has to have courage and the one man who epitomised this was Jack Crapp. Although not a Gloucester man he wasn't far out, being a Cornishman and a 'pirate' who loved his adopted county as any true-blooded Gloucestershire man does. His professionalism, dedication and courage were a shining light to one and all, and perhaps this story will illustrate why I and many others respected him so much. Unfortunately for him, whilst touring South Africa with the MCC he contracted a rare skin disorder which left his hands in a horrible mess. They were never clear of trouble because the skin on them would never heal—no sooner did it look as though it was beginning to heal it would peel off again leaving his hands red raw. For any batsman this was a terrible handicap, yet the old boy soldiered on and not once did he complain. It was courage one could only marvel at, especially in one particular game against Lancashire at Stanley Park, Blackpool. Here he played an innings against Statham and company on a very fast bouncy pitch where each time the ball hit his bat it must have jarred his hands terribly. When he was eventually out for nearly a hundred, and sitting alone in the dressing room, I went and got him a cup of tea, knowing he liked one, but when I handed it to him, I saw that the palms of the white muslin inner gloves which he used to wear continually because of the skin complaint were badly bloodstained. Knowing the Lancashire team's doctor was in the home team's dressing room, I went and asked for his help, and this was against Jack's wishes I can tell you. When the doctor saw the trouble, the poor man could hardly believe his eyes, and as with a pair of scissors he slowly cut the gloves away from Jack's hands he was dismayed at what he saw. After he had dressed and cleaned Jack's hands he advised him to miss, at least, the next couple of games; yet like the magnificent trouper he was Jack took his place in the side for the next game.

Gloucestershire cricket was, as you can see, very, very good to me. I was encouraged to enjoy the game, yet at the same time the discipline there was probably the severest of all counties. However, with the likes of Grace, Hammond, Jessop, Barnett, Goddard, Parker, etc., as the backcloth to one's career there was a great deal to play for.

Finally, I could not end this personal view without mentioning my favourite character in the Gloucestershire side, namely Cecil Cook, called 'Sam' for a reason I honestly never got to know. He was loved and admired by not only the Gloucestershire supporters but all the game's players, those of his own side and the opposition. One never heard him moan on the field. He simply got on with his job, and his accuracy as a slow left-arm spinner rates with any it's been my pleasure to watch. He could drop the ball on the proverbial sixpence and, god forbid, if he did bowl a bad ball, that warranted a discussion after the game! Sam was a person of whom one would have to rack one's mind to remember him having a meal of any kind. Yet he could bowl 20 or 30 overs on the trot each day and except for a cigarette and a few pints of bitter afterwards, I still cannot remember him going anywhere to have a bite to eat as everyone else did.

Possibly, Cook and Wells might well be best remembered for their running between the wickets. This was at times a farce, so much so that at one time we were threatened with a fine of half-a-crown for each time we were run out. When I asked George Emmett why, I was told that he was fed up with listening to the opposition bowlers moaning about it, because a wicket is a wicket no matter who. I always maintained the only reason Sam went in before me was that he was that much older. This he always stoutly denied, but if I tell you that at one stage of his career he had taken more wickets than he had scored runs, you can draw your own conclusion. When he retired and turned his attention to umpiring, he brought to that the same sort of love he had given to the game as a player and in doing so he earned respect from all and sundry.

Sam Cook was a Gloucestershire man through and through, and the Tetbury 'Twirler', as he is known in his own town, is a Gloucestershire player who will be for ever remembered. Not for the many times he played for his country but because he was a man of the people. As I said earlier, they adored him; he was a lovely, gentle character, a great friend and companion and if I say I have never had a better bowler to bowl in tandem with that is saying a great deal and I hope it shows the respect I have for this truly wonderful person. Lastly, as he said to me one day after about the sixth near run-out: 'For crying out loud, say something if it's only goodbye, Bomber.'

EARLIEST TIMES

THE ORIGINS OF CRICKET will be debated as long as scholars and antiquarians exist to contend over them. It is not the purpose of this volume to debate them. There is however a general consensus that the game began to flourish and spread in the second half of the 17th century, and, though the first written reference to cricket in Gloucestershire is not to be found until well into the 18th century, cricket in the county cannot be placed in its context without a brief examination of the earlier period.

The game was sufficiently established, at least as a pastime for the young, for the boys of Stonyhurst School, founded in 1593 at St Omer for the children of English Catholics, to bring across a version of it when the threat of the French Revolution caused their return to England. Earlier still, John Derrick had stated in a court case that he had played at 'Krekitt' among other sports at Guildford as a boy, his age and the date of the court case placing cricket as an acknowledged game some time in the 1550s.

Through the middle years of the 17th century there are numerous records of prosecutions against groups of people for playing cricket on Sunday. The geographical extent of other references indicates that the game was by then spreading rapidly from what scholars agree was its original cradle, The Weald, that tract of land including portions of Kent, Sussex and Surrey, which lies between the North and South Downs.

It is difficult to argue with H.S. Altham's reasons, which he sets out in his magisterial 'History of Cricket', for the game's development from a sport played by 'the yeomen of The Weald' to one with truly national status. Mr Altham contends that, with the success of the Puritans against King Charles I and the establishment of the Commonwealth, it is likely that the nobility and gentry would tend to retire to their country seats, there to find the game being played by their servants and tenants, and to be taken themselves by it. Certainly the Sackvilles of Knole Park and the Richmonds of Goodwood were involved as players and patrons shortly after the Restoration, in the year of which—1666—a cricket club was founded at St Albans.

From the Restoration onwards interest in cricket increased and the press makes regular reference to it. The game's early involvement with betting is confirmed by *The Foreign Post*'s announcement in 1697 of a match in Sussex, eleven-a-side and for 50 guineas. In 1705 an XI of Chatham played an XI of West Kent. In 1709 comes the first county match between Kent and Surrey at Dartford. When William Bedle, born in 1679, died nearly 90 years later he was referred to as: 'Formerly accounted the most expert cricket player in England', an indication of the importance of cricket in the days of his prime, which would have been the earlier years of the 18th century.

Gloucestershire and cricket are fortuitously linked in 1706 when William Goldwin, shortly to be appointed Headmaster of Bristol Grammar School after attending Eton and King's College, Cambridge, wrote a Latin poem describing a rural match he had seen played in Kent some years before. However, the first certain knowledge we have of the game being played in Gloucestershire comes from *The Gloucester Journal* of 16 September 1729 announcing a forthcoming match played, as so many were throughout the 18th century and well into the 19th century, for money 'upwards of 20 guineas'. Twenty-three years later *The Bristol Journal* announced a match between an XI of Bristol and an XI of London, to be played at Durdham Down for 20 guineas. The long gap between these two publicised contests should not be taken as an indication that cricket was not being played regularly in these parts but it must be doubtful whether there were many 'organised' matches such as the two referred to above. Elsewhere the loss of three of the game's great patrons in the early 1750s—Frederick Prince of Wales and the Duke of Richmond died and Lord John Sackville went mad—led to something of a recession. In 1771 a report spoke of 'the expiring fame of cricket', a jeremiad heard constantly through its history and up to the present day. However, the foundation of the Hambledon Club in Hampshire (though it was clearly of London origin) stimulated a revival. New patrons like Sir Horace Mann and the Duke of Dorset, with other backers, provided the impetus.

Undoubtedly the fame of Hambledon over the couple of decades when it was supreme, the manner in which it attracted the greatest players of the day to play under its banner and send them, admittedly not too far afield but to other counties like Kent, brought about a renewed interest in the game. Certainly the number of reports of cricket matches in Gloucestershire increases around the turn of the century and by the early years of the 19th matches were being arranged throughout the county. These took place not merely at the larger centres of population—Bristol, Cheltenham, Gloucester, Cirencester—but at St Briavels in the Forest of Dean and at Minchinhampton and Stow-on-the-Wold, an indication of cricket's continued hold on country folk which would have kept it alive during the pre-Hambledon decline in the number and reputation of the 'Great Matches' of the mid-18th century.

This period is followed by the formation of clubs with regular fixture lists: Clifton in 1819, Lansdown in Bath in 1825 and Gloucester in 1829. By the 1850s clubs which exist, and, in many cases flourish today, had been founded: Bedminster, Bitton, Frenchay, Knowle, Shirehampton, Westbury-on-Trym and The Schoolmasters in the Bristol area, with Cheltenham, Stroud and Chipping Sodbury starting up to the north and east. It is during this period that the Grace family, which was to be the *Fons et origo* of Gloucestershire cricket, makes its appearance in the person of Dr Henry Mills Grace, born 22 February 1808, who married Martha Pocock of Bristol on 3 November 1831. They were to produce four daughters and five sons, one of whom, William Gilbert, was to be by some distance the greatest player of his era and was to have claims to be the greatest in the game's history. W.G.'s two brothers, Edward Mills, born seven years before him in 1841, and George Frederick, born two years after in 1850, were also players of very high quality who were to have much to do with the establishment of the Gloucestershire County Club.

However, that is to run a little ahead of the story. Henry Mills Grace and his new bride lived originally at Long Ashton, but moved to Downend House, Downend, after Henry had qualified as a doctor at the age of 28 years. All their children were born at Downend House. By 1850 eight children had blessed their singularly happy marriage, the eldest, Henry, then being 17 years and the youngest, William Gilbert, not yet two. Accordingly, with space now somewhat cramped, they moved across the road to larger accommodation at The Chestnuts, where George Frederick was born.

W.G. set down in his 'Cricketing Reminiscences and Personal Recollections' how The Chestnuts had two orchards, in one of which his father laid a cricket pitch, on which E.M., already thoroughly taken by cricket, also worked tirelessly. W.G. recalled:

> My father, my brother Henry and my Uncle Pocock (his mother's brother Alfred) practised at every spare moment, and we youngsters fielded for them from the time we could run about. Then they would give us a few balls, so I soon learned how to handle a bat. Uncle Pocock took great pains with me, and helped me a great deal, by insisting on my playing with an upright bat even as a child.

A little earlier than this, Dr H.M.'s love for the game and desire for its wider propagation in the Bristol area had prompted him to initiate in 1844 the formation of the Mangotsfield Cricket Club, Mangotsfield being only a mile or so from Downend. When Mangotsfield amalgamated with Coalpit Heath two years later the West Gloucestershire Club was formed. Some eight years later W.G., then six years old, was to see his first important cricket match, in which XXII of West Gloucestershire, organised by Dr H. M. himself, played William

Clarke's All England XI in a field behind The Full Moon Hotel in Stokes Croft, Bristol. W.G. recalls that this field, originally ridge and furrow, had been relaid during the previous autumn, and that, although the pitch was very good, the outfield was rough and uneven. Clarke's team was very powerful, including as it did Clarke himself, one of the greatest of lob bowlers, George Anderson, George Parr, Caffyn of Surrey, Box the famous wicket-keeper and Willsher of Kent. As W.G. said: 'It is doubtful whether nine of the eleven could have been excelled in all England', and not surprisingly the West Gloucestershire XXII were beaten by 149 runs. Dr H.M. captained the side and his eldest son Henry and Alfred Pocock also played.

This is an appropriate juncture to look at the influence of the great travelling sides of the mid-19th century and their contribution to the game. The founder of these was Clarke, born in 1798 at Nottingham and a bricklayer by trade. He was only 18 when he first played in the Notts Eleven of which he was to be a member for 20 years. He was subsequently engaged as a practice bowler by the Marylebone Club where he soon established himself as the county's premier slow bowler. The increasing, though admittedly irregular, organisation of the game on a County basis prompted Clarke to organise a team representing English cricket's flower and to play matches, if necessary against odds, up and down the country. This he did between 1846 and his death ten years later. In 1852, his notorious tight-fistedness over money caused a schism and John Wisden formed the United England Eleven as a rival to Clarke's All England XI. The two sides were not to meet till after Clarke's death.

Clarke's long-sightedness over the prospects of his venture cannot be gainsaid. As H. S. Altham has said:

> The Eleven were the focus of attraction wherever they went. It was every cricketer's ambition to see them play, still more to be chosen to do battle with them, and a double figure with the bat or a wicket or two with the ball, against the acknowledged champions of England, would win a man local renown for ever.

It is not surprising, therefore, that Martha Grace kept a scrapbook of the scores and results of the 1854 All England v West Gloucestershire game in which her family took part, or that the young W.G.'s next recollection of cricket should be the visit of Clarke's side the following year, when All England again won, by 165 runs this time. West Gloucestershire were all out for 48 and 78, W.G.'s brother Henry being top scorer with 13 in the first innings and his Uncle Pocock with 16 in the second, no other double figure score being recorded. On this occasion Alfred Grace, then aged 15, and E.M., 13, also played. E.M. made such an impression with his work at long stop that William

Clarke presented Mrs Grace with a copy of a book to which he had contributed: 'Cricket; Notes by W. Bollard, with a letter containing practical hints by William Clarke'. This he inscribed as follows: 'Presented to Mrs Grace by William Clarke, Secretary All England XI'.

County organisations were now springing up rapidly, among them Sussex (1836), Nottinghamshire (1841), Kent (1842), Cambridgeshire (1844) Surrey (1845), Hampshire (1849) and Yorkshire (1861) and it was not surprising that Dr H. M. Grace, the driving force for cricket within the county, turned his attention toward the setting-up of a Gloucestershire side. As a first step towards this end, and while continuing to encourage the activities of the West Gloucestershire Club, he had by 1862 begun to turn his attention to Gentlemen of Gloucestershire games. His work bore fruit when this side met and defeated the gentlemen of Devon by an innings and 77 runs on Durdham Down, Bristol, on 8 and 9 July 1862. E.M. played in this match, as did Henry and Alfred, E.M. making 57 runs in an opening partnership of 113 with J. J. Sewell, the father of that C. O. H. Sewell who was to play for Gloucestershire 158 times between 1895 and 1919. W. G. reckons this to be the first county match played in Bristol.

Around this time E. M. Grace was, in his younger brother's words, 'doing great things all over the country'. W.G. cites as an example the Canterbury week of August 1862 which his parents customarily attended. Dr Grace agreed to summon E.M. to make up the sides, on provision that he played not just in the first match, but also in the second, for MCC against Kent. This was agreed and E.M. duly arrived, retrieving the failure of a first innings duck by scoring 56 in the second. In the following match E.M. carried his bat through MCC's innings for 192 not out and followed up by taking all ten Kent wickets in the second innings. In W.G.'s words: 'A score of 118 in the same year, made at Lord's for South Wales against the MCC, established E.M.'s reputation in first-class cricket and at that time he was as well-known on cricket grounds all over the country as I am now' (W.G. was writing in 1899). So highly was E.M.'s skill regarded that he went as a member of George Parr's team to Australia in 1863 where, according to W.G.'s account, he did 'fairly' though handicapped by illness and a whitlow on his finger.

E.M. then, and for some time afterwards, was regarded as one of the most daring and brilliant batsmen of the age. Eyebrows were constantly raised at his fierce pulling of fast bowling into the vacant spaces behind mid-on. He attacked from the moment he reached the crease, and never with more panache than when things were going badly for his side. Such methods are not always as effective in later years, when the eye has lost its keenness, and it is not altogether surprising that E.M.'s record for the County is modest. In fairness, he was 55 when he played his last match, in 1896, and his appearances were not always regular. In any event, the blazing successes of his youth, as batsman, medium-pace or lob bowler and fielder are sufficient to justify his fame.

The year 1863 saw two county fixtures against Devon and also the first match against Somerset at Sydenham Fields, Bath, which Gloucestershire won by 87 runs, the 15-year-old W.G. making 52 not out in the first innings. W.G. recalls with pleasure a match in the same season between Parr's All England XI and XXII of Bristol and District. W.G. was down to bat at number 10, the lunch interval arriving just before he was due to bat. During lunch Tarrant, the great fast bowler, gave young W.G. some practice, a kindly gesture from one whose character, according to H. S. Altham, 'cannot have been lovable'. W.G. then 'knocked him about so freely' when he got to the middle that he was taken off and replaced by the lob bowler Tinley, who soon caused the budding champion to hit over a straight one. Nonetheless he had made 32 against extremely powerful opponents, and his reputation was growing. The England XI, moreover, were beaten by an innings.

W.G.'s fame was enhanced during the following season, 1864, when he and his brother Henry were invited to join the South Wales team on their annual tour. At the Oval W.G. took four first-innings wickets and made 5 and 38 with the bat. The South Wales captain then said that he did not require W.G. for the next match at Brighton. But, just as Dr Grace two years before would not agree to E.M. returning from Canterbury after just one game, so now, in W.G.'s words: 'My brother Henry would not have me left out of the Brighton match, and insisted that I should play.' Going in first wicket down, he made 170 in the first innings and 56 not out in the second. A few days later W.G. played his first match at Lord's, for South Wales against MCC and Ground, and made 50. And all this, let it be said, before his 16th birthday!

W.G.'s performances in 1865, when he made his first-class debut, were encouraging: a batting average of 28 and a bowling average of 13 were healthy enough for a raw-boned lad who reached 17 years of age only in the July of that season. It was, however, in 1866 that his majestic presence was first fully felt in the first-class game. He had just turned 18 when he made 224 not out on the first day of the match between an England XI and Surrey at the Oval, this being the occasion on which he was given leave of absence by his captain, V. E. Walker, to compete in a 440-yards hurdle race at Crystal Palace, which he duly won. In that same season he made 173 not out for the Gentlemen of the South versus the Players of the South at the Oval.

*E. M. Grace, who played for Gloucestershire from 1870 to
1896, and was secretary from 1873 to 1909. (NCCC)*

In this same season the youngest of the brotherhood, George
Frederick, made his debut, playing for South of the Thames *v* North
of the Thames at Canterbury. W.G.'s admiration for his young
brother's skill shines through his written words. He recalls a match at
Beeston, between the Gentlemen of the South and the Gentlemen of
the North, in which Fred scored 189 and I. D. Walker 179. W.G.'s
innings of 77 was, he says: 'quite overshadowed by the brilliance of my
brother and Mr Walker'. G.F.'s record for the Gentlemen against the
Players, in those days as important as a Test match was soon to
become, was outstanding both with bat and ball. He was also one of
the greatest outfielders the game has known, and the skier he caught to
end the Australian Bonnor's innings at the Oval in 1880, a few days
before his tragically early death, has gone down in legend, the batsmen
having already turned for the third run when the catch was held.

In 1868 a Gloucestershire team defeated MCC and Ground at Lord's

G. G. Grace, a fine all-round cricketer and a great outfield,
he died tragically young, just short of his 30th birthday.
(GCCC)

by 134 runs on the first visit of a west country side to the game's headquarters, but it was not until two or three years later that the County Club was actually formed. I say 'two or three' because there is some controversy over the matter. Gloucestershire certainly played as a first-class county in 1870, which leads many to favour that date. However, the eminent authority Rowland Bowen contends that there is no written record indicating that the Club had been formed prior to 1871, so it is perhaps safer to accept that date.

There had been earlier, if feeble, attempts to set up a county club. In 1842 the County of Gloucestershire and Cheltenham Cricket Club had been established, a grandiose title implying confusion over objectives, and it is not surprising that the enterprise was wound up in 1846. In 1863 a further attempt was made in the north of the county, this time under the title of the Cheltenham and County of Gloucester CC. This had Lord Fitzhardinge as its President but attracted no

W. G. GRACE

W.G., the Champion, was the greatest figure the game has produced. Born at Downend, Bristol on 18 July 1848, he came to maturity as a cricketer very early. He had made a half century at Lord's, playing for South Wales against MCC before his 16th birthday, and by the time he was 18 the heaviness and regularity of his scoring was already pre-eminent. His first first-class century was made in 1866, his last in 1904, when he was 56 years of age.

He was the first true 'all-round' batsman, favouring neither the back foot nor the front, as happy playing on the off-side as the on, equally prepared to attack or defend, though, having the aggressive cricketer's instinct, he much preferred to attack. 'I don't like defensive strokes,' he is reported to have said, 'because you can only get three off them.' He mastered every type of bowling, from the tearaway fast round-armers on the often horribly rough pitches of the 1860s and early 1870s, to the great bowlers of the golden age, Tom Richardson, George Lohmann, J. T. Hearne, Bobby Peel and company. Only four batsmen have made more than his 54,896 runs. He made 126

W.G. as seen by 'Spy' in Vanity Fair. (GCCC)

centuries, a staggering number for those days (among his contemporaries, the next highest is Arthur Shrewsbury's 59).

He was, too, undoubtedly a great bowler, at first fastish, later slow and devious. Again only five bowlers have exceeded his tally of 2,876 wickets. In his younger days he was a magnificent outfield with a powerful throw (at the Oval in 1875 he threw the ball 111 yards and then back the same distance). Later he fielded closer to the wicket, where very few chances escaped those huge hands. In the words of Ranjitsinhji's Jubilee Book: 'He revolutionised cricket. He turned it from an accomplishment into a science, he united in his mighty self all the good points of all the good players and made utility the criterion of style . . . he turned the one-stringed instrument into a many-chorded lyre.' Massively built, dominant and tireless, he broke bowlers' hearts. As J. C. Shaw, the feared Nottingham fastish left armer of the 1860s and early 1870s, said of him: 'I puts 'em where *I* wants 'em, and then 'e puts 'em where '*e* wants 'em.'

notable cricketers, the quality players and opposition sides being drawn to the Bristol area through Dr H. M. Grace's unstinting efforts. Attempts to suggest that the Cheltenham and County of Gloucester CC should in some way take precedence over the Bristol-based County Club of 1871 have been thoroughly demolished by Rowland Bowen. He notes that Lord Fitzhardinge became a vice-president of the Gloucestershire Club and argues convincingly from this that the Cheltenham and County of Gloucester CC must therefore have been disbanded earlier. 'One can imagine Lord Fitzhardinge's answer,' says Mr Bowen, 'to become Vice President of The County Club while he was still president of another club called the County Club.' Mr Bowen's argument for the 1871 date for the formation of Gloucester-shire CC is strengthened by the fact that the Cheltenham and County of Gloucestershire Club was wound up in March 1871.

At this point, with Gloucestershire poised to start their career as a first-class county, it may be useful to examine what the game itself was like at that point. There is a tendency to assume that, with the legalisation of over-arm bowling in 1864 (round-arm having been accepted in 1828 when a Gloucestershire man, Robert Kingscote, was MCC president) the game has altered only in detail. Equipment certainly has changed, bowling tactics too, and batting styles, we say to ourselves, but broadly speaking, if we were transported by time-capsule to a cricket ground in 1870 we should find very little unfamiliar to us. In fact, there seems little doubt that we should have seen any bowling method that we do not recognise. Changes in laws do not constitute the sudden end of one compartment in the game's history and the beginning of another. Certainly things change, but not swiftly or suddenly. After 1828 it was some time before the high noon of the fast round-arm bowlers arrived. Alfred Mynn was admittedly their precursor, but it was not until the 1850s and 1860s with John Wisden, John Jackson of Notts, George Tarrant and Edger Willsher that they truly ruled the roost.

Similarly with 1864: the great English bowlers of the following decade or so undoubtedly bowled what we would call round-arm, with the hand no more than a fraction above the shoulders. W.G. himself bowled round-arm all his life, at first briskly in the fashionable tearaway style, later slow and very foxy. There is a famous photograph by George Beldham of W.G., by then grey-bearded and carrying much weight, in the act of launching one of these deceptive slows in a manner which makes it most unlikely that the hand will at any time be higher than the shoulder. The great medium-pacer Alfred Shaw of Notts, who took 2,027 wickets between 1864 and 1897 at an average of 12.12, was likewise a round-arm bowler, and such an accurate one that of the 24,700 (4-ball) overs he bowled in his career,

16,922 were maidens. It was not until the visit of the Australians in 1878 that England saw over-arm bowling as we know it.

Pitches, which had been very rough through the 1860s and previously, improved greatly from 1870 onward, though batting averages generally—W.G.'s and later Arthur Shrewsbury's apart— are low enough to suggest that they were not as good as they were to be in the later 1890s, the early years of cricket's 'Golden Age'. Batting methods differed in that the pads were not used as a second line of defence—a wise approach in view of their frail construction!—and also, as H. S. Altham states, players tended to have but one method, playing back or forward habitually and also tending either to defend or attack. It was to W.G.'s triumph that he gathered together these separate threads and wove of them one cloth, fashioning a method and an execution which dominated cricket for 35 years.

With regard to the status of County Cricket itself, it needs to be stated that inter-county matches were by no means the most important part of the domestic season. Indeed, with less than a dozen counties playing first-class cricket and not all of them playing each other, it could not be otherwise. Certainly there was an unofficial championship, dating back to 1864, but there was no official competition until 1890. In 1873, when Gloucestershire were deemed to have shared the title with Nottinghamshire, they played only six county matches, meeting Yorkshire, Surrey and Sussex twice each. Not surprisingly, games like Gentlemen *v* Players (of which there were four annual contests at Lord's, the Oval, Princes and Brighton) and North *v* South took precedence for many years, as did games between MCC and the various counties. The great weight of W.G.'s cricket, and indeed of any of the major cricketers, was played in these matches, as statistics make very clear. In 1870 W.G. made 366 first-class runs for Gloucestershire, but 1,808 in all. In 1871 the figures were 435 and 2,739 (that was Grace's first *annus mirabilis*), in 1872, 497 and 1,561 and so on. It was not until 1885, when Gloucestershire's county programme had expanded to 14 matches, that W.G.—or anybody else—made 1,000 runs in a season for the county alone.

W. G. Grace aged 22. At this time, in addition to being the greatest batsman of the time, he was a formidable fastish bowler and an outfield scarcely inferior to his brother G. F. (GCCC)

GLOUCESTERSHIRE, THE 'IRRESISTIBLE'

IN THAT FIRST SEASON of 1870 Gloucestershire played only three matches against first-class opposition, all three being won with various degrees of comfort. In the first, played at Durdham Down on 2, 3 and 4 June, Surrey were defeated by 51 runs in a match of modest scoring, Gloucestershire making 106 and 167 to Surrey's 134 and 88. The famous Surrey and England bowler James Southerton had match figures of 14 for 111, but W.G., who made 26 and 25 with the bat, took nine for 92 and G.F. seven for 87, with R. F. Miles, the very slow left-armer, nipping in with one for 1 and three for 23.

The return match at the Oval was won by an innings and 129 runs, W.G. making 143 and Frank Townsend 89 in Gloucestershire's 336 and Miles taking six for 86 and six for 20 as Surrey were humbled. In the third match, against MCC at Lord's in August, Gloucestershire again won by an innings, having scored 276 batting first. Of this W.G. made 172 and C. S. Gordon 53. W.G. and Miles bowled MCC out for 76 in the first innings and, with the assistance of G.F., repeated the trick in the second, this time for 114. At this time, it should be remembered, the Lord's pitch was the most dangerous in England. This was not the first occasion on which W.G. had demonstrated his extraordinary skill on untrustworthy surfaces. In 1868, playing for the Gentlemen v Players on that same Lord's pitch, he made 134 not out in a total of 201, an innings he always considered to be his best.

All the Gloucestershire players were amateurs, among them being Frank Townsend, a headmaster and father of the great all-rounder C. L. Townsend and grandfather of D. C. H. Townsend, who played three Tests for England in the West Indies in 1933–34. Other notable Gloucestershire amateurs were J. A. Bush, wicket-keeper and rugby international, the slow left-armer R. F. Miles, whose County record of 175 wickets at 15 apiece marks him as a very capable performer, and T. G. Mathews, who was to make a double-century against Surrey at Clifton the following year.

In 1871 Gloucestershire played five first-class games, again beating the powerful Surrey side twice, on each occasion by an innings, defeating MCC by five wickets in a low-scoring match at Lord's, and losing to and drawing with Nottinghamshire. This year was darkened by the death, on 23 December, of Dr H. M. Grace, father in every sense of Gloucestershire cricket. In 1873 Gloucestershire shared the Championship with Nottinghamshire by virtue of four wins and no losses to Nottinghamshire's five wins and one loss. Unfortunately, the clubs did not meet that season owing to a still-simmering row between them which had prevented the fixture being played in 1872. This was due to Nottinghamshire's reluctance to confirm the date of the Trent Bridge match until they could be sure that W.G. would play in it. W.G., however, had promised to play in a benefit match for Joseph Rowbottom in Yorkshire on the proposed date. E.M., Club secretary then and right up until 1909, suggested an alternative date but the committee refused. W.G. would not break his promise to Rowbottom and the fixture was suspended, and not resumed until 1875.

The year of 1873 was a good one for the Graces, W.G. making 2,139 runs and taking 106 wickets in all matches, the first ever performance of the 'double', while G.F. and E.M. both averaged well over 30 in County matches, with G.F. heading the bowling averages with 27 wickets at 15 apiece. Yorkshire were beaten twice, G.F. making a marvellous unbeaten 165 at Clifton College to set up the second win. In addition, on 9 October 1873 W.G. was married to Agnes Nicholls Day at St Matthias' Church, South Kensington, his old friend and County colleague J. A. Bush being best man.

Season 1874 saw Gloucestershire outright Champions, W.G. averaging 85 in county matches and G.F. 46. W.G. took 60 wickets at 11.53 apiece, so evidently his gruelling tour of Australia during the winter had only served to whet his appetite. The debt the County owed to the Graces during those first five years of county cricket can be measured by a few simple statistics. During them, W.G. scored 2,176 runs at an average of 68, G.F. 1,199 at 36 and E.M. 814 at 26. Only two other players, Frank Townsend and T. G. Matthews, scored more than 500 runs in this period.

The next season, 1875, a season of wet wickets, saw the County slip back with only three wins from eight matches, but in 1876 and 1877 they again carried off the Championship outright, W.G.'s contribution with bat and ball being massive in both seasons. In fact 1876 was his second *annus mirabilis*, for he scored in all matches 2,622 runs at 62.22 and took 129 wickets at 19.05. He had comfortably achieved the more modest double of 1,000 runs and 100 wickets in 1874 and 1875, as he was to do four more times in all, with several near misses—on three occasions being less than ten wickets short and in three more less than 50 runs short. In 1876 he made 890 runs for Gloucestershire at an average of 81, including a score of 318 not out against Yorkshire at Sheffield, the third score in a sequence which brought him 839 runs, the others being 344 for MCC *v* Kent at Canterbury and 177 against Nottinghamshire at Cheltenham. W.G., curiously, did little else at Cheltenham College, in contrast to his heavy scoring on the Clifton College ground, to which the County had moved in 1871 since they could charge admission there, which was not possible on Durdham

GLOUCESTERSHIRE *v* YORKSHIRE

Played on the College Ground, Clifton, 17 18 and 19 August 1876

MATCH DRAWN

GLOUCESTERSHIRE

1	*Mr W. G. Grace	not out	318
2	Mr E. M. Grace	c sub b Armitage	5
3	Mr W. R. Gilbert	b Armitage	40
4	Mr F. Townsend	st Pinder b Armitage	0
5	Mr G. F. Grace	b Emmett	0
6	Mr W. O. Moberly	c Myers b Emmett	103
7	Mr R. E. Bush	c Lister b Clayton	0
8	Mr C. R. Filgate	b Clayton	1
9	Mr E. J. Taylor	run out	1
10	Mr R. F. Miles	b Clayton	4
11	#Mr J. A. Bush	b Ulyett	32
	Extras	b 12, lb 8, w 4	24
	Total		528

1-9, 2-166, 3-167, 4-168, 5-429, 6-430, 7-446, 8-449, 9-466

BOWLING	O	M	R	W
Hill	16	2	64	0
Eastwood	12	4	21	0
Armitage	31	3	100	3(1w)
Ulyett	25	7	64	1
Emmett	51	18	94	2(3w)
Myers	4	2	4	0
Lockwood	14	2	35	0
Clayton	57	18	122	3

YORKSHIRE

1	*E. Lockwood	hit wkt b W. G. Grace	23
2	M. Myers	not out	46
3	B. Lister	c J. A. Bush b Miles	1
4	D. Eastwood	c W. G. Grace b Miles	4
5	T. Emmett	b Gilbert	39
6	G. Ulyett	c Filgate b W. G. Grace	4
7	T. Armitage	c G. F. Grace b Gilbert	1
8	A. Hill	run out	6
6	A. Champion		
10	R. O. Clayton		
11	#G. Pinder		
	Extras	wides	3
	Total (7 wickets)		127

1-39, 2-40, 3-44, 4-110, 5-119, 6-120, 7-127

BOWLING	O	M	R	W
W. G. Grace	36	17	48	2
G. F. Grace	17	7	34	0
Miles	15	8	23	2(3w)
Townsend	8	0	10	0
Gilbert	8	5	9	2

Umpires: C. K. Pullin and J. Rowbotham.

County Champions 1877. Standing (l to r): W. O. Moberly, W. Fairbanks, G. F. Grace, F. G. Monkland, W. R. Gilbert, W. Midwinter. Seated: Captain H. B. Kingscote, F. Townsend, R. F. Miles, W. G. Grace, E. M. Grace. (GCCC)

Down. Other notable contributions in that season came from G.F. and Miles with the ball and Frank Townsend and G.F. with the bat.

In 1877, eight out of nine matches were won and the other drawn. W.G. for once did not head the batting averages, being second to E.M., who averaged 32.70 to W.G.'s 30.58, but in compensation he took 88 wickets at less than ten runs apiece, his tally in all first-class games being 179 at 12.78, the highest of his career. This year marked the first appearance, and pretty successful ones, of the powerful all-rounder W. E. Midwinter, whom W.G. had met when touring Australia in 1873–74 and had persuaded to come to England on

---

Gloucestershire won the toss. Close of play: 1st day: Gloucestershire 353/4 (W. G. Grace 216★, Moberly 73★); 2nd day: Yorkshire 39/1 (Myers 16★).

W. G. Grace batted just over 8 hours and hit a seven, 2 sixes, 3 fives, 28 fours, 12 threes, 30 twos and 76 singles. He gave one chance when 201.

Only two hours play on Saturday the 19th, due to rain.

Pinder injured his thumb and could not keep wicket through the whole innings.

W. G. Grace hit record individual score for Gloucestershire.

discovering that he had been born in St Briavels in the Forest of Dean. Midwinter was the first Gloucestershire professional.

The high-water mark of Gloucestershire cricket came in 1877. Up to the end of that season they had lost only seven matches of the 52 played since 1870 and won 33. In the next two seasons their extended fixture list—for the first time the number of their first-class games was into double figures—proved too much for their almost entirely amateur resources. The best players could no longer afford the time to travel to distant away venues, and recruits were inferior. The results— seven losses in 22 games against only five wins—told the whole story. There was, however, much of interest in 1878, notably the establishment of the Cheltenham Festival, which still delights cricket-lovers annually at the College Ground, and the furious row between

Match poster, Gloucestershire v Nottinghamshire. August 1878, at Cheltenham College. (GCCC)

26

W.G. and the touring Australians over Midwinter. Taking the least controversial of these issues first: the first game on the College Ground had been initiated by the former Sussex bowler James Lillywhite, then coach at the school, who managed the game against Surrey in 1872 for a fee of £10. In 1878 he proposed that there should be two matches played, and after some haggling it was agreed that Lillywhite should pay £140 to cover the costs of the week and make his profit out of the receipts, taking his chances with the weather—a harsh bargain driven, one would think, by the County, but with admission charged at a shilling a day he would have had to be very unlucky not to break even. An average daily paying gate of 500 would suffice to put him in pocket.

The Midwinter business makes strange reading in those days of cast-iron contracts. His selection for the Australian party for the 1878 tour was not altogether a wise one, for though there is no reference in the Gloucestershire Club's minutes to his arrival, payment, or departure (in 1882), it seems likely that he had a contractual obligation to the Club: why else would he have crossed the globe each year from Australia to England and from England to Australia? In any event, sparks flew when he did not turn up for Gloucestershire's first match of the season against Surrey at the Oval. W.G. and J. A. Bush flew across London in a four-wheeler to Lord's, where the Australians were playing Middlesex. Sure enough, there was Midwinter padded up, waiting to go in to bat. W.G. and Bush persuaded him to return with them to the Oval, whither an Australian deputation, consisting of Dave Gregory, the captain, H. F. Boyle, and Mr Conway, the manager, sped to seek an explanation of W.G.

Now there had been some bad feeling between W.G. and Mr Conway in Australia in 1873–74. High words were exchanged, and the Australians demanded an apology from W.G., who was prepared to make his peace with Gregory and Boyle, but not with Mr Conway, at whom his remarks had been aimed. The Australians then threatened to cancel their fixture with Gloucestershire if this was not done. In the event, W.G. relented and sent an appropriate letter in which he offered, 'without going further into the matter, to let bygones be bygones', and promised the tourists a warm welcome and a good pitch at Clifton.

One's sympathies in this case lie rather with W.G. If Midwinter had no prior contractual obligation to the County how did W.G. and Bush 'persuade' him to come across to the Oval with them? Midwinter, after all, was 6 ft 2 in (1.88 m) tall and a brawny enough fellow to be dubbed 'the Australian W.G.', and his team-mates were surely within hailing distance. Furthermore, the fact that he appeared in seven of Gloucestershire's 12 matches that season makes it more than ever likely that he was contracted, and that the tourists induced him to break his obligations. Midwinter continued his commuting, returning finally to Australia in 1883. He played for England in four Tests against Australia, in 1881–82 when Alfred Shaw was captain, and in eight for Australia against England between 1876 and 1884; no other cricketer has represented each country against the other.

Though four matches were lost in 1878, four were won, and Gloucestershire were still a great draw, with W.G. the greatest of all. The County's first match against Lancashire, which took place at Old Trafford, provoked tremendous excitement, with 16,000 present on the Saturday and another 2,000 reckoned to have clambered over the boards in vexation with the huge queues at the four entrances. Altogether 28,000 people were reckoned to have seen this match, which was the inspiration for cricket's best-known poem, Francis Thompson's 'At Lord's'.

The most quoted section of this poem is the stanza which commences: 'It is little I repair to the matches of the Southron folk' and finishes:

> As the run-stealers flicker to and fro,
>> To and fro,
> O my Hornby and my Barlow long ago!

Thompson wrote this many years after 1878, by which time he was living in London. That opening verse is repeated as the fourth and final one. The two middle verses are less often heard, but for me they encapsulate as nothing else does the high early renown of the County and the Graces, its three heroes:

> It is Glos'ter coming North, the irresistible,
>> The Shire of the Graces, long ago!
> It is Gloucestershire up North, the irresistible,
>> And new-risen Lancashire the foe!
> A Shire so young that has scarce impressed its traces,
> Ah, how shall it stand before all resistless Graces?
> O, little red rose, their bats are as maces
>> To beat thee down, this summer long ago!

> This day of seventy-eight they are come up North against thee,
>> This day of seventy-eight, long ago!
> The champion of the centuries, he cometh up against thee,
>> With his brethren, every one a famous foe!
> The long-whiskered Doctor, that laugheth rules to scorn,
> While the bowler, pitched against him, bans the day that
>> he was born:
> And G.F. with his science makes the fairest length forlorn;
>> They are come from the West to work thee woe!

When W. G. qualified as a doctor in 1879 it was assumed that his cricket career was, to all intents and purposes, at an end. A National Testimonial Fund was launched, and testimonial matches played both at Lord's (Under 30s v Over 30s) and at Clifton College (Gloucestershire v Yorkshire). There was something of an upheaval over the Yorkshire match, because E.M., as secretary, unilaterally doubled the entrance charge from 6d to 1/-. This led to five resignations from the committee—four later withdrew their resignations and rejoined—but E.M., every bit as determined a man as W.G., had his way and the charge remained at 1/-. The Testimonial Fund raised almost £1,500, a large sum in those days, which was presented to W.G. after the Lord's match by Lord Charles Russell, together with a marble clock and two bronze obelisks.

From the great peak of 1877 decline was inevitable. Though W.G. was to continue until 1899 to lead the County, and had many mighty deeds left in him, G.F, had died tragically within a few days of taking the famous skier from George Bonnor, from congestion of the lungs consequent to sleeping in a damp bed. He was not yet 30. His contribution to the County's early successes had been great. His batting average of close to 30 was by some way better than anyone else's, W.G.'s apart. His 160 wickets at 18.93 each proclaim him a very useful bowler, while as an outfielder he was supreme—Richard Daft, indeed, considered him the best he ever saw. The early stalwarts, Frank Townsend, J. A. Bush, T. G. Matthews, played less and less or disappeared entirely and E.M.'s secretarial duties increasingly restricted his appearances. Though there was some amateur talent coming through, batsmen W. O. Moberly, W. F. Pullen and J. H. Brain, for bowling the County was turning gradually towards professionals. Of these W. A. Woof from Gloucester, an accurate medium-paced left-armer whose spin from leg was to serve Gloucestershire well until 1892, was engaged in 1880, having made a single, ineffective appearance in 1878. Jack Painter from Bourton-on-the-Water, was engaged in 1881 and though eventually he was to play as batsman rather than bowler, he had his moments of glory as the latter. In 1887 Fred Roberts, a strong fast left-arm bowler from Mickleton, on the borders with Warwickshire and Worcestershire, made an auspicious debut, taking seven wickets in each innings against Yorkshire at Dewsbury (Yorkshire, however, won the match). Roberts was to do yeoman service for the County until 1904, taking almost 1,000 wickets.

James Cranston, a left-hander who played a few games when only 17, developed slowly until 1883 when, having averaged almost 30, he dropped out of the game, returning in 1889 and playing a Test match against Australia in 1890. The bowling should have been reinforced by the signing of the great Australian left-armer J. J. Ferris, whose name will for ever be linked with that of C. T. B. Turner, 'the Terror', but his performances here did not match his reputation.

In summary, the story of the 15 or so years onwards from the peak of 1877 is one of only moderate achievement. When there were dips, they tended to be abysses, like 1879 when only one match was won, as also happened in 1884, 1887 and 1892. The peaks, by contrast, were minor ones. The best season up to 1895, W.G.'s third *annus mirabilis* when the County finished fourth, was 1888 when of 16 matches played there were seven wins against nine losses. There were notable individual achievements: W.G., though not quite so dominant as of yore, was still capable of performances which, had any other man achieved them, would have made the cricket world resound with his fame. In 1879, that first disastrous year, Gloucestershire could hardly complain at his 596 runs, average 49.66 or his 67 wickets, average 12.56. In 1885 he made over 1,000 runs for the County, averaging 43, and took 68 wickets, achieving the 'double' comfortably in all matches. This season was Woof's best, his 92 wickets at 16.51 helping to secure six wins from 14 matches. Seven, though, were lost, and looking at the figures it is not difficult to see why. There was no-one near W.G. as a batsman and no-one near Woof and W.G. as bowlers. Only one other batsman, Gilbert, topped 500 runs and the next highest bag of wickets was 26.

Season 1887, Queen Victoria's Jubilee Year, was celebrated too by W.G. who made 1,405 runs for the County at an average of 63 and took 64 wickets at 22. In all matches he again topped 2,000 runs, averaging 54, and was only three wickets short of the 2,000 runs and 100 wickets 'double' which he, and only he, had reached before. C. L. Townsend and Gilbert Jessop were to perform this feat in 1899 and 1900 respectively, it being the province solely of Gloucestershire players until George Hirst did it in 1904. And yet, as we have seen, so moderate was the rest of the County side in 1887 that only one victory was recorded.

Season 1888 was notable for the acquisition of a piece of land at Ashley Down, on which was founded Gloucestershire's headquarters, where they remain today. In 1887 the County committee's attention had been drawn to this land, which at the time seemed a long way from the city; however, it was cheap enough, and level, and it was resolved that representatives of the Club should treat with the owner for rental or purchase of the whole 25 acres, the Club's overall requirement being 12 to 13 acres. The purchase was effected early in 1888 for £6,500 and progress in enclosing the ground, much of it supervised by W.G., who had been appointed to serve as a director on the board of management, proceeded so swiftly that a Colts match was played on it in May, in which W.G. opened the innings for the County against the Colts.

It was in this match that W.G. spotted J. H. 'Jack' Board, who was to give yeoman service as wicket-keeper-batsman up to the First World War, and who would play six Test matches for England on two separate tours of South Africa. Such excellent recruits were too infrequent to satisfy some members of the County committee, who were disturbed at Gloucestershire's continued mediocrity in the field and ascribed some of it, at least, to the sole control exercised by W.G. over matters of selection.

W.G. had a great, and certainly unfounded, fear that a preponderance of professionals in the game would be to its detriment, leading to an attitude governed by money rather than love for the sport, and also, he suggested, 'to betting and all kindred evils'. In fact, there was never more betting on cricket than in the 18th century among its aristocratic and undeniably amateur patrons. W.G.'s preference was for products of the public schools and universities, and this caused some indigation around the county generally and in Bristol in particular, where it was felt that local club cricketers were not being given their chance. Gloucestershire's moderate performance strengthened the hand of these objectors, and it is possible to deduce from E.M.'s sparse minutes that a proposal was made in 1892 for the formation of a selection committee, and that this led to W.G.'s resignation from the committee and from the captaincy of the XI. Further attempts to patch up the rift were finally successful, W.G.'s letter to the committee saying '. . . as it is the wish of the committee, I will withdraw my letter of resignation. With regard to the selection committee, I will have nothing to do with it.'

It is probable that W.G. was right in his stand; his knowledge of local cricketers was extensive, and his judgement, though not infallible, was good enough to recognise the gifts of C. L. Townsend, who first played for the County when only 16, and of G. L. Jessop, with whom he kept faith despite the cricketer's very ordinary early performances. Local cricketers, after all, would only be able to play the occasional game, given that they were good enough to be selected, whereas men with public school and university backgrounds could, in those days, be expected to have the means to devote the greater part of their summer to cricket. Around this period, from 1890 to 1894, Gloucestershire were a poor side. Their Championship positions in those years were 6th, 9th, 7th, 9th and 9th (in a table containing only 9 teams). The bowling was as ineffective as it has ever been, for Woof fell away after 1891 and with W.G. bowling less and less the attack depended increasingly on Fred Roberts, supported by Bill Murch who had been signed in 1889 to bowl to members in the nets at the

31

C. L. TOWNSEND

The son of Frank Townsend, who had played for Gloucestershire from 1870 to 1891, C. L. Townsend first played for the County in 1893 when he was 16 and still a pupil at Clifton College. A tall, slender leg-spinner and left-hand bat, he made an early impact that season with a hat-trick against Somerset at Cheltenham, all stumped by W. H. Brain, a unique feat. In 1895, though he had played only one match before his school term ended in July, he finished the season with 131 wickets at 13 runs each. He took 16 for 122 against Notts at Trent Bridge and 13 for 110 against the same opponents at Cheltenham, and also took 12 wickets in each of the matches with Sussex at Bristol, Surrey at Clifton and Somerset at Taunton. In the month of August he took no fewer than 94 wickets.

If his bowling was never quite so devastating again, he took 113 wickets in 1896 and 92 in 1897. In 1898 his graceful batting brought him 1,270 runs, average 34 and he took 145 wickets. The following season he made 2,440 runs including his highest score of 224 not out against Essex, took 101 wickets, and played twice for England against Australia. He bowled at quite a brisk pace, spinning the ball fiercely and took many wickets with one that skidded straight on. After 1900 he played little owing to business commitments but was still capable of marvellous batting, making 129 in two hours against the 1909 Australians at Cheltenham. In his all too brief career he made 9,390 runs and took 725 wickets.

Charlie Townsend, an adornment to cricket's Golden Age. (NCCC)

G. L. JESSOP

Described as 'the human catapult, who wrecks the roofs of distant towns when set in his assault', G. L. Jessop was born in Cheltenham on 19 May 1874. He first played for the County in 1894 as a fast and hostile bowler and a dangerous, if erratic, long-handled slogger with an astonishing eye. Within a few years he had applied his keen intelligence to batsmanship and, having shortened his grip on the bat in order to have greater control, he became a player without equal in cricket history in terms of the combined rapidity and regularity with which he scored his runs.

Gilbert Jessop—truly a phenomenon. (GCCC)

Wisden lists nine 'fastest hundreds', two of which were obtained when the fielding side were offering up cannon fodder to produce a declaration. Of the remaining seven, two are by Jessop, 101 in 40 minutes against Yorkshire at Harrogate in 1897 and 191 for the Gentlemen of the South against the Players of the South at Hastings in 1907, in which he reached three figures in 42 minutes.

Two of the fastest five double-hundreds in history were scored by him, one in two hours against Sussex at Hove in 1903, his final score of 286 being made in well under three hours, and the other in two hours ten minutes against Somerset at Bristol in 1905, his final score being 234. No one who scored with comparable speed throughout his career has matched Jessop's 26,698 runs, average 32.63, or his 53 centuries.

Stocky and very strong but amazingly lissome and quick-moving, Jessop's swift advances up the pitch, followed by powerful driving which was only lofted if he intended to hit the ball out of the field, inevitably induced a shortened length, which he would then punish with ferocious pulling and cutting. If he had never played another innings his 102 in 75 minutes for England against Australia at the Oval in 1902, which enabled them to make the 263 they needed for victory on a dangerous pitch after he had come in at 48 for five, would have placed him among the game's immortals. His bowling brought him almost 900 wickets and in addition he was among the very greatest of cover-points.

1894 side. Standing (l to r): H. Wrathall, J. Painter, Smith (scorer), G. W. Murch, F. Roberts. Seated: E. M. Grace, Captain A. Newnham, W. G. Grace, J. J. Ferris, S. A. P. Kitkat. Front row: W. Troup, J. H. Board, H. W. Brown. (GCCC)

new Ashley Down Ground. The batting, too, was unreliable and it seemed to all that the Champion's days as a first-class cricketer were drawing to their close. In 1891 he made only 440 runs for the County, averaging less than 21, recovered to average 36 in 1892, but in 1893 dropped back to 27, while in 1894 it was below 20. He did not score a century for the County in those four seasons. However, one of W.G.'s greatest seasons was just around the corner, and in addition the advent of two great cricketers was to assist greatly in reviving the County's fortunes.

In 1893 Charles Lucas Townsend, son of Frank Townsend, a tall leg-spinner who was later to become an outstanding left-handed batsman, made his debut in August. His success was immediate and rather startling, for he still had two years left as a pupil at Clifton College. In that handful of games he took 27 wickets at 21 runs apiece, taking five for 70 in the Australians' first innings at Cheltenham College and six for 56 in Surrey's first innings at his own school ground, assisting materially in the County's 33-run victory. In the following season he played in seven matches, taking 32 wickets and then, in 1895, he electrified the cricketing world by taking 124 wickets at an average of 12.58 *in only 12 matches.* He played in the first match of

Fred Roberts, who took 967 wickets with fast left arm 1887–1905. (GCCC)

C. L. Townsend: aged 18, he took 94 wickets in the month of August 1895. (GCCC)

the season, against Somerset, doing little with the ball but making a handsome 95. Returning to the side on 22 July, at Old Trafford, he entered upon a spell of wicket-taking unequalled for its intensity in the history of the English game. His figures make staggering reading: five for 47 in Lancashire's first innings, eight for 52 and eight for 70 against Nottinghamshire, five for 36 in Yorkshire's first innings at Bradford, five for 78 and five for 51 against Warwickshire at Gloucester, five for 59 and seven for 28 against Sussex at Bristol, eight for 64 and five for 109 against Middlesex at Clifton, six for 51 in Kent's first innings in a rain-ruined match at Bristol, five for 43 and eight for 67 against Nottinghamshire at Cheltenham, where he also took eight for 130 and seven for 54 against Yorkshire, seven for 80 and five for 95 against Surrey at Clifton and seven for 122 and five for 103 against Somerset at Taunton. Not surprisingly, five of those 11 matches were won.

Townsend's bowling was never quite so spectacularly successful afterwards, though this is very much a matter of degree. He was, after all, to take 107 wickets for the County in 1896, 130 in 1898, and 101 in 1899, when his batting had developed to such an extent that he made 2,440 in all matches, and played twice for England against Australia.

Townsend was to play only irregularly after 1900, owing to the demands of his solicitor's practice but he did not play his last match until 1922. The statistics of his brief Gloucestershire career are impressive: 7,754 runs at an average of 30.28 and 653 wickets at 21.92 in only 161 matches.

The second great cricketer to arrive was Gilbert Laird Jessop, born in 1874 at Cheltenham. His name will for ever be linked with rapid scoring, in which field some of his feats stretch credibility, and with brilliant fielding and throwing. He was also for some years a notably hostile fast bowler; indeed his first England cap was earned for his bowling. Though only 5 ft 7 in (1.70 m) tall and somewhat stockily built, Jessop was spring-heeled and lissom, with the agility of a gymnast and possessing great speed over the ground and phenomenal reflexes. He is the only great hitter, Ian Botham possibly apart, who could combine a breakneck speed of run-getting with consistency. The great hitters of the 1880s and 1890s, C. I. Thornton, W. J. Ford

G. L. Jessop. Note the crouched stance and low bottom-hand grip. (NCCC)

and the Australians George Bonnor and J. J. Lyons, scored only 12 centuries between them. Jessop made 53. In 1900 he was to score 2,210 runs with six centuries, in 1901 2,323 with five centuries, and in 1911, 1,907 runs with seven centuries. In 1897 and 1900 he was to take over 100 wickets, and in his whole career he dismissed 873 batsmen.

His total tally of runs was 26,698 at an average of 32.63. His overall rate of scoring is impossible to ascertain, since the scorers' methods in his time were not sophisticated enough to reveal it. However, the times of his scores of 50 or more have been researched by Gerald Brodribb, from whose fascinating biography, 'The Croucher', these facts have been culled. Mr Brodribb states that his 127 scores of 50 to 99 were made at an average of 76.32 runs per hour, while his 53 centuries were scored at 82.70 runs per hour. Among his amazing feats of scoring a few may be picked out:

286 in 175 minutes, Gloucestershire *v* Sussex at Hove, 1903
233 in 150 minutes, Rest of England *v* Yorkshire at Lord's 1901
206 in 140 minutes, Gloucestershire *v* Nottinghamshire at Trent Bridge, 1904
191 in 90 minutes, Gentlemen of South *v* Players of South at Hastings, 1907

He was not merely a destroyer of weak bowling: six of his centuries came against Yorkshire, who in Jessop's time had the best attack in England, with bowlers of the calibre of Wainwright, Peel, F. S. Jackson, Rhodes, Hirst and Schofield Haigh. In the match at Bradford in 1900 Jessop made a century in each innings (104 and 139), a feat he would perform three more times.

In addition to all this, he was among the very greatest cover-points in cricket history, so fast that he would stand yards deeper than his rivals and still prevent singles, and with a whippy side-arm throw that registered countless direct hits on the stumps. From 1900 to 1912 he proved himself a most inventive captain whose skill in handling limited resources was constantly remarked on.

The virtues of Jessop's batting were those of any great player: he watched the ball as closely as anybody ever has, he scored with equal facility on both sides of the wicket and he was as happy playing off the front foot as the back. In addition, partly through the ungainly stance which earned him his nickname, which in his own view had the advantages of the crouch of a sprinter awaiting the gun, he was extraordinarily quick on his feet, both to move back or to 'charge' the bowling. He thus induced more errors in length than most batsmen which, with his steely wrists and heavy bat (around 3 lb or 1.4 kg) gripped low on the handle, provided deliveries he would despatch to all parts of the ground. Though he drove, cut and hit to leg in the orthodox way, he was always likely to pull the good length ball on or outside off stump far around on to the leg side. C. L. Townsend has said that in his early years Jessop was a 'slogger', if a very gifted one, until around 1899, when he really began to study batting. From that point on, Townsend 'looked upon Jessop's batting as a great art . . . unless he was going to hit it out of the ground, he hit it along the ground . . . no one could bowl him a ball he could not score off'.

Those days of Jessop's mastery were some way away in 1895, one of the most dramatic seasons in the Club's history. We have already touched on the County's poor record in the preceding seasons, and on the sad decline in the batting of the Champion, for whom 1894 had been the nadir of his career. In 1895, however, the years fell from his heavy shoulders and, in his 47th year, he batted as he had a quarter of a century before. At the start of that season his tally of centuries was 98, a figure none of his contemporaries had approached (Arthur Shrewsbury, who retired in 1902, was to finish with 59, a long way behind W.G.'s final tally of 126). A century in the second innings of the match between MCC and Sussex increased the figure to 99. Innings of 18 and 25 for MCC v Yorkshire followed, after which W.G. travelled down to Bristol for the Championship match against Somerset, who batted first making 303, W.G. taking five for 87. With W.G. 38 not out overnight the crowd next day was large, and included Mrs Grace and her daughter Bessie. With C. L. Townsend at the other end W.G. moved smoothly on to 98, at which point Sammy Woods bowled a leg-side full toss which W.G. struck to the square-leg boundary. There was a wild outburst of cheering and a magnum of champagne was brought out on a tray. W.G., very much in the groove, went on to make 288, batting only $5\frac{1}{2}$ hours for this huge score and, according to the Reverend A. P. Wickham, who was keeping wicket for Somerset, permitting only four balls to pass his bat during his whole innings!

That match was won by nine wickets, as was the next, against Kent at Gravesend, in which W.G. was last out in Gloucestershire's first innings for 257 and, making 73 not out of the 103 runs needed for victory in 75 minutes, was on the field for every ball bowled in the match. In between these two games W.G. made 52 for A. J. Webbe's XI against the University at Cambridge. W.G. then made 18 in W. W. Read's testimonial match at the Oval, which meant that he still needed 153 to take him to the coveted four figures. The first day of Gloucestershire's match with Middlesex at Lord's was 30 May. W.G. duly won the toss and, after a cautious start, sailed past his century and on to 149, when the Middlesex spinner E. A. Nepean sent down a long hop which was duly cuffed to the boundary. W.G. went on to make 169. He was, therefore, the first batsman ever to make 1,000 runs in May, having scored 1,016 runs at an average of 112.88 between 9 and

30 May. Only twice since has this feat been achieved, by W. R. Hammond in 1927 and Charlie Hallows in 1928. The five other times that 1,000 runs have been made before the end of May, i.e. in April and May, were by Tom Hayward in 1900, Sir Donald Bradman in 1930 and 1938, W. J. Edrich, also in 1938, and G. M. Turner in 1973. Only Sir Donald, in 1938, reached the target in fewer visits to the crease than W.G., who had ten innings.

A glittering Testimonial was launched by the *Daily Telegraph* to commemorate the twin achievements of the 1,000 in May and the 100th century. This realised £4,281 9s 10d, which donations from other sources swelled to £9,073 8s 3d. This was a colossal sum in those days and it is small wonder that the ability of W.G., nominally an amateur, to attract such sums to himself caused resentment among some of his contemporaries. It should be said, though, that the minutes of the Gloucestershire Club detailing expenses payments made to him during his career indicate either a singular lack of avarice on his part or his calm acceptance of the County's inability to pay more, for they always seemed to be in financial straits.

The 1895 season also saw the emergence of talented amateur batsmen in F. H. B. Champain, C. O. H. Sewell, son of that J. J. Sewell who had played for Gloucestershire and Middlesex years before, and R. W. Rice. A fine professional bat emerged in Cheltenham-born Harry Wrathall and, with Jessop bowling and batting with more effect and C. L. Townsend carrying all before him in July and August, the County recovered from a poor patch in that season to finish fourth (out of 14 now) in the Championship. W.G., though adversely affected by the wet pitches of June and July, was in fine form again later on and, hitting nine centuries altogether, finished with 2,346 runs at an average a fraction over 50, being just edged out of first place in the national averages by Archie MacLaren.

This was, however, far from W.G.'s swan-song, for he topped 2,000 runs again in 1896 in all matches and had over 1,500 runs, at an average of around 40 in 1897 and 1898. Though the County slipped to 10th place in 1896, when the bowling depended too much on Townsend, they were fifth and third respectively in the following two seasons, and once more clearly a power in the land. Sadly though, there were upheavals round the corner.

The 1899 season opened, as for some seasons past, with the County XI playing a Colts team. This match was invariably against odds, in this case the Colts had 24 players. W.G. did not play, Gloucestershire being led by his vice-captain, Walter Troup, a product of Cheltenham College who had first played for the County in 1887. W.G., however, took the side on the southern tour, playing against Sussex, Kent, Surrey and Middlesex. Meanwhile, it appeared that some members of

MIDDLESEX *v* GLOUCESTERSHIRE

Played at Lord's, 30, 31 May and 1 June 1895

GLOUCESTERSHIRE WON BY 5 WICKETS

GLOUCESTERSHIRE	FIRST INNINGS		SECOND INNINGS	
1 *Dr W. G. Grace	b Thornton	169		
2 H. Wrathall	b Rawlin	23	b Thornton	15
3 J. R. Painter	b Stoddart	21		
4 Mr S. A. P. Kitcat	c Lucas b Nepean	36	c Philipson b Thornton	0
5 Mr A. J. Dearlove	c Webbe b Stoddart	23		
6 Mr G. L. Jessop	b Thornton	5	not out	14
7 Capt A. J. H. Luard	c Hearne b Thornton	64	c Stoddart b Thornton	0
8 Mr E. L. Thomas	c Philipson b Thornton	0	c Philipson b Thornton	1
9 Mr F. C. Bracher	c Thornton b Rawlin	3	not out	2
10 †J. H. Board	c Hayman b Nepean	6	c Stoddart b Thornton	12
11 F. G. Roberts	not out	1		
Extras	b 11, lb 4	15	b 1, nb 1	2
Total		366	(5 wickets)	46

1st inns: 1-36, 2-73, 3-156, 4-229, 5-262, 6-347, 7-, 8-, 9-361
2nd inns: 1-, 2-27, 3-, 4-, 5-

BOWLING	O	M	R	W		O	M	R	W
Hearne	41	21	71	0		11	1	24	0
Nepean	34.4	9	109	2					
Rawlin	31	8	75	2					
Stoddart	14	4	44	2					
Thornton	30	16	52	4		10.3	5	20	5(1nb)

MIDDLESEX	FIRST INNINGS		SECOND INNINGS	
1 Mr A. E. Stoddart	b Jessop	2	c Kitcat b Painter	2
2 *Mr A. J. Webbe	lbw b Jessop	33	c Board b Painter	22
3 Mr H. B. Hayman	b Jessop	11	b Roberts	1
4 Mr R. S. Lucas	c Dearlove b Jessop	9	b Painter	70
5 J. T. Rawlin	c Thomas b Roberts	11	c Board b Painter	83
6 Sir T. C. O'Brien	b Jessop	28	c Board b Painter	4
7 Mr G. F. Vernon	c Wrathall b Painter	62	c Board b Painter	11
8 Mr E. A. Nepean	c Luard b Painter	26	c Kitcat b Painter	0
9 †Mr H. Philipson	c Bracher b Painter	8	c Kitcat b Jessop	1
10 Dr P. G. Thornton	b Painter	0	b Painter	4
11 J. T. Hearne	not out	0	not out	2
Extras	b 5, ln 5	10	b 3, lb 4, nb 1	8
Total		200		208

1st inns: 1-6, 3-48, 4-69, 5-89, 6-107, 7-187, 8-, 9-
2nd inns: 1-2, 2-8, 3-47, 4-47, 5-169, 6-, 7-200, 8-, 9-

BOWLING	O	M	R	W		O	M	R	W
Roberts	36	20	60	1		24	4	65	1(1nb)
Jessop	48	24	88	5		30	12	68	1
Painter	12.3	4	42	4		45.2	16	67	8

Umpires: Jas Lillywhite jun and J. Street.

Gloucestershire won the toss. Close of play: 1st day: Gloucestershire first innings completed; 2nd day: Middlesex (2)154-4 (Lucas 61*, Rawlin 61*).

the committee—not all of whom were well disposed towards W.G., as the 1892–93 row over selection clearly showed—had heard rumours that W.G. had been invited to manage the new ground at the Crystal Palace and captain the London County Club which was to be based there. Accordingly a brusque resolution appeared in the minutes 'that the secretary write to Dr W. G. Grace immediately, asking him from the committee to state exactly what matches he intends playing in for the County during this year'. This was, to say the least, tactless, particularly in view of W.G.'s proven devotion to the County's interests, and also his known dislike of interference from the committee.

W.G.'s response in a letter written on 28 May was immediate and typically direct and forthright. After stating that his intention had been to play in nearly all the games that season, he handed in his resignation as captain. He expressed his regret in moderate terms but the last two sentences of his letter show how deeply he had been affronted: 'I have always tried my very best to promote the interests of the Gloucestershire County Club . . . I have the greatest affection for the county of my birth, but for the committee as a body, the greatest contempt.'

The committee took umbrage at these strong words, and it was soon evident that the rift was too great to be healed this time. It was sad that the County and its greatest cricketer—possibly *the* greatest cricketer—should part company in this bitter manner. However, calm eventually prevailed and three years later W.G. was elected a Life Member of Gloucestershire, and the County played matches against London County, whose offer W.G. had perforce accepted. Walter Troup captained the County for the rest of the 1899 season which, unsurprisingly after such upheavals, was not a particularly successful one. It did, however, see the meteoric arrival of A. J. Paish, a slow left-armer with an odd action, who captured 125 wickets at 19 apiece. Though he took plenty of wickets in the following two seasons they cost nearly 30 runs apiece and, with increasing concern being voiced over the legality of his action, he dropped out of sight after the 1903 season.

Season 1899 was Townsend's great batting year, but though he took 101 wickets in all games, it was not a vintage season for him with the

---

Grace batted 310 minutes and hit 24 fours in his 169—he also completed 1,000 runs in first-class cricket before the end of May, during this innings.
Dearlove, a recruit from the Bohemians C.C., Bristol, batted 60 minutes for his 23.
'Painter's success as a bowler was the most noteworthy feature of the game. This player is now in his thirty-seventh year, and his suddenly coming to the front as a bowler is one of the most remarkable events of this year's cricket.' (Cricket).
W. G. Grace became the first player ever to score 1,000 runs before the end of May.

ball. Indeed his 72 wickets for the County cost over 26 runs apiece, clear evidence that his great gift was declining.

With Gilbert Jessop now down from Cambridge—he left without taking his degree—he was appointed captain for 1900, a position he was to hold until 1912. These were not good years for the County, seventh position in his first year being the highest they reached under the Croucher, but contemporary judges did not blame his energetic captaincy for this.

In that season of 1900 Jessop scored 1,733 runs for the County, averaging 44, and took 86 wickets at under 18. In all matches he made 2,210 runs and took 104 wickets to emulate Charlie Townsend's 'double' feat of the previous season. Highlights of Jessop's season were his 179 in 105 minutes against Sussex at Hove and his 104 in 70 minutes and 139 in 85 minutes against Yorkshire at Bradford. Against the touring West Indians at Bristol in June, in a match not given first-class status, Jessop put on 201 in an hour with Townsend, of which he made 157 himself. Since suffering a back strain in his Test debut of 1899, when he was England's only fast bowler and consequently sadly overbowled, Jessop had cut down his pace but was still a very effective performer, as he moved the ball both ways.

Jessop's innings of 104 for England against Australia in the fifth Test at the Oval in 1902 will be remembered as long as cricket itself. England, needing 263 to win on an awkward pitch against Trumble, Saunders, Noble and Armstrong, were 48 for five when Jessop came to the wicket. He made 102 out of 139 in 77 minutes, from which point George Hirst, who made 58 not out, shepherded England to victory by one wicket.

During this period there were some notable new faces. Among amateurs the Robinson cousins, F.G. and D.C., members of the great Bristol paper manufacturing company, appeared as did two future captains in W. H. Rowlands and M. A. Green. Jessop himself discovered George Dennett, a great slow left-arm bowler, playing in Bristol club cricket. Dennett was to play from 1903 to 1926, during which period he was to take 2,147 wickets, 2,082 of them for Gloucestershire. Of the 33 bowlers to pass the 2,000 mark, all of whom were qualified to play for England, only three, Dennett, Jack Newman of Hampshire and Don Shepherd of Glamorgan were not chosen to play for their country.

Charlie Parker, born in Prestbury near Cheltenham, who was to take more wickets than anyone in the game's history apart from Rhodes and Freeman, appeared as early as 1903, but at that time he was bowling quickish left-arm with only moderate success. He did not completely switch to slow left-arm, at which he has had few peers, till after the First World War, so his story really belongs to another chapter. Percy Mills, who began as a medium-pacer but later turned successfully to off-spin, first appeared in 1902. A. E. Dipper, the famous on-side nudger, who was to score nearly 28,000 runs for Gloucestershire, first appeared in 1908, but again, the years of his plenty did not come until after the war.

The County's bowling relied far too much on Dennett, who took 100 wickets for the first time in 1904 and did not fail to exceed this total, often by large margins, right up to the war. In 1907 he became the first Gloucestershire bowler to reach 200 wickets in a season, taking 201 at 16.05. Only the presence on the England scene of such very great bowlers as Wilfred Rhodes and Colin Blythe, and a little later of Frank Woolley, who in 1914 had 2,272 runs to add to his 125 wickets, denied Dennett the chance to show his skill in Test matches. By now Roberts had retired, Jessop was bowling less and less, and Gloucestershire lacked what the moderns term 'strike bowlers'. In one sense Jessop was a team in himself, but it should be remembered that at this period English cricket was as powerful as it has ever been. Of the successful sides of that era, Yorkshire had Rhodes, Hirst and Haigh to bowl and Tunnicliffe, Denton and F. S. Jackson to bat; Lancashire could call on MacLaren, Spooner and Tyldesley to bat, and had bowlers like Brearley, Harry Dean and Jimmy Heap, while Kent had Blythe, Woolley, Fielder, Hardinge, K. L. Hutchings and Bill Ashdown.

In this sort of company Gloucestershire's resources look distinctly thin. Amateurs like F. H. B. Champain, C. S. Barnett (father of the Test player C. J. Barnett) and C. O. H. Sewell had their moments but were rarely consistent, a matter for little surprise since their appearances were generally intermittent. Board, a fine wicket-keeper whose tally of 1,207 dismissals is the ninth highest in the game's history, had become a reliable bat, and Dipper's skills were developing, but the chances of the County making a formidable score depended largely on whether Jessop came off.

Nevertheless, despite the County's lack of playing success, these years were happy ones. Jessop recalls that his relations with the committee over 13 seasons were 'always of the friendliest'. The chairman, H. W. Beloe, was greatly admired by Jessop. 'There can never have been a keener supporter of county cricket than Harry Beloe, nor a chairman so bountifully endowed with ready tact.'

Gloucestershire's dependence on amateurs, who generally were not able to find time to play with any sort of regularity till the later part of the season, prevented them from really challenging for the Championship, but at full strength, and with Jessop in form, they could challenge the best and, in 1900, won five of their last eight matches.

Jessop's contributions in that year were prodigious. Against Sussex

Alf Dipper: 27,948 runs, 53 centuries.
(GCCC)

at Brighton in early June he made 179, the first 50 coming, sedately for him, in 45 minutes, the second in 20, and the final 79 in 40 minutes, 115 minutes in all. There must have been some batsmanship on show in this match, for K. S. Ranjitsinhji made 97 and 127. Ten days later, at Lord's Jessop made 109 off J. T. Hearne and Trott, among others, in 65 minutes and, in the second innings, with Gloucestershire on course for a win, made 58 not out in 37 minutes. In the match already referred to, against Yorkshire at Bradford, Jessop came in with his side 116 for five, Yorkshire having made 409, and scored 109 off Hirst, Rhodes and Haigh in 70 minutes. In the second innings he came in when Gloucestershire, chasing 327 for victory, were 105 for five, and made 139 out of 182 in 95 minutes 'quite ten of which according to Lord Hawke, were spent in recovering the ball'. In the end, however, with Lord Hawke, according to C. L. Townsend, 'at his wits end', Jessop was marvellously caught one-handed in the deep by Tunnicliffe off Rhodes, and Yorkshire, unbeaten that season, won by 40 runs after experiencing a very nasty fright.

In those days, the ball had generally to be hit out of the ground for six to be awarded. At Bradford six was given if the ball was struck over the football stand at the bottom end of the ground, where Jessop actually hit Rhodes four times, but if, as with one blow off Haigh, it landed on the roof of the stand, only four was given. In this innings Jessop scored 76 off 27 consecutive balls from Rhodes including seven sixes and eight fours. Eye-witness accounts attest that he cleared the ropes 20 times in all. It should be noted, too, that this was Rhodes' greatest season, in which he took 261 wickets at 13.81. Though Jessop considered that Bobby Peel had the more puzzling flight, he greatly admired Rhodes. That season of 1900 they met 14 times—four times in the Championship, plus Gentlemen *v* Players, North *v* South and other Festival games. Rhodes, Jessop said, 'however hard he was "punched", came up smiling for more', and was rewarded with Jessop's wicket eight times in those encounters. Jessop, though, scored

647 runs, so honours were about even.

The retirement of C. L. Townsend at the end of the 1900 season was a severe blow to Jessop's hopes of maintaining Gloucestershire's improvement. Townsend was subsequently able to play only during his holidays, but some notable feats were still to come from him. In 1909, for instance, playing for the County against the Australians at Cheltenham, his 129 helped his side to total 411 after the tourists had been dismissed for 215, and only Vernon Ransford's 121 enabled the Australians to save the match in the face of fine bowling from Dennett, who took six for 40. In 1906, also at Cheltenham, Townsend made 214 in Gloucestershire's total of 523 against Worcestershire, after which Dennett took 15 wickets for 140, the County winning by an innings and 230 runs.

Jessop's best season with the bat was 1901—he made 2,323 runs in all, just under 1,600 of them for the County—but, Wrathall apart, there was little else of substance to the batting, and only three matches out of 24 were won. There was no discernible improvement until 1904 when five out of 18 matches were won and ninth position achieved in a Championship of 15 counties. In 1905 George Dennett came to the fore, taking 131 wickets, an advance which counter-balanced the retirement of the faithful Fred Roberts, and the County finished eighth out of 16, Northamptonshire having entered the Championship that year. Neither 1905 nor 1906 were vintage batting years for Jessop, or for any of the regular batsmen for that matter, but Dennett had a marvellous season in 1906, his 160 wickets in the Championship helping greatly in securing six victories and a respectable ninth place.

However, from that point up to 1912, when Jessop relinquished the captaincy and also the secretaryship of the County, which he had held since E. M. Grace's retirement, Gloucestershire were never higher than ninth. In 1909, for much of which Jessop was absent through torn back muscles, they were bottom, as they were in 1914 in the second year of C. O. H. Sewell's captaincy.

Throughout Jessop's stewardship Gloucestershire's finances had been in a perilous state. They had had a healthy credit balance of £2,726 in 1879, which had been eroded to £296 in 1904 and declined further to £88 in 1911. In this lay the principal reason for their struggles on the field, for they simply could not afford the strong nucleus of talented professionals on which, even in that golden age of amateur cricket, other counties increasingly relied. Of the great sides of that era Yorkshire generally fielded eight professionals, as did Surrey and Nottinghamshire, while Kent fielded seven. Gloucestershire would often have six or seven amateurs and they were not of the calibre of Lancashire's nap hand of MacLaren, Spooner, Brearley, H. G. Garnett and L. O. S. Poidevin. It is somewhat ironical that

GLOUCESTERSHIRE *v* ESSEX

Played at Bristol, 6 and 7 August 1906

ESSEX	FIRST INNINGS		SECOND INNINGS	
Mr F. L. Fane	ct Jessop b Dennett	11	b Roberts	2
Mr J. W. H. T. Douglas	b Dennett	14	ct Townsend b Dennett	25
Mr P. A. Perrin	ct Brownlee b Dennett	22	st Board b Dennett	1
Mr C. P. McGahey	ct Brownlee b Dennett	17	st Board b Dennett	1
Mr W. M. Turner	st Board b Dennett	0	ct Goodwin b Dennett	8
Rev F. H. Gillingham	ct Spry b Dennett	4	ct Thomas b Dennett	20
Major A. J. Turner	ct Thomas b Dennett		lbw, b Roberts	9
W. Reeves	ct Brownlee b Dennett	4	b Roberts	7
C. P. Buckenham	lbw, b Dennett	5	not out	4
†A. E. Russell	not out	0	b Roberts	4
W. Mead	ct Goodwin b Dennett	2	ct Sewell b Roberts	0
Extras	lb 2	2	b6, lb 4	10
Total		84		127

BOWLING	O	M	R	W	O	M	R	W
Dennett	19.4	7	40	10	31	12	48	5
Roberts	19	8	42	0	30.2	7	69	5

GLOUCESTERSHIRE	FIRST INNINGS		SECOND INNINGS	
Mr C. O. H. Sewell	st Russell b Mead	21	b Douglas	14
Mr E. P. Barnett	b Reeves	17	not out	20
Mr G. L. Jessop	ct and b Douglas	75		
Mr A. F. M. Townsend	ct Fane b Mead	23		
†J. H. Board	lbw, b Douglas	0		
Mr F. E. Thomas	b Douglas	4		
Mr L. D. Brownlee	b Mead	6	not out	5
Mr H. S. Goodwin	ct McGahey b Douglas	6		
Mr F. B. Roberts	b Reeves	10		
E. Spry	ct Reeves b Douglas	6		
E. G. Dennett	not out	0		
Extras	b 4, lb 1	5		
Total		173		39

BOWLING	O	M	R	W	O	M	R	W
Mead	19	3	72	3	4	0	12	0
Douglas	14	3	50	5	3.5	0	27	1
Reeves	10	1	46	2				

Umpires: A. E. Clapp and F. W. Marlow.

This match furnished a second instance during the season of 1906 of a bowler taking all ten wickets in one innings of a first-class match. The feat was performed by Dennett who disposed of the ten Essex batsmen at a cost of only 40 runs, and followed this up in the second innings by obtaining five more wickets, his record coming out at 15 wickets for 98 runs. He and Roberts bowled unchanged in the two Essex innings. Dennett's bowling triumph was followed up by some very skilful and judicious batting on the part of Jessop who—at the wickets an hour and a half—gave no chance until he had made 60. Before the first day's cricket came to an end Essex in their second innings had lost four batsmen for 63. Less than two hours' play on Tuesday sufficed to finish off the match, Gloucestershire gaining a brilliant victory by nine wickets. Dennett, it should be added, received splendid support in the field, Brownlee bringing off three brilliant catches in the first innings of Essex.

Gloucestershire, who possessed in W.G. and Gilbert Jessop two of the greatest draws in cricket history, men whose presence in a match could be expected to have a massive effect on the gate, should have found themselves in such straits. However, as we shall see, such problems have recurred regularly throughout their history.

Jessop's intention had been to play some cricket in 1919—he had appeared in 12 games in 1913, and nine in 1914—but, having volunteered for active service in 1914, he suffered a bad accident two years later. He was undergoing treatment for lumbago at a clinic in Bath. This involved being 'steamed' in a lidded container, the lid being for the patient to lift if he became too uncomfortable. The catch unfortunately stuck, so that Jessop endured great heat, and his heart was thereby severely damaged. Though eventually able to play a little golf (he had rapidly made himself a scratch player) he was never strong again. His brain, though, remained as sharp as ever until his death in 1955, just before his 81st birthday.

Nothing, however, signified so finally the end of an age—or, to be more exact, of three ages—than the death on 23 October 1915 of W.G. Following his acrimonious departure from Gloucestershire in 1899 he had, as we have seen, accepted the offer to run the cricket at the newly formed London County Club, based at the Crystal Palace. He was during this final period to take his tally of centuries to 126, scoring one for South v North at Lord's in 1900 and the other seven for London County at Crystal Palace. The penultimate one, 150 made in 1903 against Gloucestershire, must have given the Old Man enormous satisfaction.

He had truly eclipsed in fame any cricketer before him, and, in all probability, since. His 1,000 in May 1895 resulted in a letter from the Prince of Wales, whose keenest interests, it is well known, lay in other directions than cricket. He mastered the fast round-armers on the rough pitches of his youth, he coped with the new methods of Spofforth and Boyle, and he made plenty of runs off the new-fangled swingers when well into his 50s. It is the nature of each generation to pour cold water on the achievement of its predecessors but 54,896 runs, 2,876 wickets and 874 catches admit of little denigration.

As a batsman he was orthodox and methodical, two characteristics that are rarely associated with destructive power; however, when they are, as also with Sir Donald Bradman and, though less regularly, with W. R. Hammond, the results are spectacular. The pace at which W. G. scored was related to the condition of the pitch and the quality of bowling and fielding, but above all, to the needs of his side. Hence, if he was in form he would score with great rapidity and certainty, the rapidity being due to his recognition of the fact that runs scored at a good rate are more valuable than those accumulated over a long period, and the certainty owing itself to his marvellous eye, his solid technique and the tirelessness of that powerful frame. His pure batting ability was extraordinary. Once, on that dreadful Lord's wicket in the late 1860s, he stopped four shooters in succession from a fast bowler, and the crowd, recognising that any one of those balls would almost certainly have uprooted any other batsman in the land, rose to him as if he had made a century.

As a bowler, he was among the very best for the 20 years from 1870 to 1889, initially bowling fastish round-arm but later, as his bulk increased, preferring to bowl quite slow, with flight, a little spin from leg, great accuracy and considerable cunning. During this later period he kept his mid-off pretty straight, himself moving across, as soon as he had delivered the ball, to a shortish mid-off position where he picked up countless return catches, often from extremely fierce drives. A contemporary has recalled that the ball went into those great hands 'like a pea into a top-hat'.

His fielding, indeed, was remarkably fine until he was past 40 years of age. In his youth he was a magnificent outfield, swift and sure and able to throw well over 100 yards. Lord Charles Russell, in his speech at Lord's in July 1879 when he presented W.G. with the proceeds of his Testimonial, professed never to have seen fielding to equal W.G.'s (though, like all old gentlemen, he felt the game had not gone forward in all departments, bowling generally being better in his youth). W.G. was later a fine point, though not in the class of E.M., who is reported to have caught a batsman when fielding there and handed the ball to his wicket-keeper without moving a step.

As a man, W.G. had in some quarters a reputation for sharp practice, if not for outright cheating. Francis Thompson, in the poem quoted from earlier, talks of: 'The long-whiskered Doctor, that laugheth rules to scorn'. Yet I am persuaded, by Bernard Darwin who knew him well and wrote the definitive biography of him, and by other reading, that this is precisely what he didn't do. Even those Australians with whom he'd had disputes on the 1873–74 tour do not claim this. A contemporary Australian report said:

> Now it may be confessed, if only in a shame-faced fashion, that in Australia we did not take kindly to W.G. For so big a man he is surprisingly tenacious on very small points. We duly admired him at the wicket but thought him too apt to wrangle in the spirit of a duo-decimo attorney over small points of the game.

This view accords well with that of Darwin, who said that right to the end of his life W.G., though by nature the kindest hearted of men, had an almost childish dislike of having anyone 'put anything over on him'. With this cast of mind, and with cricket so important to him, it is hardly surprising that he defended his and his side's position to the very limit of the law. Had he gone beyond that, he would hardly have earned the affection and respect of his contemporaries, amateur and professional, of whom the latter in particular would surely have been quick to cavil if they were being denied their just rewards by a cheat. As it happens, the reverse is the case. The great Yorkshire fast bowler George Freeman, writing many years later of an innings of 66 W.G. played for MCC against Yorkshire on a dangerous pitch at Lord's in 1870, said:

> A more wonderful innings was never played. Tom Emmett and I have often said it was a marvel the Doctor was not either maimed or unnerved for the rest of his days or killed outright. I often think of his pluck on that day when I watch a modern batsman scared if a medium ball hits him on the hand. He should have seen our expresses flying about W.G.'s head, ribs and shoulders in 1870.

The great bowler Alfred Shaw, who played against W.G. from 1865 to 1897, almost venerated him, and was exceedingly proud of having bowled him more times—21—than any other bowler in first-class cricket.

W.G.'s influence on cricket was enormous. Such was the prestige that he, particularly, and his brothers E.M. and G.F. brought to Gloucestershire in their early years that it could even distort historical perspective. Francis Thompson, in his famous poem, refers to Lancashire, who had taken part in the very first unofficial Championship of 1864 as 'new-risen', whereas Gloucestershire, who did not compete as a first-class county till 1870, are by 1878 already 'the irresistible'.

The County has only infrequently approached the glories of those early years, but with and after W.G., as we have already seen, came remarkable men in C. L. Townsend and G. L. Jessop and there were many more to come. If Gloucestershire has not always been among the leading counties, it has still had its share of good times and, to the joy of its supporters, has rarely failed to produce cricketers of fascinating character and high skill.

CHARLIE PARKER AND WALLY HAMMOND

FOR GLOUCESTERSHIRE, AS FOR EVERY OTHER COUNTY, the first post-war season of 1919 had something eerie about it. The golden age, with its air of sunlit tranquillity enlivened and embellished by the stirring deeds of grand and heroic men, had departed for ever. As four years of mud and slaughter dragged to a close men raised weary eyes to a new and utilitarian era. Cricket was to some extent to reflect the values of this altered context, but because of its innate capacity for producing the heroic achievement or the gallant failure, and because its very existence stirred memories of other and, for some, happier times, it was to flourish greatly after an uncertain period of adjustment. Gloucestershire, however, were not to benefit too much in monetary terms, finances remaining in their familiar and precarious position up to and beyond the Second World War. There is no doubt, though, that the cricket played by the Club between 1920 and 1939 was as inventive and attractive as playing resources allowed. It may seem curious to talk of 'limitation of resources' in the age of Charlie Parker's prime, of Walter Hammond and Charles Barnett, of Tom Goddard and Harry Smith, but I trust that the unwinding tale will justify the phrase.

With a new spirit abroad there were proposals of varying degrees of sense or otherwise about what should be done with first-class cricket, among them the shortening of boundaries and penalties for the batting side if they permitted maiden overs to be bowled or if their run-scoring dropped below a certain rate. These ideas were plainly designed to produce bright cricket which would enliven the drab post-war world—as if the 'Golden Age' had produced dull cricket—and the MCC turned a deaf ear, unsurprisingly.

However, MCC did agree to the suggestion to reduce County Championship matches to two days' duration, an experiment generally agreed to have been disastrous. Certainly there were few bright spots for Gloucestershire. The king-pin of their attack, George Dennett, had been commissioned from the ranks and was still serving in India. Parker had yet to convert wholly successfully to the slow to slow-medium left-arm spin that was to earn him renown, and though he was within striking distance of his 100 wickets, they were somewhat expensive. Percy Mills hardly played at all and, under F. G. Robinson's captaincy, only four Championship matches were won, though eighth place was secured. Dipper, who had made his 1,000 runs in 1911, 1913 and 1914, albeit at modest averages, broke through to score 1,329 runs for the County at 45.82, announcing himself after a longish apprenticeship as one of the most consistent run-scorers in the English game.

There were important developments on the administrative front at this juncture. First, it should be recorded that it had been necessary to sell the Ashley Down ground to a local company, Messrs J. S. Fry and Sons in 1915, a move that was in the longer term found to be disadvantageous, although under the conditions of the sale the County retained the right to buy back the ground at the same price Fry's had paid for it.

Meanwhile, spurred on by the need to revive the Club, whose activities had entirely ceased in 1914, there was a concerted effort by pre-war committee-men, former and current players, together with local business men, to set up a constitution for the Club which would satisfy all those who had its interest at heart. Prime movers in this were the Chairman, R. E. Bush, brother of J. A. Bush, the County's former wicket-keeper, the former chairman, Harry Beloe, a local sugar-broker and a cricketer himself, and other cricketers in W. S. A. Brown, C. Troup and H. V. Page, a very useful player whose son was to take over the captaincy from B. H. Lyon in 1935. Further support came from younger men in A. E. S. Hill, E. W. L. Olive, F. O. Wills, the Robinsons, F. G. and D. C., and W. H. Rowlands. Under the agreed constitution the Club was to be run by a general executive committee which had finance, match and selection sub-committees. This executive committee was itself elected from the main body of the committee, which was first called the 'council' of the Club in 1921. This council comprised the 18 members elected from Bristol, with representation, also totalling 18, coming from other parts of the county in proportion to their membership. For example, there were four each from Gloucester and Cheltenham but only one apiece from Thornbury, Wotton-under-Edge and Cirencester. There was also one representative from J. S. Fry.

This constitution, broadly speaking, still operates today, with the full council responsible for electing the chairman, the captain and all officers of the Club and for ratifying the membership of sub-committees. Indeed, when it comes down to brass tacks, the council, which meets quarterly, can withhold its approval from any action of any sub-committee whose chairman it has appointed and whose constitution it has ratified. In such circumstances, and in the absence of any motivating force applied to the council, the desires of the executive can be, and have not infrequently been, thwarted by the full vote of the council itself. There is strong argument to this day as to whether such a system, not so much of checks and balances as of built-in inertia, can permit the effective operation of so diverse and unwieldy a composite as a county cricket club. There can be no doubt, however, that the organisation was established with the best intentions and may well have been specifically designed to avoid some of the resentment caused among members when W.G. and E.M. appeared to run the Club themselves without any great regard to the County's membership. The council, being directly elected by Club members from their various districts, was no doubt specifically designed to act as rudder and brake, thereby preventing the abrogation of power into a few pairs of hands.

In 1920 the Championship reverted to three-day cricket. Gloucestershire's position in the table was identical with the previous season, at eighth, but their cricket was generally considered to have improved. Mills played regularly and, now bowling more off-spinners than seamers, took 52 wickets for the County at 14.38 apiece. George Dennett had now returned from military duty and, though not the force he had been—he was now 40—took 52 wickets at an average of 24. The batting, Dipper and some occasionally effective hitting from F. G. Robinson apart, was wretched. The prime cause of the County's improvement was the breakthrough made by Charles Parker who, at the age of 37, leapt to the forefront of English slow bowlers, taking 125 wickets at an average below $14\frac{1}{2}$. That year Gloucestershire won eight matches out of 20 against four out of 16 the previous season.

This is an opportune moment to look at the remarkable career of Charlie Parker in some detail. If ever patience and perseverance were finally justified, it was so in Parker's case. He made his debut for the County in 1903, against London County, when he did not take a wicket, and had to wait for another two years before playing in his first Championship match, against Lancashire, when he bowled Reggie Spooner in his first over. If anyone thought that this feat presaged instant stardom for the tall fastish left-armer they were much mistaken. He did not play again till 1907, when he took only 14 wickets, but he established himself the following season, taking 65 wickets. Thereafter he held his place comfortably enough without doing anything particularly startling. His best pre-war tally of wickets for the County was in 1909, when he took 71, his best in terms of average 1910, when his 61 wickets cost 19 apiece. However, in both 1913 and 1914 his bowling average was above 30. In all, his pre-war wickets numbered 454 and cost between 25 and 26 runs each, respectable but not startling. When cricket began again in 1919 Parker was 36, an age when most cricketers have half an eye on retirement. When Parker finally did retire in 1935, a month or so before his 53rd birthday, he had reaped a harvest of 3,278 wickets, a total exceeded only by Wilfred Rhodes and 'Tich' Freeman. He took 100 wickets in a season 16 consecutive times, i.e. from 1920 until he retired, and five times captured over 200. Given that Rhodes' great years were prior to the First World War, and that Woolley's bowling had by 1924 become secondary to his batting, Parker's claims to be the best left-arm spinner of the time are very strong. Yet he was to play in only one Test, against Warwick Armstrong's Australian side at Old Trafford in 1921, a fact which must make him one of the game's unluckiest players.

Charles Warrington Leonard Parker was born on 14 October 1882 at Prestbury on the outskirts of Cheltenham. His father was a labourer, with a large family— Charlie was one of nine children. He was a clever enough scholar to win a place at Cheltenham

Charlie Parker: 3,278 first-class wickets, 200 or more wickets in a season five times, six hat-tricks. (GCCC)

Grammar School, where Gilbert Jessop had been educated, and it was here that his passion for reading, which never left him and which his parents encouraged, was fully nurtured. Charlie was to a large extent self-educated, for his reading took him far outside the parameters of a pre-1914 grammar school syllabus into the world of political ideas. David Foot, who has written fascinatingly of Charlie in his book 'Cricket's Unholy Trinity', has described Charlie as a radical rather than a socialist. He was certainly too much of an individualist to relish the collective solutions of socialism, just as he had too much personal pride to defer to a person's views because that person was of noble or wealthy descent. To Charlie, Jack was certainly as good as his master, and if anyone wanted to argue about this Charlie would accommodate him and, through his wide reading and the logical strength of his mind, invariably win the day.

Inevitably, therefore, he was destined to come into conflict with the rulers of the game. In his single Test he was far from a failure, taking two for 32 in 28 overs and bowling the great C. G. Macartney for 13. He was in the England party for the Headingley Test of 1926 against H. L. Collins's Australian side but was left out despite the fact that the pitch was wet and, as was agreed by most present including the Australians themselves, one which would have suited the Gloucestershire man. The England selectors, however, had got themselves into a tangle, not for the first time and certainly not for the last. Woolley and

CHARLES PARKER

Born at Prestbury, near Cheltenham, on 14 October 1882, Charles Parker first played for Gloucestershire as a fastish, left-armer in 1903 and continued in that method right up to the outbreak of the First World War, the County's slow left-arm requirements being in that period admirably met by George Dennett. In 1919, with Dennett still serving as a commissioned officer in India, Parker switched to slow left-arm, and met with enough success during that season to persevere.

From 1920 to 1936 he never failed to take 100 wickets in a season. On five occasions, in 1922, 1924, 1925, 1926 and 1931, in which year he was rising 49 years of age, he took over 200 wickets. He performed the 'hat-trick' six times—only Doug Wright of Kent has done so more often—and captured in all 3,278 wickets, average 19.46. He was a fierce spinner of the ball and though he bowled a little quicker than most of his type he still

Charlie Parker, pre-eminent among English slow left-armers from 1920 until the arrival of Hedley Verity. (NCCC)

possessed a puzzling flight and was a most destructive bowler, in his most prolific seasons taking a wicket every six or seven overs, a remarkable striking rate.

Astonishingly, he played only once for England, against the Australians in 1921. It is said that his somewhat radical political views, which he was seldom loth to express with all the articulacy of a highly intelligent, self-taught man, may not have endeared him to the powers-that-were in English cricket. If true, this would be very sad, but it must be admitted that he had powerful competition in the 1920s from Rhodes, Woolley, Jack White and Roy Kilner. It would be difficult, though, to argue that at that time any were his superiors purely as a bowler. Whatever the rights and wrongs of it, his greatness is not in doubt. He is remembered, too, as a man whose sometimes crusty exterior could not conceal an essentially kind and helpful nature.

Yorkshire's Roy Kilner were also in the party, and likely to play because of their batting, Woolley being a great batsman and Kilner a very useful one. Had Parker played, there would have been three left-armers in the side, so the selectors, understandably, went for balance and included Yorkshire's off-spinner George Macaulay. That Macaulay was hammered by Macartney, who made 100 before lunch, was not the selectors' fault, though the initial choice of such an odd-shaped party certainly was. Parker was again in the 12 for the fourth Test at Old Trafford and again omitted, this time in favour of Greville Stevens, the Oxford University all-rounder who bowled leg-breaks and googlies. For the final Test Rhodes was recalled, and his bowling had much to do with the victory which regained the Ashes.

Parker was to be recalled once more, for the final Test of the 1930 series against Australia, but was again omitted on the morning of the match. These experiences confirmed Parker's already jaundiced view of the brain power, and indeed honesty, of those responsible for the selection of England teams. It is known that Charlie blamed P. F. Warner for his constant omission. David Foot elicited from Charlie's county colleague, the late Reg Sinfield, an eye-witness account of the incident in the lift of the Grand Hotel, Bristol, following the Gloucestershire dinner of 1929, at which Warner and Parker had both made speeches. In a moment of considerable drama Parker, having been asked by the lift attendant to 'make room for Mr Warner', grasped that eminent gentleman's lapels with his large countryman's hands, and delivered a broadside of invective to the effect that Warner alone had blighted Charlie's Test career. Fortunately no actual blow was struck, though according to Sinfield: 'Mr Warner was white as a sheet.' In the circumstances one can understand Charlie's frustration, but it may also be to Pelham Warner's credit that, with all the influence he wielded in the game, he did not prevent Charlie's name from coming up before the selectors afterwards, as was proved by the Gloucestershire man's ultimately fruitless journey to the Oval the following season. On this occasion the decision to omit Charlie was entirely that of the England captain R. E.S. Wyatt, who confirmed this in print in his book 'Three Straight Sticks', and also in a telephone conversation with David Foot in 1984.

Parker was undoubtedly unfortunate in terms of Test selection, but nonetheless his deeds on the field will speak for his great skill as long as cricket records are kept; certainly, in terms of Gloucestershire cricket between the two wars, he and Hammond are the pre-eminent figures. In 1921 his advance continued, his Championship wickets numbering 156 at an average of 16.54. George Dennett also took 100 wickets, for the last time in his career, and with Dipper getting greater support, particularly from the little left-handed wicket-keeper Harry Smith, who passed 1,000 runs for the first time, the side looked much stronger. Smith, a product of the Frenchay club in Bristol, had first played in 1912 as a batsman and occasional leg-spinner. His wicket-keeping talents developed quickly, and he was good enough to gain Test match recognition, against the West Indies in 1928. He was the second in the line of Gloucestershire keepers which runs as follows: J. H. Board (1891–1914, 1,016 victims), H. Smith (1912–34, 705 victims), A. E. Wilson (1936–55, 585 victims), B. J. Meyer (1957–71, 826 victims) and, after a slight gap, Robert 'Jack' Russell. In this year 12 out of 24 Championship games were won, and the side secured seventh position in the table.

In 1922 they slipped to 13th, the batting, apart from Dipper and Smith, being totally unreliable. Though Parker took 206 wickets in all games, and 195 for the County at 13.17 each, Percy Mills had 90 wickets at 18 and George Dennett 81 at 20.60. With few runs to bowl at, regular defeats were inevitable, 17 championship games out of 28

Percy Mills, an effective medium-pacer and off-spinner between 1902 and 1929. (NCCC)

being lost against seven wins.

In the following season there emerged the cricketer who was to transform the County's batting and with, B. H. Lyon, its fielding also, so that it became equipped, despite the lack of a bowler of any pace right up until 1939, to challenge seriously for the Championship on several occasions.

Walter Reginald Hammond was born on 16 June 1903 in Dover, the son of an Army corporal who served in France throughout the First World War and by 1917 had reached the rank of major. During Walter's father's absence on military duties his mother took the decision to send him to Cirencester Grammar School, feeling that the opportunity to board would provide him with the friendship he was presumably finding it difficult to strike up at Portsmouth Grammar School. Walter arrived at Cirencester Grammar School on 18 April 1918. Less than three weeks later his father was killed in action.

The young Hammond's exploits as a schoolboy cricketer attracted widespread local notice and it was logical that he should be approached by the Gloucestershire Club. He played his first games for the County as an amateur, shortly after leaving school and only a few weeks after his 17th birthday. He made only 27 runs in four innings but even then there was no mistaking the quality of this powerful, beautifully balanced young athlete. He became a professional in 1921, appearing twice against the Australians but scoring only two runs in three innings. From such unpromising beginnings emerged the man who was to be, for an all too brief period, the world's finest batsman. Sir Donald Bradman's arrival a few years later would remove that unquestionable primacy, but there are still those, Sir Leonard Hutton among them, who contend that Hammond was the best player they have seen. In his introduction to Gerald Howat's sensitive biography of Hammond, Sir Leonard says:

> Walter Hammond on all wickets was the finest batsman against whom I played. He could hit the ball as though it had been fired from a gun. He could make spin bowlers on a turning wicket look inept.

He was to be sixth in the all-time list of run-getters with over 50,000 runs, in addition to which he was among the game's very greatest fielders, initially away from the wicket but increasingly at slip and gully, where he took 819 catches. As a bowler, there seems little doubt that he would have aspired to Test match status in that area of the game alone had he so wished. This, however, is to run ahead of the story. In 1921 it was discovered by Lord Harris that Hammond had no birth qualification for Gloucestershire, and he therefore endured two years on the sidelines while this oversight was rectified.

Hammond dropped at slip when 0, Oval test v West Indies, 1933. (NCCC)

His first full season was 1923 and, though regarded as impetuous, he still totalled 1,313 runs in Championship games, averaging just under 30. Mr H. Roslyn, writing on Gloucestershire's season in the 1924 *Wisden*, was in no doubt as to the potential of young Hammond: 'Here we have in all likelihood one of the best professional batsmen of the future. Irreproachable in style and not yet 21 years of age, Hammond has all the world before him, and there is no telling how far he may go.' Prophetic words indeed.

Though Harry Smith, who once again comfortably exceeded 1,000 runs, was picked to play for the Players against the Gentlemen at Lord's—Hammond being picked for the Players in the slightly less prestigious game at the Oval—Gloucestershire were still a side of modest achievement, improving marginally to 11th place. That this was so was no fault of Dipper, who was close to 2,000 runs in the Championship, or to Parker, who once again carried the attack, taking 167 wickets.

It was the old story—Gloucestershire now possessed a nucleus of gifted professionals in Parker, Dipper, Smith and Hammond, supported by Dennett and Mills who were still making useful contributions. That, though, was all they could afford, for membership, which had leapt briefly to 3,000 just after the war, was now little over 1,000 and gates, the golden summer of 1921 apart, had been moderate. In these circumstances a few gifted amateurs were essential but Gloucestershire's unpaid men, though capable of occasional good performances, were not really up to the mark. However great the contribution to the club of D. C. Robinson, F. G. Robinson, P. G. Robinson, P. F. C. Williams and W. H. Rowlands may have been—and very great it was in some areas—the plain fact is that none of them averaged 20 with the bat, and all played as batsmen.

In 1924 the captaincy, which had been in the hands of F. G. Robinson for the first three seasons after the war and of the Old Etonian P. F. C. Williams for the next two, was assumed by Lt Col D. C. Robinson. His first season, a wet one, saw Gloucestershire advance to sixth position, with ten wins out of 28 Championship matches. Dipper was again consistency itself but Hammond was still over-committed to attack before he was set. In consequence his figures were much the same as the previous season's, though something of the controlled majesty to come was foreshadowed in his marvellous 174 not out against Middlesex at Bristol. Parker revelled in the condition, taking 184 wickets at 13.51 in the Championship, Percy Mills had a good season with his off-spinners, taking 81 wickets at 19 apiece, and with Dennett taking 54 wickets the bowling was more satisfactory than the batting. It was a similar story in 1925, though Hammond made a definite advance. He scored 1,571 runs in the Championship and though these runs included only one three-figure score, this was a brilliant 250 not out at Old Trafford. This season Parker took 200 wickets in Championship games alone, and 222 in all games, the second successive season he had passed 200, and the third in four seasons. His greatest support came from Dennett, who took 71 wickets, and Hammond, who bowled mainly medium-fast swingers and captured 61.

In the winter of 1925–26 Hammond was invited to tour the West Indies with F. S. G. Calthorpe's side. It was then that he incurred an infection, possibly as a consequence of a mosquito bite, as a result of which he came close to death. Gerald Howat states that 'for a time his life hung in the balance and surgeons contemplated amputating his leg'. The pleas of his mother that this would end his livelihood spurred the doctors to seek other means of preserving his life and, though so ill that he was to miss the whole of the 1926 season, he eventually made a full recovery. In the winter of 1926–27 he was sent by the County to South Africa, where he built up his strength, and whence he was to return like a giant refreshed.

Hammondless, Gloucestershire finished 15th in 1926. Parker once again exceeded 200 wickets in all matches, a remarkable hat-trick. It is an adequate comment on the standards this extraordinary cricketer had set himself that his 198 Championship wickets at 17.68 apiece could cause H. G. Roslyn to write in *Wisden*'s comments on the County's season that Parker 'had more bad matches than usual'. In fairness, Roslyn had early on pointed out the possibly deleterious effects of the vast amount of work that Charlie was perforce undertaking year after year, and was yearly worried about the consequences of such prodigious over-bowling. Mills had something of an Indian summer, taking 100 wickets for the first time at the age of 43. Though the batting, Dipper and Harry Smith apart, was unreliable there were some good omens. B. H. Lyon, a product of Rugby School who had been awarded cricket blues at Oxford in 1922 and 1923, and had turned out occasionally for the County since 1921, appeared with more regularity and made an excellent impression with his dashing strokeplay and fearless close fielding. F. J. Seabrook, of Haileybury and Cambridge, also made some telling contributions and though, sadly, he was to play less in the future, in him and Lyon the County now had a couple of amateurs who were truly worth their place as players.

A further indication of future success was the performance of the all-rounder Reg Sinfield. A Hertfordshire man, born near Stevenage, he had made his Championship debut against Worcestershire at Cheltenham in July 1925. A solid batsman and an off-spinner who bowled the out-floater and the leg-cutter with great effect, he was a slow developer, but became a cricketer of immense value to the County. He was to perform the 'double' twice, in 1934 and 1937, and his Gloucestershire carer record of 15,561 runs and 1,165 wickets confirms his effectiveness as an all-rounder. These deeds were foreshadowed in that 1926 season when he took 48 wickets, he and Tom Goddard, then in his fast-medium guise, providing the support for Parker and Mills.

In 1927 W. H. Rowlands, whose career stretched back to 1901, took over the captaincy. Though a batsman of modest talents he had scored two centuries for the County, the first in 1902 and the second 19 years later. He was greatly respected by the players for his knowledge and enthusiasm, and this, combined with the improvement in the quality of the players he led, brought about an upward swing in their playing fortunes. This was the first season in which Hammond's performances truly confirmed his greatness as a batsman. In all matches he was only 31 runs short of 3,000, and averaged just over 69, hitting 12 centuries, ten of which were scored in the Championship, the other two being for Gloucestershire against Cambridge University at Bristol and for the Players against the Gentlemen at Folkestone. His greatness as a slip fielder had become apparent in 1925, when he made 65 catches in deadly alliance with Parker. His 1927 tally of 46 was still formidable enough. The batting was stronger than for some time, with Dipper again passing 2,000 runs and Reg Sinfield advancing to make 1,000 runs for the first time, a target also reached by Harry Smith. Billy Neale, who had been at school at Cirencester with Hammond, to whom he was closer personally than most, also improved. He was not to become a professional until 1929 and continued to play until 1948. It was in 1927 that he made his highest score, 145 not out against Hampshire at Southampton. He reached 100 in his next innings against Essex at the Ashley Down Ground, known as Fry's since the sale in 1915.

For once the bowling was the weakest department. Parker was again the leading light, taking 183 Championship wickets at 18.9, but Percy Mills' bag dropped to 64 and Goddard, who had taken 60 wickets at 30 apiece in 1926, took only 24 at 60 runs each. This disastrous season had far-reaching consequences for, having been not surprisingly sacked, Goddard was sent by the County committee at Bev Lyon's instigation to the nets at Lord's to work at converting himself to an off-spinner. This he did with such success that, in an era in which England's selectors rarely considered off-spinners for home Test matches, let alone abroad, he forced himself to their attention by the sheer weight of the wickets he took, and was to play in five Tests in England and three in South Africa on the 1938–39 tour.

After attaining 12th place in 1927, the County advanced further the following year and, in this second year of Harry Rowlands' captaincy they came fifth, winning nine and losing six of their 28 Championship matches. This year was Hammond's greatest as an all-rounder. In all matches he made 2,825 runs at an average of 65 (2,474 in the Championship, including nine centuries, average 82.46), took 84 wickets (63 in the Championship, average 22) and caught 78 catches, still a record number. Against Worcestershire at Cheltenham he produced one of the most remarkable performances ever seen in a first-class match. On an awkward pitch, *Wisden* relates that he 'made the ball turn appreciably and swing through the air' as he took nine for 23 in the visitors' first innings of 35 all out. With the pitch still posing problems he made a majestic 80 and finally, on a surface by now much more benign, took six for 105 to bowl Gloucestershire to an innings victory. In the previous match, also at Cheltenham against Surrey, he had scored a century in each innings and caught ten catches, the latter a record he still holds.

The batting was now looking much more solid. Apart from Hammond's enormous contribution Dipper, to whom the County had owed almost everything in their lean years after the First World War, scored six Championship centuries and averaged only a fraction under 50. Sinfield again passed his 1,000 runs, and some fine forceful innings were played by C. J. Barnett, son of C. S. Barnett, who had played as an amateur each side of the First World War. C. J. had first played for the County in 1927 when still a schoolboy at Wycliffe College. At this time he was something of a hitter, batting down the order, but, being a great thinker about the game, he gradually matured into one of the most formidable opening batsmen the English game has known, harnessing his innate aggression to an excellent technique with such success that, on his day, he could destroy any attack in the world. He was a tall powerful man and when he hit the new ball through and over the field, it flew like 'a driven pheasant downwind'—to purloin a simile I heard H. S. Altham use 30 years ago to describe the drives of K. L. Hutchings.

On the bowling front Parker was again the mainstay, with 143 Championship wickets, though their cost rose to 22 each. Sinfield, with 77 wickets at 25 apiece continued his unspectacular advance but Mills, despite a remarkable analysis of five for 0 against Somerset at Bristol, fell away further and appeared only rarely after 1928. Nonetheless, the County were poised for one of their most exciting periods. Harry Rowlands had done much in his two seasons of captaincy to mould together the pre-war stalwarts—Charlie Parker, Alf Dipper, Harry Smith—with the new men like Wally Hammond and Reg Sinfield, and the amateurs like B. H. Lyon, F. J. Seabrook and C. J. Barnett. It was under the first-named of these amateurs, Bev Lyon, that Gloucestershire were to lift themselves so tantalisingly close to the very summit of English cricket.

BEV LYON AT THE HELM

THOUGH BEVERLEY HAMILTON LYON actually took up the captaincy in 1929 he had acted as Harry Rowlands' deputy when the latter dropped out towards the end of the 1928 season. He was born at Caterham in Surrey on 19 January 1902 and from his very early years there was a strong sibling rivalry between himself and his brother, Malcolm Douglas Lyon, known curiously as 'Dar', who was four years older. Both were educated at Rugby but thereafter their paths diverged. M.D., a batsman-wicket-keeper, went up to Cambridge, where he was awarded blues in 1921 and 1922: B.H., a batsman who bowled a bit, went to Oxford, where he was a blue in 1922 and 1923. M.D. played for Somerset and eventually captained them, so it was, in a sense, inevitable that B.H. should play for Somerset's most deadly rivals, and captain them also.

B.H., who first played for the County in 1921, was in his early days a furious and somewhat uncontrolled hitter, so it is not altogether surprising that it was 1928 before he made his first century. That was against Surrey at the Oval when he and Wally Hammond, who made 205 not out, put on 285 at over 80 runs per hour, Lyon's contribution being 131. Once that first hurdle had been surmounted Lyon harnessed his power with increasing discrimination, though he remained essentially an attacking player. Greater consistency brought its rewards for he was to score three centuries for the County in 1929, four in 1930, and four again in 1934, in which season, when business commitments severely restricted his appearances, he made just over 1,000 runs in only 20 completed innings.

Lyon was from the start a very fine and brave close fielder, whether at slip or at short-leg, in which latter position he contributed greatly to Tom Goddard's success. Most of all, however, he was a brilliant leader, whose instinctive grasp of the game's basic principles did not inhibit a propensity for the inspired and, apparently, illogical move, with which he was to revive many a moribund match. E. W. Swanton has written in his 'History of Cricket' that 'his tactics were so daring and unorthodox that Gloucestershire and their leader soon found themselves surrounded by a glamour rivalling that of Yorkshire'. His greatest hatred was reserved for drawn games, and he would far rather take a great risk of defeat, given the faintest chance of victory, than permit a match to drift away to an inconclusive result. Unfortunately, as we shall see, the points system in operation in the Championship in those days did not wholly favour such an approach, for while eight points were awarded for a win, there were five for achieving first innings lead in a drawn match. There was, therefore, good reason for sides to grind on for first-innings lead and then merely seek to avoid defeat, for a defeated side, even if it had led on the first innings, scored no points. It is no criticism of B. H. Lyon to raise this point, but rather of the system itself. Lyon played cricket as it should be played, rightly paying little heed to a set-up which could offer disproportionate rewards for stodgy play.

Season 1929 may properly be termed a watershed for Gloucestershire, though this is a retrospective judgement. At the time the County's strengths were known to rest almost entirely in the greatness of Hammond, the solidity of Dipper, the maturing all-round skills of Sinfield and the slow left-arm of Parker. True, there was the promise of Charles Barnett, but his maturity lay some years ahead, while Parker, now 46, was showing signs of declining skill, as was only to be expected. As far as Tom Goddard was concerned, nobody really knew what to expect. He had been a very ordinary, fastish bowler; why should he return, after a mere season at the Lord's nets, as a good off-spinner? Certainly he had big hands and long fingers, and at 6 ft 2 in he had plenty of height, but there is more to bowling than mere physique.

In the event Goddard was to jump straight into the very highest bracket of spin-bowlers, taking 154 wickets in the Championship at 15.97 runs each. Parker, who now did not have to work quite so hard, reduced his bowling average by five runs per wicket to 17.33, taking 130 Championship wickets. Sinfield provided useful support, finishing with 63 Championship victims. The batting was certainly adequate with Hammond making 1,730 Championship runs, average 66.53—it is a measure of the expectations that he had so swiftly aroused that *Wisden* reported, rather querulously, that 'his aggregate and average fell away'. Dipper passed 2,000, while Bev Lyon and Sinfield comfortably exceeded 1,000, with Harry Smith not far away. Fifteen matches out of 28 were won, the highest tally of any county, against 14 by Nottinghamshire, the eventual Champions. The fact that Gloucestershire lost six matches, against Nottinghamshire's two for instance, pushed them back into fourth place, though they certainly had their chances of finishing first.

The campaign started poorly for the County, 'Dodger' Whysall's 244 enabling Nottinghamshire to total 396 at Trent Bridge and win by an innings. Sussex won by the enormous margin of 374 runs, Ted Bowley having a *Boys' Own Paper* sort of match, making 74 in Sussex's first innings, 280 not out in the second and then skittling Gloucestershire out in their second innings with six for 31. However, the wins soon began to come and of the first 17 matches played 11 were won against three defeats. An example which may be cited of Lyon's aggressive and inventive approach is the second Middlesex match, which came after second innings centuries by Dipper and Hammond and Goddard's match return of 13 for 120 had earlier earned a handsome victory at Lord's. At Gloucester, in a match badly affected by rain, Lyon declared at 185 for six in the County's first innings, one run ahead of Middlesex, and with Hammond 104 not out. Most people's expectation had been that he would get something of a lead and then hope to bowl Middlesex out cheaply. That, however, was not his way: he wanted constantly to be harrying his opponents. Charlie Parker responded by taking seven for 35 and Gloucestershire, needing 122 to win in two hours, made them in 85 minutes for the loss of two wickets. In the final session, incidentally, with defeat staring them in the face, Middlesex bowled 33 overs, a rate of over 23 per hour! In those slightly more quixotic days it was not necessary to devise laws to prevent the fielding side cheating batsmen of their fair allowance of bowling.

This surge of form took the County to the top of the table, from which perch they were removed when Nottinghamshire came to Bristol and won an intensely exciting match by six runs. Nottinghamshire, having gained a first-innings lead of 51, were bowled out for 116 in their second by Parker, who again took seven for 35. In their turn, Gloucestershire found batting very difficult against Voce and Staples and with only Dipper (43), Lyon (36) and Barnett (41) reaching double figures the task was just too great for them. No team led by Lyon would be likely to fade away because of one reverse, and the County duly clambered to the top again, only for Sussex to beat them at Cheltenham by one run in circumstances very similar to the second Nottinghamshire match. On this occasion Sussex gained a first-innings lead of 49, after which Parker again got amongst the opposition, taking seven for 49. Gloucestershire needed 165 for victory but, despite an immensely valuable 69 from Dipper, were denied again. Had these two narrow defeats been reversed, the County would have more than regained the 13 points by which Nottinghamshire finished ahead of them.

If 1929 constituted a near miss, it was as nothing to 1930 when Gloucestershire finished second to Lancashire. The northern county finished three points ahead despite having won only ten matches to Gloucestershire's 15, the next highest tally of wins being 12 by Kent, who finished fourth. While the previous season's performance had confirmed that Gloucestershire were once more a side to be respected, their success in 1930 was a little startling, for England duties caused Hammond to miss 12 matches, Parker missed nine through injury and Lyon six through business commitments. In the event, despite his injury, the season was a triumph for Charlie Parker, who in only 19

WALTER HAMMOND

Born at Dover on 19 June 1903, Hammond was in his early seasons a beautiful if impetuous stroke-maker whose performances did not always reflect his enormous talents. Nonetheless, so manifest were his gifts that he was picked to tour the West Indies with MCC in 1925–26, where he was struck down by an infection which all but cost him his life. Having missed the 1926 season as a consequence, he emerged in 1927 as a batsman of such mastery that only Sir Jack Hobbs, Sir Len Hutton and Denis Compton of 20th century English players, may be mentioned in the same breath as him.

His 50,551 runs, average 56.10, and his 167 centuries place him in the very top rank of batsmen. He could play any stroke, but maturity brought a discipline which caused him to forego the hook, the short ball being forced back past the bowler with a straight bat. The power and grace of his off- and cover-driving has surely never been surpassed.

Strong, deep-chested and perfectly balanced, Hammond was the supreme athlete. Though a reluctant bowler, he could bowl anything from fast through medium-fast swingers to off-spin and leg-breaks and googlies. A marvellous outfielder in his early days, he became one of the greatest of slip-fielders. His 78 catches in 1928 is still a record. Ask Englishmen who played with or against him 'who was the greatest cricketer of your time?' and, 100 to 1, the answer will be simply 'Wally'. He played in 85 Test matches, scoring 7,249 runs, average 58.45.

Hammond sweeps to leg: balance, control, concentration. (NCCC)

matches captured 162 wickets in the Championship at less than 12 runs each. Never had he bowled more destructively. In Warwickshire's first innings at Cheltenham he took nine for 44, the sixth and last time he would take nine wickets in an innings (he had taken all ten for 79 against Somerset at Bristol in 1921). At Cheltenham he took 16 for 109 against Middlesex and 15 for 91 against Surrey.

There was certainly no talk of fading powers now. Goddard again played his full part, with 131 wickets at under 19 each, and Sinfield had 88 at below 20. Of the batsmen, Hammond's contribution was almost mortal compared with previous seasons. In his 23 completed Championship innings he scored 1,168 runs at an average just over 50, with only three centuries, though he also made an unbeaten double hundred at Oxford and 113 in the third Test against Australia. B. H. Lyon had his best season, averaging over 40 for his 1,355 Championship runs. His four centuries included 115 and 101 not out in the match against Essex at Bristol, his second innings hundred coming up in only an hour and a quarter. Sinfield, reliability itself, again passed his 1,000 while Charles Barnett, who had had a wretched time in 1929, was only a few short of that mark.

An important plus was the arrival of the New Zealand hitter Charles Dacre, who had toured England in 1927 with Tom Lowry's side. Though New Zealand were not a Test match country until 1929, Lowry's side had some pretty useful performers in it, among them Dacre, who began the tour with innings of 101 and 107. Later, playing for New Zealand against Gloucestershire at the Cheltenham Festival, he went in first and scored 64 in half an hour, hitting five sixes. He was persuaded to come and qualify for the County and arrived in 1928. For two seasons he worked with young cricketers at the Nursery at the Fry's ground, first as assistant to Percy Mills, and then as chief coach after Mills had gone to coach at Radley School. Stocky, very strong in the chest and shoulders, and extremely nimble, Dacre hit the ball immensely hard and with complete abandon. He was to play until 1936, during which period he made over 8,000 runs at an average of 28, and scored 16 centuries, most respectable figures for a player so single-mindedly committed to attack.

In 1930 Dacre made almost 1,300 runs in the Championship and averaged 32, a performance which helped to overcome Dipper's fading form. For the first time the years told on this great servant to the Club: his season's figures of 1,071 runs at an average below 25 were his worst since well before the war, and though the side would not seem the same without his solid presence he was too immobile a fielder to be 'carried' if he was not scoring runs. Sadly, his days were numbered.

Gloucestershire started their campaign uncertainly, and were not helped by the fact that their first two matches were against Lancashire, the first at Gloucester, where they were comfortably beaten, and the second at Old Trafford, where they could only draw. However, they once again recovered with commendable spirit under Bev Lyon's dynamic leadership, and were challenging strongly again by early August when business commitments forced Lyon to hand over the captaincy to F. J. Seabrook, which he did with these words: 'We have five matches left and we must try to win them all. We must look for eight points, five are no good to us.' To his credit, Jim Seabrook led the County to victory in four of them, only the rain-affected game against Derbyshire at Chesterfield being drawn. Gloucestershire had won seven out of their last eight Championship matches, collecting 59 points out of a possible 64, but it was not quite enough. It was small consolation to the County to reflect that under almost any other points system that has been used to decide the Championship they would have won in a canter. In any event, the manifest unfairness of the existing set-up prompted a rapid rethink at Lord's and from 1931 there were 15 points for a win rather than 8, with the arrangements for first-innings lead in a drawn game remaining the same.

During this exciting tussle for the Championship the County played one of the most remarkable matches in its history against the Australians, who, having beaten England at the Oval by an innings and 39 runs, had regained the Ashes, which they had lost there in 1926 and which Percy Chapman's side had retained in 1928–29 in Australia. The tourists had evidently not celebrated in too abandoned a manner for, after the start—on Saturday 23 August—had been delayed by heavy rain till 4 pm Victor Richardson put the County in and Grimmett, the slow left-armer Hornibrook and Harwood dismissed them for 72 in 2¼ hours. When play restarted on Monday morning the pitch was still damp, but the Australians did not seem unduly embarrassed. Though Archie Jackson went cheaply Bill Ponsford and the young phenomenon Don Bradman carried them to 78 for one. Then Bradman left for 42, caught by Sinfield off Parker, and though on paper the Australians had plenty of batting left, with Ponsford well set and Kippax, McCabe, Richardson and A'Beckett to follow, their innings fell away. Goddard took five for 52, Parker three for 72, Sinfield snapped up a couple and the Australians led by only 85. At close of play Gloucestershire were 62 runs ahead at 147 for three with Hammond still there on 76.

An estimated 18,000 crammed into the Fry's ground on the Tuesday, the queues stretching far down Nevil Road and Ashley Down Hill. Alas for their hopes, Hammond, who had played a truly marvellous innings, added only 13 more runs before Hornibrook bowled him. Dacre and Harry Smith resisted for a while but Hornibrook bowled Smith and McCabe caught Dacre off Grimmett and the remaining wickets fell with a clatter, Gloucestershire's score of 202 all out meaning that the Australians needed only 118 runs for victory. This did not appear to present too great a problem when Jackson and McCabe gave their side a good start, putting on 59 before they were parted. But 59 for none became 67 for three, and then the veteran Parker, rising 48 years of age, dismissed the 22-year-old Bradman who, in the Test series just ended, had eclipsed Walter Hammond's series record total of 905, set in 1928–29 in Australia, by making 974, and the odds favoured Gloucestershire as their opponents slipped to 86 for seven. Grimmett offered unexpected resistance and the score had crept to 115 before the ninth wicket fell. A leg bye and a single to Hornibrook brought the scores level. Goddard and Parker bowled 14 balls between them without conceding a run in almost indescribable tension. Then Goddard's big fingers spun one into Hornibrook. The ball struck his pad, Goddard's famous appeal boomed out and umpire Buswell's finger was raised. The crowd surged on to the field, acclaiming the Gloucestershire players, and gathered in front of the Pavilion to demand speeches from the two captains. Victor Richardson and Bev Lyon responded suitably, after which, still accompanied by hordes of excited spectators, the Gloucestershire players dashed off to Temple Meads station to catch the train to Swansea. Hammond recalls, in his book 'Cricket my Destiny' how there was '. . . vast confusion . . . the approach to the station, the booking office, the platforms, seethed and thundered with hilarious mobs . . .'

Charlie Parker, who made no secret of his unhappiness at being continually excluded from the England side, must have taken some wry satisfaction from his match figures of ten for 124—seven for 54 in 35 overs in that nerve-tingling second innings, during which Goddard bowled 34.2 overs to take two for 54. From 60 years on, this tied match, the only one the Australians have ever played in England, seems like a sort of compensation for the County's desperate luck in playing such fine cricket throughout the season without carrying off the main prize. Though they were not to come so close again until after the Second World War, they remained a most attractive side, particularly after Charles Barnett had really jumped into the front rank of English players in 1933, and between 1931 and 1939 they only had two poor years.

In 1931 Gloucestershire again finished second, this time to Yorkshire, but this season there was no complaint, the tykes winning 16 Championship matches to Gloucestershire's 11. This was Charlie Parker's last great season, the Championship matches yielding him 205 wickets at 14.44 each, his tally in all games being 219 at 14.26. He was then in his 49th year. Goddard had another thoroughly satisfactory

TOM GODDARD

Born in Gloucester on 1 October 1900, Goddard played for Gloucestershire between 1922 and 1927 as a very ordinary fast bowler. Persuaded by B. H. Lyon to spend a season at the Lord's nets with a view to converting himself into an off-spinner, a role for which, with his height, big hands and long, powerful fingers he was physically suited, he returned to the County in 1929 to take 184 wickets. Thereafter he never failed to take 100 wickets in a season until 1951, when, in his 51st year, he was struck down with pleurisy and appeared only infrequently thereafter.

Four times, in 1935, 1937, 1939 and 1947, he captured over 200 wickets, 1937 being his most prolific year when his bag was 248. Like Charlie Parker, who, sadly, was nearing the end of his career when Goddard—as a spinner—was starting. Tom was an attacking bowler who never considered maiden overs to be of any great importance. A big spinner

Tom Goddard: first, ordinary fast bowler, then off-spinner extraordinary. (NCCC)

of the ball, he looked constantly for the inside edge into the short-legs, or the batsman's pads in front of the wicket, in which latter case his bass-baritone roar 'How wuz 'er?' would echo round the ground. His striking rate in some seasons was stupendous. In 1937 he took a wicket every six overs and in 1939, allowance having been made for the fact that eight-ball overs were used that year—every $5\frac{1}{2}$ overs. Only Wilfred Rhodes, Tich Freeman, Parker and J. T. Hearne have exceeded his total of 2,979 wickets and he shares with Parker the distinction of having achieved six hat-tricks, one fewer than Doug Wright, whose seven are unique.

Harry Smith and 'Dick' Stephens going out to bat at the County Ground, Bristol. (GCCC)

year, with 122 Championship wickets at 18.22, but Sinfield, curiously, was used little, despite his success in 1930, and no bowler apart from Parker and Goddard took 40 wickets. Hammond again headed the batting but though he hit five centuries his average dropped below 50. Dacre again played some splendid forcing innings, hitting four centuries and scoring almost 1,400 runs for the County and Harry Smith, Sinfield and Neale all made useful runs. Dipper fell away further, again averaging below 25.

With the Championship race virtually a one-horse one, with Yorkshire out front and the rest nowhere, it was interesting to see the shifts and stratagems to which Lyon resorted in an attempt to keep Gloucestershire somewhere in the hunt. In these days, when contrived declarations are commonplace, indeed actively encouraged, one's eyebrows do not shoot into one's hair at Lyon's deeds; but then, and for many years after, collusion between the two captains was not allowed, so that the challenging gesture of declaring a hatful of runs behind could well rebound if the opposing captain would not play ball. Fortunately for Bev Lyon, one or two would and when, after rain had badly interfered with the Surrey match at the Oval, Lyon declared 83 runs behind on first innings with just over three hours to go Percy Fender picked up the gauntlet. Surrey had a quick slog and left Gloucestershire 110 minutes to make 144 on a pitch now helping bowlers. Hammond and Charlie Dacre, by a mixture of slog and tip and run, ensured that they got there, but it was only in the final over that they succeeded. Moreover, seven wickets had been lost and both Hammond and Dacre had been missed in the field.

Later on in a very wet season the match with Yorkshire at Sheffield never looked like starting at any time on the first two days. According to Walter Hammond's account Bev Lyon spent most of this time rummaging through the laws of the game, after which, before play started on the third day, he went to the Yorkshire captain, Frank Greenwood, with a proposition. Lyon suggested that, in order that the two teams should play for 15 points rather than for the 8 available for a match played on a first-innings basis—which was what they seemed condemned to—each side should bowl four wides and then declare, thereby getting the first innings out of the way. Greenwood agreed that there was nothing in the laws against this and consented to take part. He won the toss and, after the farcical bowling of four wides per side the real contest got under way. Frank Greenwood must have been happy enough when Hedley Verity, making a tremendous impact in this, his first full season, took seven for 64 as Gloucestershire were bowled out for 171. However, with $2\frac{1}{2}$ hours to get the runs Yorkshire struggled throughout against Goddard, who took five for 21, and were bowled out for 124. This was the only defeat suffered by that very powerful Yorkshire side during 1931, so there can be no doubt that they fully deserved the title. Lyon's ploy alerted the legal men of the MCC, and the loophole he had exploited was blocked up for 1932.

The years from 1928 to 1931 were among the most successful, in playing terms, in the Club's history. Successive Championship positions of fifth, fourth, second and second had been achieved and the side, first under Harry Rowlands' kindly hand and then under the restless, inventive Bev Lyon, had played excellent cricket. If the next eight seasons are not quite so successful, they still contain the maturing, truly majestic Walter Hammond, the flashing blade of Charles Barnett (the 'Guv'nor' to his fellow players), the fiercely spun off-breaks and stentorian appeal of Tom Goddard and, a little later in the decade, the men who were to help to carry the side through to the 1950s, Andy Wilson, Jack Crapp, George Emmett, George Lambert and Colin Scott.

In 1932 Gloucestershire declined to 13th in the Championship for reasons not all that easy to discern, except that Bev Lyon was prevented by business commitments from playing in more than nine matches. The batting was at least as effective as in 1931, perhaps more so, if only because Hammond's Championship runs increased from under 1,400 to over 2,000, his average from 46 to 62, and his tally of centuries from three to six, which included an innings of 264 against Lancashire at Liverpool. Dacre, Sinfield and Neale all did pretty well, but Harry Smith fell ill with heart problems, and his batting was missed, as well as his wicket-keeping. Indeed, though Smith eventually recovered sufficiently to play again in 1935 the wicket-keeping position was not satisfactorily filled until the arrival of Andy Wilson from Middlesex in 1936, or strictly speaking, 1938 for he had to qualify by residence for two years before he could appear in the Championship. Meanwhile the wicket-keeping gloves passed between Bernie Bloodworth, who had been engaged in 1919 as a batsman, Bert Watkins, professional and groundsman at the Gloucester Club, P. I. V. van der Gucht and, later Vic Hopkins of Dumbleton.

The bowling remained much as in the previous year: Parker's bag was smaller, 128 Championship wickets at 21 each, but Goddard advanced to 159 at 19 each, significant progress, and from now on it was to him rather than the ageing Parker that Gloucestershire looked when pitches were taking spin. Hammond, for this season officially appointed Bev Lyon's vice-captain, bowled more than for some years, taking 46 Championship wickets.

In this season appeared two young amateur batsmen in Grahame Parker and Basil Allen who were in their different ways to contribute greatly to the Club's well-being in the future. Grahame Parker, a product of the Crypt School, Gloucester, was to win his blue at Cambridge in 1934 and captained the side the following season. Meanwhile he made irregular appearances for the County as a batsman who also bowled medium pace, and did not make his last appearance for them until 1951. A very talented games player, Parker won rugby blues in 1932, 1933, 1934 and 1935, and, as a member of the famous Gloucester Club, was twice capped by England at full-back in 1938. He was later to become Gloucestershire's first secretary-manager, a post he held from 1968 to 1976, and later still the president.

Basil Allen, a Cambridge blue in 1933, became a most effective left-handed batsman, as his final tally of 13,265 runs for Gloucestershire and batting average of almost 30 amply demonstrate. He was to have two spells as County captain, the first in 1937 and 1938, after which he made way for Hammond, who had changed status from professional to amateur in November 1937. When Hammond was chosen to captain England in the 1938 home series against Australia it seemed logical for his County captain to stand down in favour of him. After the war Allen captained the side for a further four seasons, selflessly shouldering the burden from 1947 to 1950 after Hammond had announced his retirement from first-class cricket at the end of England's tour of Australia in 1946–47. He too, was president of the Club, in 1979 and 1980.

Hammond did not really enjoy his first taste of captaincy, which was thrust upon him in 1932 because of Bev Lyon's long absences. It was not an easy matter to succeed a man like Lyon. As Hammond himself said: 'The breath-taking risks he had taken, and won so many victories with, were not for any beginning in the art of captaincy to take.' There was muted disappointment in H. E. Roslyn's *Wisden* comments on Gloucestershire cricket for that year that Hammond had sometimes let matters slip in the field, and also that, compared with Lyon anyway, his approach was rather cautious. There was, though, no questioning his cricket brain, and no feeling that he would not, with experience, become a fine captain, particularly if given charge of a reasonably strong side. He did have problems in 1932, though one felt that Lyon might have found ways round them. Apart from anything else the batting depended too much on Hammond himself, as it had since 1929, Dipper's last really productive year. Season 1932 was to be Dipper's last, and it was good to see him average above 30 again, even though he finished well short of 1,000 runs.

Gloucestershire's debt to Alf Dipper cannot be overestimated. He virtually carried the County's batting from 1919 to the arrival of Hammond, whose invaluable lieutenant he then became. Some were deceived by an awkwardness of style and movement that was more apparent than real into thinking Dipper untalented, but this was far from the case, for he had a wide range of strokes and was a notably deft placer of the ball, particularly on the on-side. He had, too, a marvellous defensive technique, and carried his bat through a Gloucestershire innings 11 times, two more than W.G., his nearest rival. A final run tally of over 28,000 runs, a career average of 35,53 centuries, 2,000 runs in a season five times and 1,000 in another ten, all add up to a pretty formidable player. Having left the playing side of the game to be a first-class umpire, he was greatly missed by his team-mates for his solidity and dependability.

The County finished 13th in 1932, a disappointment after their successes over the previous four years, but there was to be an improvement later in the decade as new talents forced their way forward. Before passing on to those events, however, the tangled saga of the Ashley Down Ground, which had been sold to Fry's in 1915 and had borne their name ever since, needs to be examined. Fry's had paid £10,000 for the ground, which had been used to the full by their employees for rugby, cricket, hockey, athletics, cycling, and so on. The County, however, during the course of this secession, possessed no ground of their own and therefore had no capital asset to develop or against which they could borrow in those times of financial pressure with which they were so depressingly familiar. The repurchase was not easy, for the County had to launch a special appeal fund in addition to the issuing of debentures at $3\frac{1}{2}$ per cent. The appeal, which caused Hammond to delay his benefit until 1934, raised nearly £4,300, and the debentures another £10,500, but with the annual losses increasing—even the great years from 1928 to 1931 had not brought prosperity—further appeals soon became necessary. An annual loss of £1,656 in 1931 soared to £3,691 in 1933 and £3,327 in 1934. A second special appeal, designed to raise £13,000 in 1935, fell some £3,000 short of its target. So the County's financial difficulties, though reduced by these manoeuvres, remained. At their root lay the pitifully low level of membership, which, despite the best efforts of successive committees, dogs the County to this day. Though in the euphoric days of peace after 1918 numbers briefly ran to around 3,000 they dropped swiftly thereafter. It is extraordinary to consider that during Hammond's prime, and Dipper's and Charlie Parker's and Sinfield's and Goddard's and Charles Barnett's, Gloucestershire's members rarely numbered much above 1,000.

In any event, the ground was sold back to the Club on 4 April 1933, just before the start of a season in which the County moved up slightly to tenth place, winning ten Championship games and losing 13. Bev Lyon played in 26 of the 28 matches, and there can be little doubt that his presence contributed to the improvement. Hammond was again in tremendous form, scoring 2,578 runs in the Championship at an average of 65 and hitting 11 centuries in all matches, including 264 for Gloucestershire against the West Indies at Bristol, 231 against Derbyshire at Cheltenham and 206 at Leicester. In all matches he made 3,323 runs, exceeding 3,000 for the first time. He also broke W.G.'s record for the highest number of runs in a season by a Gloucestershire player, 2,739, which the Champion had set in 1871.

The major bonus on the batting front, though, was the form of Charles Barnett who, at the age of 23, showed the form of which good judges had always deemed him capable. For Gloucestershire alone he scored 2,161 runs, average 41.55, and by the quality of his play forced himself into the England side for the Oval Test against the West Indies where he made 52 not out, batting at number 8. On the occasions when Lyon sent Dacre in to open the innings with Barnett the results could be explosive, as during this very season at Worcester when the pair were 196 for no wicket at lunch on the first day. Both made centuries, with Dacre getting another in the second innings. As

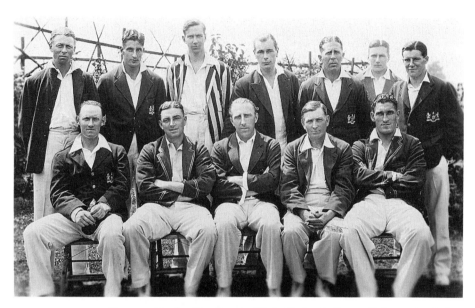

The 1933 side. Standing (l to r): W. L. Neale, A. Rogers, P. I. van der Gucht, D. A. C. Page, C. C. Dacre, C. J. Barnett, E. J. Stephens. Seated: R. Sinfield, W. R. Hammond, B. H. Lyon, C. W. L. Parker, T. W. Goddard. (NCCC)

Hammond also made centuries in each innings, it is a fair bet that the Worcestershire fielders had sore hands long before the end of the match!

The bowling this season rested largely with Goddard, who responded with 183 wickets at 17.41. Parker by now was becoming expensive; his control, now that he was into his 50s, was not always complete and though he took 117 wickets they were at a cost exceeding 30 runs each. Sinfield, given more bowling, took 65 wickets, but Gloucestershire certainly lacked, as they had since the days of Fred Roberts, an effective fast bowler.

The County improved further to seventh in 1934, despite Wally Hammond missing 13 out of 28 matches through Test calls and other duties, Goddard missing seven with broken fingers and Lyon, in his final season as captain, able to play in less than half the matches. That Gloucestershire won 12 matches was due more to their batting than their bowling, for Goddard's 119 Championship wickets cost him almost 24 each, Parker's 108 cost 32, while Sinfield, taking 100 wickets for the first time and also completing the 'double', paid nearly 23 each for his 119. Against these comparatively modest performances the batting was very brilliant. In his 20 Championship innings Hammond made 2,020 runs at an average of 126.25, and hit eight centuries of which one, 302 not out against Glamorgan at Bristol, was a triple, with

CHARLES BARNETT

Born in Cheltenham on 3 July 1910, Charles Barnett was the son of C. S. Barnett who played for the County between 1904 and 1926. Charles was educated at Wycliffe College and was still a pupil there when he made his debut as an amateur. In his early days an impatient player, he took some time to mature. His first 1,000 run season for the County did not come till 1930 and he did not fully reveal his quality until 1933 when he made well over 2,000 runs and was selected for England against the West Indies.

By this time he was opening the innings, the responsibility of doing so giving his game a new discipline without reducing the variety and power of his strokes. He played in 20 Test matches between 1933 and 1948 at the end of which latter year he abruptly left Gloucestershire to play as a professional for Rochdale in the Central Lancashire League. He made Test centuries against Australia at Adelaide in 1936–37 and at Trent Bridge in 1938. So conscious were the Australian selectors of Barnett's ability to 'destroy' bowlers that they were known to delay their own choice until they had discovered whether Barnett would be playing for the opposition. A splendid outfielder, he was also a very useful medium paced inswing bowler and took over 400 wickets. In all first-class cricket he scored 25,389 runs, average 32.71, and hit 48 centuries.

Charles Barnett, patrician opening batsman. (NCCC)

Gloucestershire take the field against Yorkshire at Scarborough, 1934. L to r: Dacre (wicket-keeper), Goddard, Sinfield, B. H. Lyon, D. N. Moore, Neale. Gloucestershire won by nine wickets. (NCCC)

three others over 200. Barnett scored almost 2,300 runs for the County, averaging nearly 46, Lyon in his irregular appearances made 1,000 runs, averaging 50, and Sinfield, Dacre, Neale and Basil Allen all batted effectively.

The season was notable for the County's double over Yorkshire, the first time this had been achieved since 1874. This was a great feat, for at the time Yorkshire, under A. B. Sellers, were as strong as they have ever been. In the nine seasons between 1931 and 1939 they failed to win the title only twice, in 1934 when they were fifth and in 1936, when they were third. Both the defeats inflicted on them by Gloucestershire in 1934 were by the very comfortable margin of nine wickets. At Scarborough, after Gloucestershire had batted consistently to make 348, Goddard, Sinfield and Charlie Parker bowled Yorkshire out for 143. Following on, Yorkshire fared better, making 262 but with the County needing only 58 for victory the rest was a formality. At Bristol Gloucestershire, again without Hammond, also lacked the services of the injured Goddard, but the off-spinner's deputy Monty Cranfield came in to take five for 58, Sinfield's five for 80 completing Yorkshire's dismissal for 247, of which Arthur Mitchell made a typically adhesive 90. The County responded with 358, of which Dallas Page, son of H. V. Page who had played alongside W.G., made 90, Sinfield 70 and Barnett a robust 58. Sinfield (four for 61) and Parker (five for 88) cut down Yorkshire in their second innings for only 190 and once more Gloucestershire knocked off the required runs without difficulty.

WAR INTERRUPTS AN UPWARD SURGE

UNDER THE CAPTAINCY OF DALLAS PAGE who, at the tender age of 23 was very much feeling his way, 1935 was a bleak year. Only six matches out of 30 were won in the Championship, though the touring South Africans were defeated at Bristol by 37 runs. Goddard had a fine season, taking 200 wickets in all matches for the first time, while Charlie Parker again took 100 wickets and at reduced cost. Hammond, inevitably, led the batting, followed by Sinfield, who exceeded 1,500 runs. Barnett fell away, his aggregate dropping to 1,354 and his average to 25 but there was modest compensation in the form of E. J. 'Dick' Stephens, a left-handed bat and fine fielder from Gloucester. Stephens had first appeared in 1927, and was to drop out at the end of the 1937 season. During that period he made only 4,593 runs at an average below 18, so 1935, when he made 1,134 and averaged 28, was by some way his most successful year.

At the end of the 1935 season Charlie Parker finished playing. In a career stretching back to 1903 he had taken 3,170 wickets for the County, and the amount of recognition his talent gained him elsewhere can be gauged by the fact that he only had the opportunity to take 108 in addition to his Gloucestershire ones. His career average of 19.46 indicates a very high quality bowler: in fact, as we have seen, he only became a slow left-arm bowler after the First World War, prior to which his 454 wickets, taken when bowling at a brisk pace, had been comparatively expensive at over 25 runs each. Purely as a slow bowler he took over 2,800 wickets at less than $18\frac{1}{2}$ runs each. he took 100 wickets 16 times in succession, from 1920 to 1935. On five occasions he exceeded 200, a tally which only Tich Freeman has bettered. Only Doug Wright exceeded his six hat-tricks, only Tom Goddard equalled it. Only Rhodes and Freeman took more wickets than Parker did. He followed his former Tewkesbury team-mate Alf Dipper on to the first-class umpires list, but returned to the County as coach after the Second World War before becoming cricket coach at Cranleigh.

He had the reputation of being a difficult man, and this is a reason sometimes advanced to explain why he played in only one Test match. Those who knew him do not bear out this view. Bob Wyatt, who captained him more than once, says he was 'quick-tempered, but not difficult'. Anyone who has played competitive sport will recognise that there is a world of difference between the two. Grahame Parker has recalled how, when he dropped a catch off his illustrious namesake, he received first a furious glare and then, a few moments later, a wry grin. Andy Wilson and Ken Graveney, both of whom he coached, remember him as patient and very knowledgeable, provided he felt he was 'getting through'. Idlers, or people who would not listen, he had no time at all for. One thing can be said about him: whatever the England selectors did or didn't do during Charlie Parker's career it is certain that, in the pantheon of the English game, he has a niche among the very greatest.

Charlie Parker's retirement left a great gap in the fabric of Gloucestershire cricket, but, such are the ironies of this curious game that, with only two bowlers to speak of, they finished fourth in the table in 1936, an advance of 11 places. The loss of Parker was covered simply enough, by doubling the work done by Reg Sinfield, whose Championship tally of wickets leapt from 77 to 146 while his average dropped from 23 to just over 19. Both he and Goddard topped 150 wickets in all Gloucestershire matches, but the new ball bowling was, as for so long, somewhat makeshift. However, with Barnett back in full form with nearly 2,000 runs for the County at an average of 40, and with Hammond averaging just under 50 in the 30 or so innings that his Test commitments permitted, the batting was solid enough, particularly as Billy Neale reached his 1,000 runs in company with a newcomer, J. F. 'Jack' Crapp, a Cornishman from St Columb Major. The prime reason for the County's advance, though, was the performance of Dallas Page as captain. After an uncomfortable first season at the helm, Page was finding his feet and gaining respect from his team and from his opponents. His death in a car crash immediately following the last match of the season, in which Gloucestershire defeated Nottinghamshire at Gloucester in Tom Goddard's benefit match, was a great tragedy. I am grateful for Grahame Parker's earlier history of the county for an account of this match.

In those days, as Mr Parker reminds us, before the high-powered promotion of players' benefits whereby income accrues from sources far removed from cricket, a beneficiary relied almost totally on gate receipts for his reward for service and it was therefore important that the match lasted three days. Beneficiaries were terrified of bad weather, which would prevent any sort of a crowd turning up, and also of early finishes, such that which Albert Trott of Australia and Middlesex engineered in his own benefit match against Somerset at Lord's in 1907. In that match Trott took four wickets with consecutive balls and later in the same innings performed a hat-trick, thereby, as a contemporary commentator said, 'bowling himself into the bankruptcy court'. In Goddard's benefit match, he, Sinfield and Monty Cranfield bowled Nottinghamshire out cheaply on the first day and Goddard looked anxious as Gloucestershire lost two early wickets and

Hammond prepared to go out to bat on a pitch taking spin generously. Had he been dismissed on the first day the effects on the second day's receipts could have been catastrophic. In Grahame Parker's words: 'as he moved away he turned to Tom Goddard and said "Don't worry, I will bat all day Monday!"' Such statements can only be supported by genius. True to his word Hammond made 317 in $6\frac{1}{2}$ hours, another huge crowd turned up on the third day, and Tom Goddard banked the highly satisfactory sum of £2,090; and, moreover, Gloucestershire won the match by an innings and 70 runs.

After triumph came tragedy. Dallas Page, driving home to his home in Cirencester, collided with a motor cyclist and drove into a stone wall. Apparently none the worse for wear, he went to the Cirencester Memorial Hospital for a check-up. It transpired that internal damage to his body was very great, and he died early the following morning.

Turning aside from that sad loss, it is time to look at the emerging younger players who were to take the County deep into the 1950s. Andy Wilson's arrival from Lord's has already been noted. He had joined the ground staff with George Emmett, who had been born in India where his father was serving. Andy Wilson and George Emmett came to Gloucestershire together in 1936. Both had to qualify for two years, but were able to play in non-Championship matches during that period. Wilson, who had played a few matches for Middlesex but was doubtful of his chances of ousting their regular wicket-keeper, Fred Price, made an immediate impression at Gloucestershire with his safe hands and determined left-hand batting which was to earn him his 1,000 runs on six occasions. George Emmett, who had been signed originally as a replacement for Charlie Parker, bowled regularly only in his first Championship season. However, his batting, which was at times quite dazzling in its wristiness and fluency, was to develop to the extent that he became an England player.

Jack Crapp, whose family had moved up from Cornwall to Bristol when he was nine years old, did not have to qualify by residence as did Emmett and Wilson. He came straight into the side in 1936 and was immediately successful, the transition from club cricket with local cricket club Stapleton presenting him with few problems. He passed his 1,000 runs that first season, as in each up to the Second World War; he had a particularly productive season in 1938, but the years of his plenty, as with Emmett, were after 1945.

In 1937 Basil Allen led the County once more into fourth position, this being the result of batting that was always reliable and often brilliant, and bowling which, though resting almost entirely with the twin prongs of Tom Goddard and Reg Sinfield, was so successful that 15 matches out of 30 were won. This was arguably Goddard's greatest

GLOUCESTERSHIRE *v*
NOTTINGHAMSHIRE

Played at Gloucester (T. W. Goddard's Benefit Match) 29 and 31 August, 1 September 1936

NOTTINGHAMSHIRE	FIRST INNINGS		SECOND INNINGS	
W. W. Keeton	b Stephens	35	lbw b Cranfield	20
C. Harris	b Hammond	6	c sub b Stephens	50
W. Walker	c Barnett b Goddard	6	b Cranfield	9
J. Hardstaff	c Hopkins b Stephens	46	b Cranfield	0
G. V. Gunn	b Goddard	5	b Goddard	12
A. Staples	c Goddard b Cranfield	58	cAllen b Cranfield	52
*Mr G. F. H. Heane	c Page b Cranfield	11	c Barnett b Stephens	18
W. Voce	b Cranfield	25	b Barnett	23
F. G. Woodhead	not out	6	c Stephens b Barnett	0
†A. B. Wheat	c Stephens b Goddard	1	c Page b Barnett	24
H. J. Butler	lbw b Goddard	0	not out	3
Extras	lb 1	1	b 3, lb 1	4
Total		200		215

1st inns: 1-29, 2-43, 3-49, 4-66, 5-142, 6-163, 7-182, 8-193, 9-196
2nd inns: 1-25, 2-43, 3-43, 4-64, 5-136, 6-154, 7-166, 8-167, 9-

BOWLING	O	M	R	W	O	M	R	W
Hammond	7	0	21	1				
Barnett	13	3	51	0	11.3	2	25	3
Goddard	28.1	9	49	4	25	6	71	1
Stephens	11	0	27	2	8	1	32	2
Cranfield	23	6	51	3	33	11	71	4
Haynes					6	1	12	0

GLOUCESTERSHIRE	FIRST INNINGS		SECOND INNINGS
C. J. Barnett	b Voce	2	
R. W. Haynes	c Staples b Voce	18	
Mr B. O. Allen	c Staples b Butler	18	
W. R. Hammond	b Woodhead	317	
W. L. Neale	c Heane b Butler	66	
J. F. Crapp	c Woodhead b Gunn	22	
Mr D. A. C. Page	lbw b Heane	8	
E. J. Stephens	b Voce	0	
T. W. Goddard	b Heane	1	
V. J. Hopkins	not out	25	
M. Cranfield	c Wheat b Staples	0	
Extras	b 6, lb 1, nb 1	8	
Total		485	

1st inns: 1-2, 2-3, 3-75, 4-239, 5-322, 6-345, 7-346, 8-351, 9-484

BOWLING	O	M	R	W	O	M	R	W
Voce	31	2	117	3				
Butler	31	5	79	2				
Woodhead	24	3	86	1				
Staples	17.4	2	69	1				
Gunn	19	3	53	1				
Heane	28	5	73	2				

Umpires: W. A. Buswell and G. Brown

season, for he took 248 wickets in all, 215 of them in the Championship at 16 apiece, including all 10 for 113 against Worcestershire at Cheltenham, and 16 for 181 in the match. Sinfield took 129 wickets at just under 23 and also completed the 'double' for the second time. In all matches Hammond topped 3,000 runs for the second time—he had performed the feat in 1933 and was to repeat it in 1939—and his batting in the Championship was once more prolific and consistent, producing 2,353 runs at an average of 66. Barnett, close to 2,000 runs in the Championship alone, and with almost 2,500 in all matches, had another splendid season. Allen made almost 1,700 runs, averaging 31. Crapp's aggregate, though not his average, increased, and Grahame Parker, though his Championship innings numbered only 15, made three centuries, the highest 210 against Kent at Dover.

The drop to tenth place in 1938 was accounted for by Goddard's season which was, by his own exalted standards, not a productive one. His Championship victims dropped in number to 107, and their cost increased to almost 23. Goddard had a tendency at times to push the ball through too quickly, a legacy doubtless of his fast-bowling days, and in his efforts to overcome the problem could find length and full control elusive. The cost of Sinfield's wickets increased and Emmett's slow left-arm bowling, though providing welcome variety, was expensive, his 43 wickets costing 36 each.

At last, however, a fast bowler had appeared in Colin Scott, a fair-haired, athletic outswing bowler from W.G.'s village, Downend. H. E. Roslyn, writing in *Wisden*, was not deceived by Scott's modest early results: 'Although Scott's record was not impressive, his fine action, height and youth suggested he would do well in the near future.'

The batting remained as strong as that of any side in the country, with seven men passing 1,000 runs in Championship matches alone. Hammond was at his majestic peak, averaging 84 in the Championship and hitting 13 centuries in only 28 visits to the crease. Jack Crapp advanced, in terms of runs to nearly 1,700 and average to 38, and Barnett and Allen had very satisfactory seasons. Billy Neale had his

---

Thanks to Hammond the county finished the season in great style. He was in really wonderful form and, putting together an innings of 317, beat his previous best score in England and surpassed the aggregate of 1,278 runs in August set up by W. G. Grace. Hammond's mastery of the Nottinghamshire bowlers and his phenomenal powers of endurance were shown by the fact that after batting five hours for his first 200 runs he hit the third hundred in just over 70 minutes. In his last stage he cast aside all restraint and exploited his superb off-drive in devasting fashion. Altogether, Hammond batted close on six and a half hours and in all that time made one false stroke. That occurred at 111 when he almost played on. He hit three 6s and 34 4s. Neale, Crapp and Hopkins aided him admirably in stands of 164, 83 and 133 respectively. Staples proved Nottinghamshire's best batsman. Hardstaff in the first innings supported him in a partnership of 76, and Harris and Staples scored 71 together on the last day when Hammond, owing to a badly bruised instep, could not play. The second day's attendance of 7,000 was the largest ever seen on the ground.

Andy Wilson, an immensely valuable wicket-keeper batsman. (GCCC)

best year, making just under 1,500 runs, and Andy Wilson and George Emmett both made over 1,000 runs in their first full season.

Hammond had, as we have seen, captained England against Australia in the 1938 series while playing under Basil Allen for the County. In 1939 Hammond took over the Gloucestershire captaincy also. So successful were Gloucestershire in that last season before the Second World War that one cannot help wondering how they might have developed in the six lost seasons between 1940 and 1945. Goddard returned emphatically to his best, taking 181 Championship wickets at 14.66 each, and he was still only 38. Hammond too was in his prime at 35, acknowledged as the best player in the world apart from the phenomenal Don Bradman. Crapp and Emmett were young batsmen of obvious class, destined surely for higher honours. Barnett, though 1939 was a poor year for him, was one of the most formidable opening batsmen in the game who, only the previous season in the Trent Bridge Test, had taken his lunch at 99 not out, and had reached his century off the first ball bowled after the interval, and he was only 29.

At last, the County had now found a pair of opening bowlers. That

Jack Crapp: powerful left-hand bat; seven Test caps. (GCCC)

season of 1939 the 20-year-old Scott took 113 wickets in the Championship, averaging just over 22. His partner, the Paddington-born George Lambert, also 20, who had arrived by way of the Lord's ground staff and had had to qualify for two years, took 68 wickets in the competition at 26 each. Though lacking Scott's cleverness as a bowler Lambert was strong and persistent, and provided an ideal foil. Reg Sinfield, who had played in his solitary Test match against the Australians during the previous season, under Hammond and alongside Barnett, could still bowl a bit, as his 56 Championship wickets showed.

The side finished third in the table, winning 18 and losing seven of their games. There was general admiration for the tactical shrewdness of Hammond's captaincy. Carpers said that he did not have Bev Lyon's flair, but then, how many captains in the game's long history have had that? Though Yorkshire carried off the title, the County had the satisfaction of once more completing the 'double' over them, the first time Yorkshire had suffered thus since Gloucestershire beat them twice in 1934. At Bradford Leyland's first-innings century earned Yorkshire a lead of 26, despite Hammond's masterly 75. Brian Sellers,

85

positive as ever, ordered a second-innings slog after rain had interfered, his declaration at 162 for seven setting Gloucestershire to make 189 for victory in two hours and ten minutes. Barnett hit 90 in an hour, with four sixes and eight fours, and the runs were knocked off in 95 minutes. In the return game at Bristol Yorkshire were bowled out for 176, Goddard taking six for 61, but the awkwardness of the pitch was demonstrated as Hedley Verity took seven for 47 to earn his side a lead of eight runs. Goddard responded by taking seven for 38 after which Basil Allen saw Gloucestershire home by six wickets with a violent innings of 56, the only half-century of the match. *Wisden* records that 'a cheering crowd would not disperse till Hammond gave a short speech'.

This, then, was Gloucestershire in 1939, a powerful, confident side with the potential, in Jack Crapp, George Emmett, Andy Wilson,

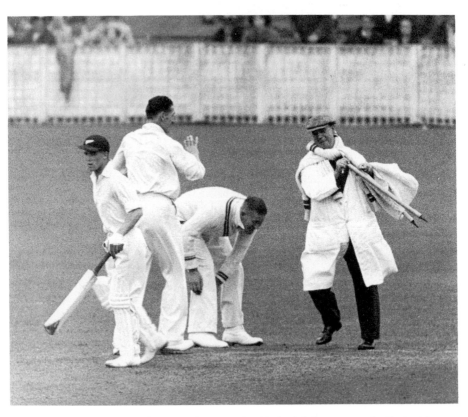

The end of the Second Test v New Zealand, July 1937, won by England by 130 runs. The batsman is Martin Donnelly. Bowler Goddard and fielder Jim Smith of Middlesex, seeking souvenir stumps, are foiled by umpire 'Tiger' Smith. (NCCC)

The 1939 side. Standing (l to r): B. Bloodworth (scorer), V. Hopkins, C. J. Scott, Col. H. Henson (secretary), G. Lambert, J. F. Crapp, A. H. Mills. Seated: G. Emmett, C. J. Barnett, W. R. Hammond, T. W. Goddard, W. L. Neale, A. E. Wilson. (GCCC)

Colin Scott and George Lambert, to develop and improve. With them, as with the other counties, some careers were to be blighted utterly by the loss of six years: others would pick up threads without apparent problems, but even for them, nothing would ever be quite the same.

HAMMOND AND GODDARD RETIRE

DURING THE SECOND WORLD WAR Gloucestershire County Cricket Club was run by an emergency committee chaired by F. O. Wills, of the great tobacco dynasty, which kept the Club's affairs ticking over, in contrast to the period of the First World War, during which Gloucestershire was virtually wound up, and had to be revived from a condition of total inertia at the cessation of hostilities. Between 1939 and 1945 the ground was used by the armed forces, including the Americans, for recreational purposes. A good deal of cricket was played, both locally and at a national level. In the latter matches the former Pilot Officer Hammond, now Squadron Leader, who in common with many cricketers had been involved in physical training, and served in Egypt and South Africa as well as in England, took a prominent part.

During 1944 a series of one-day matches took place at Lord's between England, Australia (in fact, the RAAF), the West Indies, the Rest of the World and the Dominions. Crowds of up to 30,000 attended, and large sums were raised for various charities. In 1945 a series of five 'Victory' Tests was arranged against Australia, in the second of which, at Bramall Lane, Hammond's century was the decisive factor on turning pitch.

When Gloucestershire players reported for duty at the County Ground in the April of 1946 there was a nucleus of tested players. The older generation consisted of Hammond himself, Tom Goddard, Billy Neale and Charles Barnett, all of whom began their careers in the 1920s, and the younger consisted of Basil Allen, Jack Crapp, George Emmett, Andy Wilson, Colin Scott and George Lambert, of whom the two last-named had just turned 20 when war broke out. Reg

Wally Hammond in Pilot Officer's uniform at the start of the Second World War. He was later promoted to Squadron Leader. (GCCC)

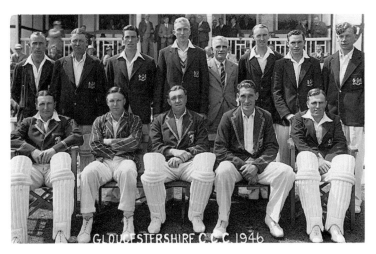

The 1946 side. Standing (l to r): C. Cook, W. L. Neale, G. Lambert, C. J. Scott, B. Bloodworth (scorer), A. G. S. Wilcox, V. Hopkins, L. M. Cranfield. Seated: C. J. Barnett, B. O. Allen, W. R. Hammond, T. W. Goddard, A. E. Wilson. (NCCC)

Sinfield, who was by then 45 but might have had a season or two left in him, had moved on to become cricket coach at Clifton College, where he was to exercise a shrewd and benign influence for many years. However, there was Monty Cranfield, who had been acting as Tom Goddard's understudy since the early 1930s. These established men were joined by a 23-year-old trialist, Cecil 'Sam' Cook, the Tetbury-born slow left-armer who was to contribute so splendidly to the County's cause over the next 19 seasons.

With no official coach yet appointed, Hammond himself ran the nets. Sam Cook, though greatly in awe of him, found him helpful and constructive about bowling, and, when lunch-time came on that first day, felt that he had made a reasonable impression on the great man. Lunch in those days was not a matter of waitress service in the dining room; Sam suspected as much, but, not knowing the form, enquired as to what it was. He discovered that the other players had brought sandwiches and therefore, having made no such provision himself, nipped out on to the Gloucester Road in search of a public house, where he might find a pork pie and, perhaps, a pint or so of beer, to which he, in common with a great many cricketers, was rather partial.

When the players reconvened Sam had bowled only a couple of balls when he saw Wally Hammond sniffing the air like a bloodhound. 'Someone's been on the beer', asserted Hammond. Finally, Sam, in some trepidation, volunteered that he had had a pint with his pork pie. Hammond then watched Sam keenly for a few minutes before

CECIL COOK

'Sam' as he was known to cricketers, was born at Tetbury on 23 August 1921. He was an accurate and cunning slow left-armer for Gloucestershire between 1946 and 1964. In his first season he took over 130 wickets. He was to capture 100 wickets in a season on eight more occasions and might well have done so another two or three times but for the presence of two other spinners in the County side from 1955 onward.

Sam was not a big spinner of the ball but could make it do just enough to find or beat the batsman's outside edge. He secured many victims, too, with the ball that dipped in with his arm. Though he was quite slow through the air his low trajectory and subtle variations of pace and spin made him extremely difficult to 'collar'. Indeed, for Gloucestershire he conceded runs at the rate of only 2.1 per over, a most miserly figure. He loved bowling for the battle of wits it involved and would peer up the pitch with a quizzical smile at the batsmen he had deceived.

In all cricket he took 1,782 wickets, average 20.52. Of that total 1,768 were taken for Gloucestershire, an indication of the lack of recognition he received outside his own County. He did play in one Test, against the South Africans at Trent Bridge, and would surely have appeared more often had he not been contemporary with Jack Young and Johnny Wardle and later with Tony Lock. He was later a highly respected umpire.

'Sam' Cook, so accurate that he conceded runs at only 2.06 per over throughout his career. (NCCC)

observing: 'Well, it doesn't seem to have done you any harm.' Hammond duly took Sam on to the staff and saw him take a wicket with his first ball in first-class cricket, against Oxford University in The Parks, and 133 at 18 each that year, a remarkable performance for a young bowler in his debut season. Cook's metronomic accuracy and clever variations of pace and spin were to bring him 1,782 wickets in his distinguished career.

Gloucestershire's fifth place in 1946 was regarded as something of a disappointment, though the reasons for it are plain enough. Only two bowlers in Goddard and Cook exceeded 40 wickets and the young pace men, Scott and Lambert, of whom so much had been expected following their impressive performances in 1939, found success elusive in the extreme. The batting, too, though deep enough, was inconsistent and, bearing in mind that the Bristol wicket was at this time as dead as any in the land, the side did extremely well to win 15 out of its 30 matches. Much of the credit for this goes to Goddard, who showed conclusively that at 45 he remained among the very top flight of English slow bowlers by taking 150 Championship wickets at less than 18 each. Cook's Championship figures of 113 wickets at 18 also represented a great achievement.

Among the batsmen Hammond, though his Championship innings were limited to 16 by Test calls and the fibrositis which had increasingly dogged him, was supreme. With those limited opportunities he scored 1,404 runs, hit six centuries and averaged 108! Though he had thickened out noticeably during the last few years, his presence was still magnetic, his power and execution masterful. His 214 against Somerset at Bristol that year remains clear in the memories of people who at the time were no more than seven or eight years old. Though Barnett hit four centuries, the highest of them his 171 against Nottinghamshire at Bristol, he had plenty of failures too, and his Championship batting average of 35 was disappointing bearing in mind the volume of runs being made up and down the country generally. Crapp, Basil Allen and Billy Neale all exceeded 1,000 runs, albeit without doing anything too startling. Andy Wilson, forced to go in first in the absence of more reliable candidates, battled gamely, but Emmett had a poor season, considering the promise he had shown pre-war.

The story of the ill-fated England tour to Australia in the winter of 1946–47 is too well known to need a detailed retelling. Sufficient to say that Hammond, himself 43, led an elderly side to heavy defeat— England lost three Tests and drew two—against what was to emerge in 1948 as arguably the greatest Australian side ever. Troubled himself by ill-health, and more and more perturbed by the treatment he was receiving personally at the hands of the Press, whose criticisms mounted as the Australians established mastery, he contemplated his cricketing future with growing doubt. He wrote to Gloucestershire at Christmas 1946, resigning the captaincy. On his return from Australia he entered business full-time, and played for the County only once more, as a help to boost membership, appearing unsuccessfully against Somerset in 1951. Shortly afterwards he left for South Africa, having divorced his first wife and married a South African, Sybil Ness-Harvey, and remained there until his death on 2 July 1965, his life undoubtedly shortened by the severe injuries he suffered in a car crash in 1960.

It is rare for a County to contain within its history two such monumental figures as Dr W. G. Grace and W. R. Hammond. It is, of course, impossible to compare cricketers from different eras in the game's development: all one can do is to concede that if a player is indisputably great in his own time he is likely to be so in any other time. Hammond, with Sir Garfield Sobers as his possible equal, was probably the finest athlete to play cricket at high level. Indeed, Charles Barnett said just this when contacted for an opinion shortly after Hammond's death: 'I played with Wally for 20 years and consider him the greatest athlete I ever knew.' In terms of cricket this meant that he could do anything, as Sobers could. I remember asking Cyril Washbrook who was the greatest cricketer of his time. He replied, as if slightly surprised that the question could be asked at all: 'Wally. Leave aside the batting, he could bowl as quick as almost anyone, he could swing it, he could bowl off-spinners and leg-breaks and googlies. There never was a better slip fielder, and before he went to field close he was a great outfielder.'

It was certainly sad for Hammond that he could not, finally, bestride his own age as Grace did his, for there had emerged, shortly after Hammond had proved his greatness by making 905 runs in the 1928–29 series in Australia, the machine-like Bradman who was to eclipse all batting records, in all probability setting in the process some marks that will stand for all time. Hammond's fuse at times could burn slowly, his power and majesty had the bloom that occasional fallibility lends. Bradman was hardly fallible at all. Only 'bodyline' rendered his performances, briefly, mortal. Hammond, of course, had days, weeks, even months, when he was completely the master. Indeed, on three occasions he made 1,000 runs or more in a month, in May 1927, August 1933 and August 1936. During such periods he could be pitiless. The old Nottinghamshire fast bowler Arthur Jepson, later a Test match umpire, said to me, only half in jest: 'We used to call him "The Beast". He was cruel—he just murdered you!'

His contempories unite in praising the aesthetics of Hammond's cricket, the beauty of his strokeplay, the ease and perfection of his bowling action, his astonishing fielding skills. I glimpsed a few seconds of his play, culled from old newsreels and included in a television programme on him produced by Peter West a few years ago. Those glimpses, together with the spoken words of men like Cyril Washbrook and Eddie Paynter, and things Sir Len Hutton has said in print, have persuaded me that, if I could see any cricketer in the past at his best for just one hour, Walter Hammond would be my choice. The statistics of his career are to be found elsewhere in this book. They set out, as an accountant might, his importance to Gloucestershire's, and to England's, cricket over a period of more than 20 years. What they cannot do is conjure up the presence—the magnetism that drew crowds of men, women and children from far afield, and has convinced those that saw his prime that there never was, and never will be, another like him.

The County's failure to win matches in 1946, a product as we have seen of frail batting and an ill-balanced attack, combined with the sudden retirement of their great cricketer, caused the County to approach the 1947 season with some trepidation. There had for some time been concern at the nature of the Bristol pitch, whose high clay content made it, in dry weather, no use at all to bowlers and, because of its generally low bounce, not suitable either for all types of batsman. Generally, though, provided batsmen did not attempt to pull or cut straight balls they had little to worry about, and consequently Bristol was frequently the scene of much high scoring and much tedious cricket. Therefore, the decision, based on the advice of the Bingley Ground-Keeping Research Unit, to mix sand with the clay top-soil in order to balance its texture, should not necessarily be seen as a cunning ruse to exploit one of the County's major strengths, the spin-bowling of Goddard and Cook.

However, if the treatment of the square had been contemplated for some time, there can be no doubt that it rebounded mightily in the County's favour. Players like Barnett and Basil Allen, who now took over the captaincy once more, had been brought up with Charlie Parker and Tom Goddard bowling to them, and knew something about playing spinners. The younger men had the advantage of practising against Goddard and Sam Cook, all this in great contrast to their opponents, who for the most part found themselves all at sea on the much-changed Bristol wickets which now turned virtually from the start, and did so more and more as each match wore on. There were still weaknesses in the County's cricket, but in this new situation they were largely masked and Gloucestershire, who won 18 and lost only five matches, finished second to Middlesex in 1947 in one of the closest races for years.

Tom Goddard gave thanks to the ground committee, taking 238

wickets, 206 in the Championship at 15.9 each. Sam Cook took 138 for the County and played in his solitary Test match, against South Africa at Trent Bridge. Barnett bowled more than for some time and, after the County had started unauspiciously by losing by an innings against Middlesex at Lord's, bowled them to an innings victory over Hampshire at Bristol, taking five for 14 and six for 46 with his inswingers. Lambert recovered his form a little, his 51 Championship wickets costing 28, but Colin Scott remained in the doldrums, taking only 15 wickets at 60 apiece. The batting this season was notably solid, Crapp making almost 2,000 runs and averaging over 40, B. O. Allen, Emmett and Barnett all making well over 1,500, Andy Wilson nearly 1,300 and Billy Neale over 1,000 again. After the win over Hampshire the County maintained their form, beating Nottinghamshire at Bristol by an innings (Goddard 15 for 81 in the match), Somerset by 78 runs at Taunton and Yorkshire by nine wickets at Bristol. This last match, Charles Barnett's benefit, was a triumph for Sam Cook, who took nine for 42 in Yorkshire's first innings, and for the beneficiary himself, who made 70 and 30 not out and clean bowled Len Hutton in the second innings. Leicestershire were beaten at Gloucester by six wickets (Goddard 15 for 134), but then there followed two drawn games, at Birmingham in Warwickshire's favour and at Swansea in Gloucestershire's. Then Worcestershire were beaten by six wickets at Worcester and Kent at Bristol by an innings and 37. Another draw at Trent Bridge was followed by victories at the Oval over Surrey by six wickets and against Derbyshire at Bristol by two wickets. In this last game A. E. G. Rhodes, leg-spinning father of Derbyshire and England fast-bowler Harold, almost bowled his side to victory but was foiled by Jack Crapp and the Gloucestershire tail. After a draw at Bristol against Sussex, the only side to top 300 runs there during the season, Worcestershire and Northamptonshire were both comfortably beaten at Gloucester. The County then returned to Bristol where Somerset were bowled out for 98 and 25 and lost by 316 runs. In Somerset's second innings Tom Goddard's final analysis was 3 overs, 1 maiden, 4 runs, 5 wickets, the five wickets coming in seven balls and including a hat-trick. It was of this pitch that the Somerset captain, R. J. O. Meyer, remarked: 'It was like batting on Weston-super-Mare beach', a statement which a future Somerset captain, the Yorkshire exile Brian Close, was to echo some 30 years later.

Then up to Bradford, where Yorkshire were beaten by eight runs. Gloucestershire twice looked a beaten side but twice George Emmett came to their rescue, his marvellous innings of 61 and 113 turning the tide so that Yorkshire needed 236 to win. They started poorly against Tom Goddard (six for 116) and Sam Cook (four for 81) but fine batting by Ted Lester and Norman Yardley, together with further

George Emmett, 'Captain Bligh': a beautiful player, later a tough and inspirational leader. (GCCC)

defiance from Wardle and Ron Aspinall, almost swung the match Yorkshire's way.

So it was neck-and-neck when Middlesex came to Cheltenham for the return match, which started on 16 August. It was to last only two days, with Middlesex deserved victors by 68 runs. Middlesex batted first, making 180. Only Bill Edrich, with 50, looked secure against Goddard (seven for 70). This score was enough to earn a first-innings lead of 27 as the County struggled in turn against the left-arm slows of Jack Young (four for 55) and the leg-spin of the veteran Jim Sims (six for 65). Goddard, with eight for 86, bowled Middlesex out for 141, only R. W. V. Robins (45), Harry Sharp (46) and Sid Brown (11) reaching double figures. A target of 169 was too high for the County and they were bowled out for 100 by Jack Young (five for 27) with Harry Sharp (three for 39) assisting with his occasional off-spin. Gloucestershire pursued Middlesex to the season's end but there was no faltering, and Middlesex thoroughly deserved their first Championship since 1921, having been runners-up for the five previous seasons.

During this season J. K. R. 'Ken' Graveney had made his first appearance. Though a back injury robbed him of his prime as a cricketer he returned as a veteran to captain the County for two seasons in 1963 and 1964 and he was later chairman of the Gloucestershire Club during one of its more severe crises, from which his good judgement helped to extricate it, and was later president. Ken's brother T. W. 'Tom', four years younger, was soon to join the Club which he was to adorn with his graceful batting until an internal conflict dictated a move to Worcestershire. Later Ken's son David was to bowl slow left-arm for the County from 1972 and to captain it with distinction and considerable success during the 1980s. Ken was then viewed primarily as a batsman, though he was to make more of a name for himself as a bowler of fast-medium outswing.

In 1948 the Bristol pitch had calmed down to such a degree that when the Australians played there they made 774 for seven, Arthur Morris making 290 (a hundred in the first session, a hundred in the second, and very nearly a hundred in the third), Sam Loxton 159 not out, and Neil Harvey 95. With such surfaces the rule rather than the exception, it was not surprising that fewer matches reached a positive conclusion. The spin bowlers took fewer wickets at greater cost, Goddard's tally being 122 in the Championship at 19.6, and Cook's 97 at 23, though he took his 100 again in all matches. Jack Crapp averaged 57 in the Championship for 1,435 runs. Emmett 38 for 1,216, and both played for England, Crapp in three Tests and Emmett for the one time in his career. Charles Barnett, who left the club at the end of the summer to play for Rochdale in the Central Lancashire League, also played in one Test at Trent Bridge (I have won a few bets over the years by giving people two guesses as to where he batted, their failure to get it right earning me a pint of bitter beer—would you believe number 6?) Barnett had a useful season, averaging 36, a point or so better than Basil Allen. The great portent for the future was the arrival of the 21-year-old Tom Graveney, who finished his debut season only 27 runs short of the 1,000-run mark and impressed good judges with his handsome strokeplay.

The match against Yorkshire at Bristol calls for comment. After Gloucestershire had struggled to avoid the follow-on, Brian Sellers' declaration asked them to score 389 for victory in $4\frac{1}{2}$ hours, an asking rate of 86 per hour against Coxon, Frank Smailes, Wardle and Ken Smales. Barnett and Emmett led off with an opening partnership of 226 in two hours. Barnett made 141, with a six and 18 fours, and Gloucestershire got home in comfort with 45 minutes to spare, having maintained an overall scoring rate of 103 per hour. Nine more matches were won against eight defeats, and the County slipped to eighth position, a not unreasonable result in view of the blander nature of the Bristol wicket.

Charlie Barnett's departure was a sad blow, for though he was by then 38 he was extremely fit, and would have been capable of playing innings like that against Yorkshire for a good few years. His enthusiasm and skill, both as player and teacher, earned him a great reputation at Rochdale, where he is still held in some awe. Later he returned to run the family fish business in Cirencester and still appears, hale and hearty, at occasional County matches. His record for Gloucestershire of 21,222 runs, average 32, 371 wickets and 274 catches is that of a very fine player, but it says nothing of the dash and excitement of his batting. When he was in full flight he was desperately difficult to halt, for unlike many aggressive players, he was particularly fallible to neither seam nor spin, and bludgeoned any type of bowling with complete impartiality.

TOM GRAVENEY

Born at Riding Mill, Northumberland, on 16 June 1927, Tom Graveney was brought up in Bristol and attended Bristol Grammar School. A tall, graceful right-handed batsman who at one time had ambitions as a leg-spinner, Graveney made his County debut in 1948 in which season he finished only a few runs short of his 1,000. So rapidly did he develop that he made over 1,500 runs in 1949 and represented the Players against the Gentlemen at Lord's. His Test debut came in 1951 against the South Africans at Old Trafford, and his first Test hundred came the following winter on England's tour of India, when he made 175 in the Bombay Test.

This swift progression seemed to presage a permanent place in the England side, but this was not to be. Graveney's deceptively languid stroke-play could give an impression of carelessness, and he was considered a little unsound. By 1960, when he parted company with Gloucestershire, he had made 48 Test appearances, compared with 62 by Peter May, whose England career had started in the same series. At that time Graveney had 2,590 Test runs, average 39, with four centuries. In his time with Worcestershire, he played in another 31 Tests, scoring 2,292 runs,

Tom Graveney returns to the pavilion, ct Benaud b. Miller 55, top score in England's first innings of 167 v Australia at Headingley, 1953. (GCCC)

averaging nearly 49, and scoring a further nine centuries.

The ease and grace of his play put a bloom on what was one of the soundest of techniques. Graveney was a beautiful player of spin and a fine and aggressive player of fast bowling, which he had the disconcerting habit of hooking dismissively off the front foot. Two of his finest innings were against Hall, Griffith and Sobers in the 1966 series against the West Indies, namely his 109 at Trent Bridge and his 165 at the Oval, the latter being one of the corner-stones of a famous English victory.

For Gloucestershire alone he made nearly 20,000 runs, average 43, with 50 centuries: in all cricket 47,793, average 45, with 122 hundreds.

Seventh position in 1949 was satisfactory for a side which still lacked the all-round bowling strength to challenge seriously the best sides. Tom Goddard was again the backbone of the attack, taking 152 Championship wickets at 18.6, Cook again took 100 wickets in all matches, his 91 in the Championship costing 23 each. Ken Graveney forced his way into the side as a swing bowler, and took over 50 wickets at an average of 27, promising figures for an inexperienced bowler, but George Lambert's 64 wickets were expensive, costing almost 35 runs each. During this season Colin Scott, whose pre-war promise as a new-ball bowler had been so sadly unfilfilled, was attempting to convert to off-spin, as Tom Goddard had done with such effect, but it was not until 1952, when he turned once more to swing bowling, by then at medium-pace, that he was again successful.

The batting was much healthier, with Jack Crapp and George Emmett both passing 2,000 runs for the first time in all cricket, Basil Allen and Wilson having satisfactory seasons and Tom Graveney

Tom Graveney batting against Pakistan in 1954. (GCCC)

showing such pedigree in only his second season that he made over 1,500 Championship runs, and played for the Players against the Gentlemen at Lord's. The Graveney family's origins are in the north-east, Ken having been born at Hexham and Tom at Riding Mill, both in Northumberland. When their father died in 1933 the family, two sisters and three brothers, moved to Bristol, where Tom and Ken attended Bristol Grammar School, which both represented at rugby, Ken as a flanker, a pugnacious one, I would imagine, and Tom at full-back, where it is difficult to imagine him ever getting a hair out of place. Ken's success with the ball in 1949 began with a return of six for 65 at the Oval in Surrey's first innings (he remembers getting some stick in the second). Later in the season he took all ten for 66 at Chesterfield: this was a remarkable performance considering that the third day pitch was expected to suit spin and, moreover, Tom Goddard wanted to bowl. Ken Graveney's success depended firstly, on his taking an early wicket, secondly on Tom Goddard not getting anyone out when he bowled, and thirdly on Ken himself getting a wicket each time he was recalled, which seems to have been on the basis of: 'Try an over this end, Ken, let's see if anything happens'. He took the first seven wickets under those circumstances, after which Basil Allen let him continue. Two more wickets fell to him quickly, but he could not part the last pair, Bill Copson and Les Jackson. A final threat of being taken off worked the oracle, however, and Copson holed out at extra cover. In that season Ken also topped 500 runs, so a promising career seemed to be beckoning him as well as his precocious younger brother.

Season 1949 should not pass without a remark on the promise shown by the 21-year-old batsman Clement Arthur Milton, Bristol-born and educated at Cotham Grammar School. He was to play soccer and cricket for England, and score over 30,000 runs for the county, in addition to which he was to take well over 700 catches. After a single Championship appearance in 1948, he played with some regularity the next year, showing an impressive technique and making almost 900 Championship runs.

The County were once more in seventh place in 1950 with six wins against seven losses, again moderate figures, though they might have been a good deal better but for the wet summer, in which rain interfered with all the home games. In these circumstances Tom Graveney's Championship performance of making 1,649 runs at an average of 38 hardly justify *Wisden's* comment that 'he did not make the progress expected'. The striking thing about Tom Graveney's career is that he never had that bad season which most cricketers, having had a good one early in their careers, frequently encounter immediately after it. George Emmett was the heaviest scorer in the

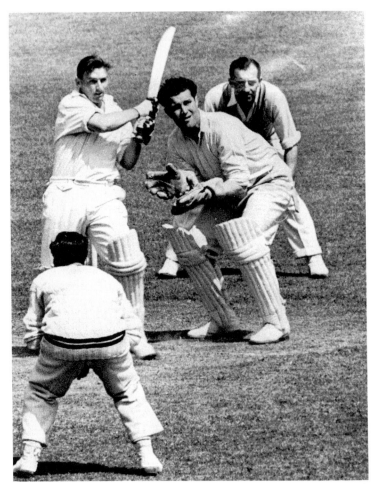

Martin Young batting against Middlesex at Lord's in 1952. Leslie Compton is wicket-keeper, Bill Edrich at slip. (GCCC)

Championship, with 1,737 runs, and it was in this season that D. M. (Martin) Young established himself as Emmett's opening partner. Born in Leicestershire on 15 April 1924, Martin Young, an alumnus of Wellingborough School, Northants, had played a few games for Worcestershire before moving to Gloucestershire in 1948. He played in a handful of games in 1949 without making any great impact but the following year he made 1,558 runs for the County, averaging nearly 34, and made the first three of his 40 centuries, among them an innings of 135 at Worcester which must have given him great satisfaction. His career for the County would yield 23,400 runs at an average of 31.53, and bring him, once or twice, fairly close to Test match honours. An attractive player, with a liking for off-side strokes, and in his youth a fine out-fielder, Martin Young's immense suavity of manner contained more than a hint of self-mockery; he was always excellent company. At the end of the 1964 season he emigrated to South Africa where he is a broadcaster and journalist.

Milton, more naturally gifted than Young—indeed few have had greater physical gifts than Arthur, whose eyesight, co-ordination, reflexes and speed of hand and foot were all astonishing—improved his average from 23 to 27, and Jack Crapp batted reliably without reaching the heights of the previous three seasons. The bowling was again largely dependent on Goddard and Cook, who each took just under 140 wickets at 20 apiece. Lambert returned to something near his best with 95 wickets in all matches, by some way the highest tally of his career to date. If they were a trifle expensive at 27 apiece, that was no reflection on George Lambert's strength and willingness to bowl, whatever the position of the game. Ken Graveney, sadly, suffered from the disc problems which were effectively to terminate his career two years later, and he took only 34 Championship wickets. Colin Scott came into the side occasionally as a second off-spinner, but his few wickets were prohibitively expensive.

This was the final season of Basil Allen's captaincy. His gritty qualities made him a most effective left-handed bat, and his brave close fielding brought him 290 catches and greatly assisted Gloucestershire's traditional spin attack. His qualities of leadership may be gauged by the fact that in the six seasons he was officially captain of the County their worst position was tenth in 1938, and their best second, in 1947, the others being fourth, seventh twice and eighth. His successor for 1951 and 1952 was to be Sir Derrick Bailey, DFC, son of the South African industrialist, Sir Abe Bailey.

Sir Derrick, educated at Winchester, had joined the RAF on secondment from the South African Air Force. Later he studied at the Royal Agricultural College at Cirencester and it was here that Tom Goddard discovered him and persuaded him to play some second team matches. Though not a gifted player, he was certainly a brave one, and earned the respect of the professionals.

Sir Derrick's first season saw the County slip from seventh position in the table to 12th, their worst finish for 19 years. The reasons for this are not hard to find. First, no bowler took 100 wickets, the first time this sort of blank had been drawn since 1902. Tom Goddard suffered a debilitating bout of pneumonia and pleurisy and retired in July; he was to return and play a few games the following year and in 1952, but his days as a great bowler were over. Second, Martin Young broke a finger playing against Northamptonshire at Rushden in mid-season

ARTHUR MILTON

Born in Bristol on 10 March 1928, Milton was a most gifted games player who represented England six times at cricket and once at soccer. He was, and is, a fine golfer who plays to a single-figure handicap without practice or apparent effort, and is a very skilful billiards and snooker player.

Milton made his County debut in 1948, at which time he batted in the middle of the order and bowled medium-paced swingers. His batting did not develop quite so quickly as that of his contemporary Tom Graveney and it was not until 1951 that he really broke through. Injury to Martin Young gave him the chance to open the innings and he responded by making almost 1,600 runs. From then on he was constantly on the fringes of the Test side, though he had to wait until 1958 for his first cap. Milton's phlegmatic temperament, excellent technique and quick reflexes made him an ideal opener though he was adaptable enough to make plenty of runs wherever he batted.

He was a great fielder in any position. At slip or close in on the leg side his suberb co-ordination made him the safest of catchers, and away from the bat his pace, athleticism and the accuracy of his throwing were outstanding. In his career he made 32,150 runs, average 33.73, hit 56 centuries and took 758 catches, the latter a tally exceeded by only seven men in the game's long history.

Milton eases the new ball off his legs at Hove in 1968. He went on to make 120. (NCCC)

and his performances consequently fell away. Nevertheless, the batting was healthy enough; Tom Graveney scoring six centuries and 1,654 Championship runs at an average close to 50 and earning selection for the Old Trafford Test against South Africa. Emmett made almost 2,000 runs for the County, averaging over 40. Jack Crapp had another excellent season and Arthur Milton, relishing the challenge of opening the innings with George Emmett in Martin Young's absence, really broke through, making just under 1,600 runs and averaging almost 40. This was an exciting time for Milton, for in the following winter he was to make his appearance for England at soccer, playing on the right wing against Austria at Wembley.

This is, perhaps, a fitting time to pay tribute to Tom Goddard, whose magnificent bowling had meant so much to the County since he switched to off-spin at the start of the 1929 season. In the 16 consecutive seasons between 1929 and 1950 he never failed to take 100 wickets, and on four occasions took 200 or more. Only Freeman and Charlie Parker took 200 wickets more often. Goddard's six hat-tricks are exceeded only by Doug Wright's seven and equalled only by Charlie Parker. His total of wickets, 2,979, is only exceeded by four bowlers in the game's history: Wilfred Rhodes, Tich Freeman, Charlie Parker again, and J. T. Hearne. Though Goddard had not the subtlety of flight which Parker commanded he was not without his variations of space and trajectory. His greatest strengths, though, were his ability to make the ball spin like a top, so that it would deviate on bland surfaces and do all sorts on damaged ones, and a deep-rooted combative instinct which made him a great trier when things were not going well for him. Not for him the 'sore spinning finger' which caused withdrawal from the attack when the stick was being dished out by the batsmen. It was typical of him that, during the Australians' mammoth first innings at Bristol in 1948, when Goddard was already 47 years old, he stood by his guns, bowling 32 overs and conceding 186 runs without taking a wicket, though I do not doubt that he expected to take one with every ball. After 1952 he returned to his furniture business in Gloucester where he died in 1966.

If the County had all but seen the last of one of its greatest servants, two new starlets twinkled in the firmament during 1951. The first, John Brian Mortimore, had played the previous season against the West Indies at Cheltenham when only 17. Bristol-born and like Milton a product of Cotham Grammar School, Mortimore's distinguished career as a notably cerebral off-spinner and hard-hitting batsman was to extend to 1975 and bring him over 15,000 runs, 1,807 wickets and nine England caps, these being earned between 1958 and 1964, a time when competition for the off-spinner's place was considerable, consisting as it did of Mortimore's Gloucestershire team-mate David Allen, Fred Titmus, Ray Illingworth and the luckless Don Shepherd of Glamorgan.

The second young star was B. D. Wells, known throughout English cricket as 'Bomber', this nickname, by all accounts, being a corruption of Bombardier Billy Wells, an English heavyweight hope of the period immediately after the First World War. 'Bomber' was certainly an appropriate nickname for Gloucestershire's Wells, for it truly reflected the unexpected nature of the man and his cricket. Born in Gloucester in 1930, Wells' rotund and bucolic exterior and abilities as a natural clown did not conceal a sharp wit, a manifest love for the game and great natural skill and variety as a not entirely orthodox off-spin bowler. The confusion caused by Bomber's calling and running between wickets has gone down into Gloucestershire legend, as have his repeated attempts, as a tail-end batsman, to hit the ball higher than it had ever been hit before. About his bowling, though, there were no jokes. Thick-set and strongly built, with powerful arms, Bomber did not really need a run-up at all, save for a couple of hops. He might extend this as the spirit moved him, or even reduce it, but the batsman was conscious that he might be ready to bowl at any time. He never took advantage of a batsman's unwariness, but it was still embarrasssing to push the ball back down the wicket to him, look around for a moment—the merest second—and look up to find him smiling courteously at you, with the air of one who has been waiting for some time for you to pay some attention so that the game can progress.

Bomber was a very fine bowler, who spun the ball sharply with a peculiar method that left a callus near the base of his spinning finger rather than near its tip. He had flight and change of pace and, unusually in a bowler of his type, a well-concealed leg-spinner with which, on one occasion early in his career, he deceived Len Hutton, only for the ball to shave off-stump. Bomber's anguished cry of: 'You lucky old man, you!' is reputed to have somewhat disconcerted the great man. Bomber was a regular member of the County side for only three seasons, in two of which he easily took 100 wickets. He took 544 wickets for Gloucestershire at an average of only 21, marginally cheaper than his off-spinning rivals Mortimore and Allen. Their greater skill with the bat and usefulness in the field, however, severely limited Bomber's opportunities and he moved to Nottinghamshire in 1960. Though the Trent Bridge shirt front pitches were less to his liking he increased his tally of wickets to 999 at which point, with his typically individual view of life and fame, he refused to play any more, on the basis that nobody else had taken that number of wickets. The statisticians' subsequent revision of his total to 998 left Bomber unmoved. He still takes a keen interest in the County's fortunes, and regularly attends the Gloucester week.

B. D. 'Bomber' Wells, highly talented off-spinner,
unforgettable character. (NCCC)

Also making his debut that season was Ron Nicholls, born at
Sharpness in December 1933. His modest beginnings—he averaged
eight in 13 completed innings in the 1953 Championship—were the
prelude to a fine career which was to bring him nearly 24,000 runs for
the County, a total bettered only by Walter Hammond, Arthur
Milton and Alf Dipper. Ron's graceful, orthodox strokeplay and his
modest and engaging personality were to be a feature of the County's
cricket until he retired in 1975, the same year as Mortimore. He
continued to play club cricket for Cheltenham, thereafter, and still
occasionally assists with bringing on youngsters in their lower sides.

That the 1952 season saw the side improve from 12th to ninth
reflected better performances both by bowlers and batsmen. A record
of seven wins against 11 losses does not look all that impressive, but
rain almost certainly robbed the County of three further wins, the
clearest cut of these occasions being against Somerset who, having
followed on, left Gloucestershire to knock off 48 runs for victory in 50
minutes. Rain limited play thereafter to two spells of eight minutes in
which Somerset bowled five overs and Gloucestershire scored 38 for

one. Three bowlers took 100 wickets for the County, George Lambert leading the way with 111 at 22.8 runs each, his best season. Sam Cook once again took 101 wickets and Colin Scott, reverting back to swing after his unsuccessful foray into off-spin, also took 101 at below 25 runs apiece. Though Tom Graveney's appearances were restricted by Test and other representative calls he still made over 1,300 Championship runs. Martin Young was close to 2,000 runs in all matches, and Jack Crapp and George Emmett both comfortably exceeded 1,500, but the averages were headed by Arthur Milton, who made 1,881 runs in the Championship, averaging 45. He hit unbeaten centuries against Nottinghamshire at Trent Bridge (146) and Kent at Bristol (117) and also reached three figures against Sussex at Hove.

Colin Scott, a gifted swing bowler whose best years were lost to the Second World War. (NCCC)

Milton's wonderful reflexes, allied to an excellent technique and beautiful footwork, made him a most difficult opponent, never more so than on untrustworthy pitches, where his ability to play—or leave—the ball very late enabled him to prosper when others were struggling. I remember playing for Lancashire against him at Old Trafford many years later—in 1965 to be precise—on just such a surface. In an innings in which Brian Statham took eight for 69, Milton came to the wicket at 20 for one and remained for four hours, making 77 and effectively winning the match for his side. First of all he took Statham, who did not seem able to get a bowl at anyone else, and when Statham rested he took Tommy Greenhough, whose leg-spinners and googlies were getting considerable purchase on the dry pitch. Tommy bowled at close to medium pace, which did not stop Milton from chasing smoothly up the pitch to him or moving swiftly back over his stumps. Tommy, who bowled well enough to have had a hatful of wickets against less talented opposition, finished with none for 60 off 31 overs, and muttered to me at one point: 'I'm getting sick of the sight of Art down there, wandering about at t'back of his blade!' And 'wandering about' is just what it looked like, for such was Arthur's balance and ease of movement that he performed, with the most casual air, manoeuvres that in other players would have looked desperately risky.

CRAPP AND EMMETT: PROFESSIONAL CAPTAINS

WHEN SIR DERRICK BAILEY relinquished the captaincy in 1952, the County broke new ground, appointing their first professional captain in Jack Crapp. The players responded well to the Cornishman's calm and kindly leadership and finished joint sixth, having won 11 matches and lost eight. They might have done better still but for a dreadful run after 9 July. At that point they stood third in the table, but then lost seven of their next eight matches and dropped into the lower half of the table before recovering their winning ways in the second half of August.

Gloucestershire's batting suffered from the irregularity of Tom Graveney's appearances owing to Test calls, and to the England selectors' understandable desire to use Milton's marvellous fielding as 12th man whenever they could. Milton must, in fact, have been very close to England honours at this stage, the England captain, Len Hutton, being known to appreciate the quality of his cricket. Unfortunately for him, England's major difficulty was less with middle-order batsmen than with finding an opening partner for Hutton. Don Kenyon of Worcestershire was tried in the first two Tests, after which Bill Edrich opened in the last three with some success. However, if Milton had been opening regularly at the time, he might well have been given a chance. Nonetheless, there were enough runs made, with Emmett making 2,000 in all games for the third time, Crapp making nearly 1,800 and Andy Wilson also well past the 1,000. Martin Young made 1,608 runs for the County, though his average dropped below 30, and his Championship runs numbered less than 1,300.

Unfortunately, in a summer that was generally considered to have favoured bowlers, Gloucestershire's did not do particularly well. No bowler, apart from Tom Graveney, averaged below 22 runs per wicket, and Graveney's now very occasional leg-spinners brought him only 14 victims. Of the major bowlers Cook took 74 wickets in the Championship at 22, Colin Scott 65 at 25, and George Lambert 76 at 28. Bomber Wells, then on National Service but released for nine matches, took 33 at 22, and John Mortimore had 24 at a similar average in his seven games. Frank McHugh, a tall fast bowler from Leeds, took 38 wickets at 30. These performances look rather bitty compared with those of the Champions Surrey, for whom Lock, Bedser and Laker exceeded 100 wickets and another bowler, Peter Loader, took 80, all at

The 1954 side. Standing (l to r): E. Mains, B. Wells, R. Nicholls, B. Creu (scorer), F. McHugh, C. Griffiths, D. Young. Seated: G. Lambert, A. E. Wilson, J. Crapp, G. Emmett, C. Cook. (NCCC)

below $18\frac{1}{2}$, or of second placed Sussex, with Ian Thomson, Robin Marlar and Ted James well past 100 wickets and Jim Wood on 79.

Despite an improvement in the bowling figures, due principally to the advance of Frank McHugh and the regular availability of Bomber Wells and John Mortimore, the County dropped to 13th in the wet summer of 1954, when only five games were won. In fairness, the County had a worse time than most with the weather, two matches, against Lancashire and Leicestershire, being abandoned without a ball bowled. However, though most players had satisfactory seasons, cohesive team work was too often absent. In this context it is, perhaps, significant that Jack Crapp, his form so badly affected by the worries of captaincy that his Championship runs dropped to 708 and his average to 23, handed over to George Emmett at the end of the season.

Tom Graveney had a wonderful season, with 1,626 runs, average 74 in the Championship and over 2,200 in all matches, and he finished second to Denis Compton in the national averages. Milton and Emmett batted reliably but Young had another quiet season, reaching 1,000 runs in the Championship but averaging barely 25. The bowling was altogether healthier, with McHugh, now concentrating on accuracy rather than pace, capturing 90 Championship victims at 20 each, and Wells and Mortimore taking 87 and 69 respectively at similar cost. Cook, at this stage in his career and for a few seasons past more accurate than penetrative, did a very useful job in taking 77 wickets at 22 apiece and though George Lambert's 51 wickets were expensive one feels that the sum of the side was not equal to the value of its component parts.

The same was true of 1955, the first of George Emmett's four seasons as captain. *Wisden* notes that: 'there were many good individual batting performances and the bowling was dependable enough, but lack of consistency and determination often allowed a game to slip away after an advantage had been gained'. In a 32-match Championship the County's number of wins increased to 10, but they lost 14 games and climbed only one position, from 13th to 12th. Tom Graveney did not quite maintain the form he had shown in 1954 but, though his selection for all five Tests against South Africa restricted his Championship appearances to 16 he still made almost 1,300 runs, averaging 44. George Emmett this season dropped down to number five in the interests of the side and at some detriment to his own performances, but there was compensation in the successful opening partnership formed by Young and Milton, the former making 2,000 runs in all matches for the first time and the latter topping 1,800. Crapp, no longer burdened by the captaincy, doubled his aggregate and improved his average, but after these five the middle and lower order looked very vulnerable, with nobody else averaging above 20. In this context it did not help that Andy Wilson, who had made his 1,000 runs six times and was a very dependable batsman, was replaced as wicket-keeper by Halifax-born Peter Rochford, a most gifted keeper but of very little account as a batsman.

The bowling was certainly adequate. Sam Cook topped the averages, taking 82 Championship wickets at below 19 each. Bomber Wells took 103 (122 in all matches) at 20 but Mortimore's bowling fell away a little, his 48 wickets costing 27 each. McHugh had another good summer, his 71 wickets at 24 representing a useful haul in a season of good pitches. It was a blow for the County when illness forced him to retire the following season. George Lambert had a satisfactory benefit year, increasing his bag of wickets to 77 and hitting his only first-class century, 100 exactly, not out at Worcester in an extraordinary match. Worcestershire made 334 batting first, after which Gloucestershire were skittled out for 108 by Jack Flavell, Roley Jenkins and Martin Horton. Only Tom Graveney, 61, and John Mortimore, 28, reached double figures. Following on 226 behind the County declared at 444 for nine, Graveney making 128, Bill Knightley-Smith, a Cambridge blue who had played for Middlesex, scoring 64, Mortimore 73 and Lambert 100 not out! Typically George Emmett wanted to do more than merely save the game, and his declaration challenged Worcestershire to make 219 at 88 runs per hour, which they did with five minutes to spare after Don Kenyon,

108, and Laddie Outschoorn, 73, had opened with a stand of 182 in two hours.

In the wet summer of 1956, in which no batsman averaged over 50 in all first-class cricket while 30 bowlers had averages below 20, the County had its best season since 1947. They finished third, only four points behind runners-up Lancashire, who won only 12 matches to Gloucestershire's 14, but 24 behind the Champions, Surrey, who won 15. Despite Martin Young's broken finger, which caused him to miss seven Championship matches, the batting was good enough, bearing in mind the general nature of pitches and the quality of the County's bowling. Tom Graveney, called on for only two Tests by the England selectors, played in 21 Championship matches out of 28 and displayed wonderful form, scoring 1,787 runs and averaging 52.5. He made six centuries, one of them a double, exactly 200 out of 298 against Glamorgan at Newport. This great innings, which was played on a pitch very helpful to bowlers, occupied five hours 40 minutes and contained three sixes and 20 fours; only Milton and Rochford of the other batsmen reached double figures. Parkhouse's 90 out of 193 in Glamorgan's first innings, though a splendid performance, paled by comparison with Graveney's, the importance of which may be gauged by the fact that, despite being bowled out for 81 in their second innings by Don Shepherd and Louis Devereux, the County still won by 37 runs. Graveney had come to the wicket with the score 9 for two and left when it was 288 for eight, at which point Glamorgan skipper Wilf Wooller, never a man to praise opponents lightly, called across to the departing Tom: 'Graveney, that's the worst bloody double-hundred I've ever seen!' Milton and Emmett, the latter opening in Young's absence and occasionally when he played, but generally batting down the order, both topped 1,400 runs and Jack Crapp, who was to go on the first-class umpires' list in 1957, wound up a distinguished career by scoring over 1,100.

It was, though as already noted, a bowlers' year, in which the chief star in Gloucestershire's firmament was Sam Cook who, now rising 35 years of age, bowled 1,125 Championship overs to take 139 wickets at 14.39 each. His total bag of 149 at 14.16 brought him fourth place in the first-class averages behind Lock, Illingworth and Malcolm Hilton. Bomber Wells was scarcely less successful, his 112 Championship wickets costing 18.5 each, and John Mortimore gave admirable support with 54 at 21. Unfortunately the quicker bowling was inadequate. Lambert by now was less penetrative and more expensive than was desirable and McHugh, having taken 25 wickets at 19 each, including a match-winning analysis of six for 41 in Nottinghamshire's second innings at Stroud in early June, was forced into retirement by poor health.

This was a curious season for Gloucestershire, for until the end of July their performances were distinctly erratic. They almost lost to Middlesex at Lord's in their first match, having been in control for two days. They lost the second to Warwickshire at Bristol by nine wickets, George Emmett, in the B. H. Lyon tradition, risking defeat for a faint chance of victory and paying the penalty as the visitors made the 122 runs they needed in 80 minutes for the loss of only one wicket. A fine century from Graveney and good spin bowling saw Somerset defeated by an innings, also at Bristol, and then at Romford, after Essex had made 356 for nine on the first day, Gloucestershire were bowled out twice on the second for 153 (Graveney 100) and 107 (Graveney 67). Then Gloucestershire beat Surrey at Gloucester by ten runs in another odd match. The County were rolled over for 52 in the first innings by Lock and Laker, Surrey establishing a first innings lead of 139 despite the steady bowling of Cook, Wells and Mortimore. However, at their second attempt, innings of 51 from Emmett, 62 from Nicholls and 94 from Crapp took Gloucestershire to 288, after which Cook (five for 23 in 25.3 overs) and Mortimore (four for 54 in 46 overs) bowled Surrey out for 139. Sussex were outplayed at Worthing, Emmett batting beautifully for 105 and 55 and Cook and Wells sharing the wickets, but rain-affected matches against Hampshire and Nottinghamshire were drawn, neither of them in the County's favour. Then followed

The elegant and productive Ron Nicholls; only Hammond, Milton and Dipper scored more runs for Gloucestershire. (GCCC)

County's favour. Then followed victory over Nottinghamshire at Stroud and heavy defeat by Yorkshire at Sheffield, despite the good batting of Milton and Graveney and the bowling of McHugh, who, in virtually his last County match, had figures of 11 for 112.

The ups and downs continued with losses to Oxford University and the Australians, easy victory over Leicestershire at Bristol, defeat at Worcester, a rain-affected draw at the Oval, heavy defeat by Middlesex at Gloucester, also the venue for the rain-ruined draw with Hampshire, and a defeat by Lancashire at Blackpool, occasioned by a disappointing second-innings collapse. Then, in a tremendous run, eight of the next nine matches were won. Essex were humbled at Bristol, Cook having match figures of nine for 80, and Worcestershire were also outplayed, with Cook again the destroyer—his match figures were: 45 overs, 24 maidens, 35 runs, 7 wickets, an example of the mesmeric power he could exert even on experienced batsmen. Wells and Cook accounted for Warwickshire at Coventry after Emmett had left them 95 minutes to make 152, another Bev Lyon-like challenge, this time joyously successful, Warwickshire being bowled out for 114. Then came the victory at Newport, followed by the only defeat in the sequence, by Sussex at Cheltenham, where a fine century by Jim Parks, together with Robin Marlar's match analysis of 11 for 114, earned the visitors victory by ten wickets. A match of declarations against Glamorgan, also at Cheltenham, ended with Wells and Cook bowling the Welshmen out for 126, 68 fewer than their target. Then in the final match of the Festival, Kent were overwhelmed. Gloucestershire made 289 for six declared (Crapp 87, Emmett 95), and then, on the second day, Kent were bowled out twice on rain-affected turf, the first time for 45 in 90 minutes (Cook six for 11, Wells four for 13) and the second for 169, Cowdrey carrying his bat for 65, and Wells taking five for 65.

Leicestershire were beaten at Leicester by six wickets, Cook and Wells taking 18 wickets between them with the latter's second innings haul of seven for 33 really deciding the match. Then came anti-climax. At Chesterfield, only $2\frac{1}{2}$ hours play was possible in the three days, but this was enough to see the County bowled out for 76 on a wet pitch by Les Jackson, Cliff Gladwin and Derek Morgan. The final match, at Trent Bridge, was again affected by rain. Though Cook's match figures were 13 for 121 Nottinghamshire held the upper hand for most of the game and Gloucestershire, asked to make 189 in $2\frac{1}{2}$ hours for victory, were hanging on at 81 for five when the rain came. Ultimately, then, the season was a disappointment, though there could be no complaint over effort expended, or of George Emmett's imaginative leadership. A glance at the averages shows that Surrey, in Loader, Lock, Laker and the Bedsers, and Lancashire, in Statham,

Hilton, Tattersall and Greenhough, possessed the greater variety in attack. It was greatly to the credit of Gloucestershire's spinners, and of their batsmen, that they got so close but, significantly, they would not challenge again for the title until they had found two opening bowlers capable of taking 100 wickets in a season.

In fact, these two young men had already played for the County. Anthony Stephen (Tony) Brown had appeared as a batsman as early as 1953, as a 17-year-old. Born in Bristol, Tony Brown was to have a distinguished career as player, captain and administrator. Though his batting never left him, as his career total of 12,684 runs testifies, it is as a medium-fast swing bowler and brilliant close fielder that he is likely to be remembered. He took over 1,200 wickets at 25 apiece, an excellent record considering that he did not use the new ball during his last eight seasons. His catching, whether at slip or close in on the leg-side, was very sure. In his career he took 489 catches, and he shares a world record with Surrey's Mickey Stewart, his seven catches in an innings, achieved in 1961 against Nottinghamshire at Trent Bridge being, with Stewart's identical bag in 1957 at Northampton, the most catches ever made by a fielder, excluding the wicket-keeper.

Tony was an excellent captain of the Club between 1969 and 1976. He could lead by example and inspiration, and also by logic and persuasion. During his tenure of office Gloucestershire were once second in the Championship and twice third, and they also won the Gillette Cup, as it then was, in 1973. On his retirement he was to take over as the Club's secretary-manager from Grahame Parker, and later to hold a similar appointment at Somerset. His administrative and managerial skills were early recognised at Lord's, for he managed the England tour to the West Indies under David Gower's captaincy in 1985–86.

The other young quickie was David Smith, also Bristol-born, who had appeared in a couple of matches in 1956 and was to make a real impact in 1957 and thereafter. In pace he was brisker than Tony Brown, with a similarly economical approach to the wicket. Basically he swung the ball away from the right-hander, with an excellent control of line and disturbingly (for the batsman) frequent changes of direction off the seam. I first saw David Smith bowl in The Parks in 1959 when Gloucestershire played Oxford University. Our Kent fast bowler, David Sayer, said to me before the match started 'Look at David Smith closely. He's got the best action in England.' And so he had. He moved in briskly but smoothly, eased into a perfect sideways-on position, after which his right arm brushed his ear before he went into a full and fluid follow-through. His physique, though as athletic as one would expect of a man who played on the left wing for Bristol City, was not robust, but the ease and economy of that action gave

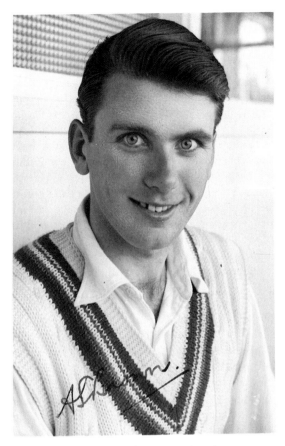

*Tony Brown in 1958; later he was captain and secretary-
manager. (NCCC)*

him firstly a great deal of 'nip' off the pitch, and secondly enabled him
to bowl a greater number of overs than one would have thought
possible. Smith was to take 1,159 wickets in his Gloucestershire career,
averaging 23.68. A superb fielder away from the bat throughout his 15
seasons, his accomplishments as a slip were also considerable, and the
bulk of his 282 catches were taken in that position. The five Test caps,
earned on the tour of India and Pakistan in 1961–62, were a modest
return for his skills.

It is worth recording that Gloucestershire cricket throughout the
later 1950s and into the 1960s was played against a background of
increasingly shaky finances. The County had, like everyone else,
profited from the post-war boom in interest in sport, and between
1946 and 1953 the Club's profits had been high enough to average

almost £2,800 per year. Unfortunately for the game, a new world was meanwhile taking shape outside it. People were finding it less and less easy to take a day off to watch cricket and, with the spread of television and the increase in the number of motor-cars the game was having to compete more and more against other attractive ways of spending leisure time. Certainly in the nine seasons from 1954 to 1962 profit turned briskly into growing losses, the smallest deficit in that period being £416 in 1953, the heaviest £8,654 in 1962, and the average just over £4,000 per year. These figures reflected a dramatic fall in both membership and gate-money. Blame was attached by the committee to poor weather, dull cricket and the negative attitude of the average Bristolian, but action was taken to set up a supporters club, whose efforts during those gloomy years were to provide the money necessary to keep the Club going. Much credit for the Club's survival should go to Col Hugh Henson, secretary from the mid 1930s until his retirement in 1956, and to a succession of wise chairmen in Mr F. Wills (1946 to 1951), Sir William Grant (1957 to 1960) and Sir Percy Lister (1961 to 1962).

Following the excitement of 1956 hopes were high for the following season, but despite a successful mid-season run only eight Championship matches were won—against 13 losses—and the County slid from third place to 13th. There were some extenuating circumstances, however. Jack Crapp, as we have seen, had become an umpire after a fine career for the County which had brought him 22,195 runs, average 34.95, 366 catches, and three Tests against Australia in 1948 and four against South Africa on the 1948–49 tour. The solidity and power of his left-handed batting and the warmth of his personality would be much missed. He died in Bristol on 15 February 1981. In addition, injury to Milton meant that he did not appear in a Championship match till July, and he was greatly missed not only as a batsman but as an all-round fielder. Graveney, though playing in only 19 Championship games, hit six centuries and averaged almost 50. Milton averaged above 40. Young had a very fair season but Emmett, now 44, struggled desperately for a long time. However, his dazzling 91 in the second innings of the West Indies match at Bristol, scored out of 111 in 67 minutes and including a six and 12 fours, and an equally brilliant 170 at Swansea in Gilbert Parkhouse's benefit match, made in only 3½ hours with four sixes and 20 fours, confirmed his great artistry. Gloucestershire won this match by an innings, and Don Shepherd's figures were 16 overs, 1 maiden, 83 runs, 1 wicket! It was rare indeed for that wonderful off-spinner to take such punishment.

The major plus in the batting was the advance of Ron Nicholls, who made 1,303 Championship runs at an average of almost 28. He batted most attractively and was also admirably consistent, his top score being 84.

Derek Hawkins, the Alveston-born all-rounder, hit a maiden Championship century, 106 against Sussex at Hove. He had first appeared as early as 1952, and though he looked for a long time capable of becoming a heavy scorer in first-class cricket, he never quite made the final breakthrough. The same could be said of the Stroud-born David Carpenter, who also seemed to have class enough but whose figures never seemed to reflect his abilities. Hawkins retired in 1962 and Carpenter, who had started in 1954, played on until 1963.

It was on the bowling front that the most significant changes took place in 1957. First, David Smith was given the new ball throughout the season, and responded by taking 94 Championship wickets at 20.64 runs each, and capturing 106 in all matches. George Lambert played only eight Championship matches, after which Tony Brown became Smith's new-ball partner. Though Brown's figures were not spectacular (he took 38 Championship wickets at 26 each) he did well enough to do more than hint at his potential. On the spin bowling front John Mortimore decisively overtook Bomber Wells. Each bowled around 650 Championship overs, Mortimore's return being 73 wickets at 18.91 against Wells' 55 at 28.50. Henceforward Mortimore's superior fielding and batting were to ensure that he took preference.

This was the first season in which Barrie Meyer kept wicket for the County. Peter Rochford had claimed the position early on but lost form and was not re-engaged, after which Meyer, born in Bournemouth in 1932, shared the duties with Bobby Etheridge from Gloucester. Both were professional soccer players, Meyer being an inside forward good enough to score over 200 League goals.

Season 1958 was another disappointing year, with only five Championship wins against nine losses and a further drop to 14th place. This was a dreadfully wet summer, and all the County's batsmen struggled with the exception of Martin Young, who made 1,755 runs in the Championship, average 38, and Graveney, though even he fell away in average and aggregate. These were the only two batsmen to average over 30. It was, however, a notable season for Arthur Milton, who, having been on the fringes of the England side since 1952, was selected to play in the third Test match against New Zealand at Leeds, and responded by making 104 not out on a wicket on which Lock and Laker had just bowled out New Zealand for 67. Curiously, Milton's opening partner was M. J. K. Smith of Warwickshire and Oxford University, who had played for England against Wales at rugby in 1956, so the same Test match created two double internationals. Milton also made a century for the Players against the

Gentlemen at Lord's. Nicholls again exceeded 1,000 runs in all matches, though at reduced average, and made a brilliant and forceful 137 against the Champions Surrey in the drawn match at Bristol.

On the bowling front Smith fell away somewhat, his 71 wickets costing over 30 each, but Brown improved, taking 78 at 22.43. Cook again took 100 Championship wickets and Mortimore had his best season so far, coming within measurable distance of the 'double' by taking 97 wickets and making 844 runs in all matches. His skills were recognised when he was flown out as replacement in November to join the MCC party in Australia.

George Emmett had struggled for form throughout the season and he now handed over the reins of captaincy to Tom Graveney. Though by the following season Emmett would be 46 he undertook to captain the Second XI and pass on something of his vast experience to the younger players. Ironically, an injured finger suffered by Tom Graveney meant that Emmett would come back for 11 matches, ten of them as captain, during the County's exciting but ultimately unsuccessful attempt to carry off the Championship title. Nonetheless,

Barrie Meyer in 1957; an excellent wicket-keeper, now a Test match umpire. (NCCC)

his departure from regular first team marks the end of another era, for he was the last Gloucestershire player to have appeared before the war.

Emmett's contribution to the County's cricket had been enormous. Reference has been made to some of the wonderful innings he played and to the quality of his strokeplay. He scored nearly 23,000 runs for Gloucestershire, averaging 31, and hit 34 centuries, but figures do not reflect his skill. Short, trim and dapper in appearance, Emmett, unusually for a small man, held the bat near the top of the handle, and employed a high backlift and full follow-through. He cut with great elegance and power, and drove wristily throughout the wide arc between square third man and mid-wicket. He had an almost uncanny command of the sweep shot which, through hitting the ball earlier or later, he could direct anywhere from mid-wicket to the finest of fine-legs. His captaincy was adventurous, his approach to his players authoritative but essentially kindly beneath a sometimes curmudgeonly exterior which earned him the nickname of 'Captain Bligh'. (This I discovered when I asked why the van, which was used for many years to transport the players' bags up and down the country and normally loaded and driven by a hapless junior professional, was always known as the 'Bounty'.)

He was the County's coach when I arrived in 1968, horribly short of confidence having just been sacked by Lancashire and rather unsure as to whether I had done the right thing in carrying on playing the game at all. I cannot exaggerate the extent of the assistance George Emmett gave me, firstly by his basic assumption that anyone who didn't want to play cricket was potty, and later by his shrewdness both in matters of playing technique and in attitude to batting. George was always a great believer in the adage that bowlers bowl well when you let them, less well when they are gettting a bit of stick, and he encouraged me to think in this way. In this he was absolutely right, for I had neither the technique nor the temperament to play long, accumulative innings. George later became secretary to the Imperial Athletic Club, whose affairs he organised with typical efficiency and style. He died in Bristol on 18 December 1976.

THE GRAVENEY AFFAIR

THERE WAS NOW ASSEMBLED the nucleus of the side which was to take the County through to the 1970s. There were some comings and goings, to be sure, but the following players were to be constant factors: Arthur Milton, John Mortimore, Tony Brown, David Smith, Barrie Meyer and Ron Nicholls, all except Meyer born within the county—in fact, apart from the Sharpness-born Nicholls, Bristolian by birth. Another Bristolian, David Allen, was to step on to centre stage in the 1959 season.

Allen, like Mortimore and Milton a product of Cotham Grammar School, had made an early impact as an off-spinner in 1953 when he was only 17. In his fourth Championship match at Bristol, he had taken three for 44 in 16 overs, impressive figures for a boy, to assist in dismissing Surrey for 213 and gain Gloucestershire a first-innings lead of 56. The County's declaration challenged Surrey to make 209 to win, but they were bowled out for 113, Allen's figures being 12.4 overs, 6 maidens, 13 runs, 6 wickets. His first five wickets were Constable, Barrington, McIntyre, Surridge and McMahon, and his sixth was Loader, whom he dismissed with the fourth ball of the last over of the game. Subsequently his appearances had been limited by the success of Wells and Mortimore, but his success in 1959 earned him an invitation to tour the West Indies, where he played in all five Tests. In all he was to play 39 times for his country, taking 122 wickets.

Though 1959 was a glorious summer, so many of Gloucestershire's home pitches took spin that their batsmen did not have so prosperous a time as those of other counties. Their leading player was Martin Young, who made 1,970 runs in the Championship, averaging nearly 43, and 2,179 in all matches. Milton ran him close, with 1,984 runs in all cricket and 1,568 in the Championship, average 39. No other player reached 1,000 in the championship, though Graveney, with 984 runs, average 39, would certainly have been around 1,500 but for his injured finger. The younger batsman disappointed, Nicholls, Hawkins and Carpenter all averaging below 20. The all-rounders compensated to some extent, with Mortimore making 836 Championship runs, Allen 696 and Brown 728, but their runs, coming as they did from the lower middle order, tended to be directed towards rectifying weak positions rather than establishing strong ones.

The bowling was another matter, for there were strong arguments for the County's being the best attack in the Championship. Though only one bowler, Brown, took 100 wickets in County matches the other tallies make their own case: Smith 99, Cook 89, Mortimore 85 and Allen 70. In all matches four took over 100 wickets, Brown and Smith having 110 each, average 23, Mortimore having 113 at 18.28 and Cook 101 at 18.31, with Allen second to Statham in the first-class averages with 84 at 15.73. Mortimore, who did the 'double' in all matches for the first time, played in two Tests against India, having played in the fifth Test against Australia and in the two against New Zealand the previous winter. With excellent support from wicket-keeper Meyer, who had 53 catches and 13 stumpings, the bowling was rarely mastered, and if big scores were made by opponents, they were not amassed at any great pace.

Gloucestershire's brittleness in batting was evident in the first Championship match, against Hampshire at Bristol. Batting first, they were soon 35 for seven, of which Derek Shackleton took six for 11, at which point Smith (42), Allen (62), and Meyer (26 not out), embarked on a rescue act that dragged the score up to 169. Roy Marshall's brilliant 150 earned Hampshire a lead of 147 and though the County fared better at their second attempt the visitors needed only 144 to win, Smith and Brown, bowling unchanged, took eight of them but Hampshire edged ahead leaving the County to contemplate what might have happened had they made another 50 or so in their first innings.

A draw against Sussex at Bristol followed, and then Somerset were beaten at Taunton, Graveney's unbeaten 69 seeing Gloucestershire home after two declarations. The County then narrowly outplayed Derbyshire at Derby, winning by 48 runs as Derbyshire chased 223 in $2\frac{1}{2}$ hours. Sussex won by nine wickets at Hove, Gloucestershire relinquishing control on the first day when they were bowled out for 175 of which Emmett, recalled through Graveney's injury, made 75. In the next match, against Worcestershire at Stroud, the County's first innings performance was again well below par—all out 150, and they lost by seven wickets. Then, also at Stroud, Gloucestershire completed a bad hat-trick as Warwickshire, having narrowly avoided following on, made 318 for six to win in the fourth innings, thanks almost entirely to Mike Smith's unbeaten 182, a wonderful innings on a turning pitch.

So far the season looked unpromising to say the least, with three losses and two wins in six matches, but after a rain-ruined draw at Old Trafford the County struck form. Leicestershire, bowled out on the first day at Bristol for 135, were beaten by an innings, being dismissed for 80 in their second attempt (Cook three for 19, Mortimore five for 7). Derbyshire also lost by an innings at Bristol after Gloucestershire had batted consistently to make 309. Smith and Brown did the damage in Derbyshire's first innings of 152, and Cook and Allen cut them down in their second for 112. Another first-innings collapse at

Edgbaston (all out 92, Roley Thompson eight for 40) surrendered the initiative to Warwickshire, who won by nine wickets. The match against Nottinghamshire at Trent Bridge was drawn in Gloucestershire's favour, Graveney making 155 not out and 85 not out in two superlative displays, and Lancashire won comfortably at Gloucester despite Milton's first innings 115 and Allen's seven for 66 in Lancashire's second innings. Thereafter Gloucestershire won six and tied one of their next ten Championship games and, also, incidentally, defeated the Indians by 192 runs, and forced themselves into contention for the prize which had for so long eluded them.

In the first of the sequence, again at Gloucester, the County declared at 365 for eight and beat Kent by ten wickets, bowling them out for 152 and 249 (Allen, now in a glut of wickets, six for 47 and eight for 63 in the match). Then Gloucestershire beat Northamptonshire in a low-scoring game at Peterborough, Mortimore having match figures of eight for 54 and Allen seven for 99. Then to Leeds, where Young made 148 out of Gloucestershire's first innings of 339. Smith and Brown bowled Yorkshire out for 223 but too much rain had fallen to permit the County to exploit this advantage. At Cowes, Gloucestershire led by only four runs on first innings but then Smith, three for 27, and Mortimore, four for 30, bowled Hampshire out for 133 in their second innings and Young and Milton knocked off the required runs without loss. There was a set-back at the Oval where Surrey's first innings of 286 proved decisive. Gloucestershire twice made horrific starts, being 31 for five in each innings. A rugged 65 by Richard Bernard, a Cambridge blue making his Championship debut, edged the County to 176 in their first innings, but they were bowled out for 116 at the second attempt and lost by 129 runs. Gloucestershire were clearly missing Graveney, who had had a recurrence of his finger injury, but they overcame Northamptonshire at Bristol by two wickets, making 195 for eight to win, thanks to Young's skilful unbeaten 108. Against Somerset at Bristol, Gloucestershire's first innings of 184 looked inadequate until Smith (six for 26) and Brown (four for 25) bowled the opposition out for 61. Milton's 121 in the second innings helped to set Somerset 400 plus for victory, and Allen's five for 56 ensured that they came nowhere near it.

Then came the tie with Essex at Leyton in Ken Preston's benefit match. Doug Insole dominated the Essex batting, making 177 not out in their first innings 364 for six declared and 90 in their second of 176 for eight declared. Gloucestershire, having made 329 in their first innings (Milton 99) needed 212 to win in 170 minutes. They were 82 for four when Tony Brown came in and 209 for nine when he was out 85 minutes later, having hit four sixes and ten fours. A wide, from Trevor Bailey of all people, and a single to Meyer levelled the scores and left Sam Cook, the Tetbury Twirler, to do or die. Alas, it was the latter, an on-side deflection off Barry Knight being scooped up left-handed by Joe Milner.

In the next match, against Glamorgan at Cheltenham, came anti-climax, the Welshmen winning by an innings after Bernard Hedges, 76, and Peter Walker, 113, had been given lives on the first day when their side scored 371 for nine. In the next match of the Festival, though, Middlesex were beaten by an innings after Gloucestershire had scored 280 for nine on the first day, thanks almost entirely to Martin Young's excellent 140. Gloucestershire's three spinners then bowled out Middlesex for 127 and 103, Cook with match figures of ten for 75, leading the rout. After overwhelming the Indians by 192 runs at Cheltenham the County travelled to Dover, where they beat Kent by seven wickets, the winning run being scored at 3 o'clock on the second day, the pitch showing itself to be a crumbler on the first day when Brown (five for 35) and Mortimore (three for 13) dismissed Kent for 119. Arthur Milton (58), and Ron Nicholls (49), were chiefly responsible for the County's lead of 75. Tom Graveney, now fit again, gave the second innings new ball to Cook and Mortimore, and they responded by taking four for 49 and six for 58 respectively to set up the win.

Then, at Bristol, the eventual Champions Yorkshire, who were without their Test players Fred Trueman and Ray Illingworth, were outplayed in an astonishing match. Gloucestershire made 294 for eight declared (Graveney 67, Mortimore 76, Smith 49 not out) after which Yorkshire were bowled out on the second morning for 35 in only 75 minutes. The pitch had 'sweated' overnight, a circumstance of which Smith and Brown took full advantage. The last six Yorkshire batsmen scored ducks, and only Brian Bolus, who came in at number five and made 12 not out, reached double figures. Smith's figures were 11-3-16-3 and Brown's 10.5-5-11-7. Bolus went in first at Yorkshire's second attempt and held on for almost four hours to make 91 but Smith and Brown would not be denied and, taking four for 68 and three for 54 respectively, ensured that Yorkshire were defeated by an innings and 77 after an hour's play on the third morning.

A crucial match against Surrey on a spinner's pitch at Stroud was one in which Gloucestershire would have dearly wished to win the toss. As it was, Surrey took first innings, making 130 (John Edrich 45, Allen five for 43, Cook three for 33). Only Graveney offered much resistance as Lock and Laker took five wickets each and gained Surrey a lead of 29. Cook then took two quick wickets before the first day's close when Surrey were 39 on. The Gloucestershire players still think they might have won this match but for Ken Barrington's masterly 49 which, despite Mortimore's four for 28 and Cook's five for 66, set

Gloucestershire 161 for victory on a pitch deteriorating all the time. It was too many, particularly after Laker (six for 27) and Lock (three for 37) had reduced the County to 27 for six. There followed some bold hitting from Allen and Smith, but the margin of defeat was a decisive 81 runs. Gloucestershire still had a faint chance of carrying off the title if they could collect a maximum 14 points from their final match at Worcester, but that evaporated when their first innings collapsed to 26 for six after they had bowled their opponents out for 205, and Martin Young's second innings 130 only served to reduce Worcestershire's margin of victory to 83 runs.

David Allen: 122 wickets in 39 Test matches. (GCCC)

After so noble a struggle, which might have been crowned with success if Graveney had been fit all summer—he missed ten Championship matches and was troubled by injury in several of the games he played in—it was disappointing that Gloucestershire should slip back to eighth position in the table in 1960. And yet the reasons for this comparative failure are plain enough. A broken finger incurred in the famous victory over the South African tourists at Bristol meant that Arthur Milton did not play after 30 June, missing 17 out of 28 county matches. Injuries also meant that Tony Brown missed nine matches and Sam Cook three, while a sore spinning finger kept David Allen, who had bowled so well in the West Indies during the winter, out of action for nine games. Graveney himself, troubled by shoulder muscles, missed four games. Even so nine matches were won, against 12 in 1959, and losses reduced to seven against 11 the previous year.

Graveney and Young, who hit four centuries, led the batting, with 1,394 and 1,462 Championship runs respectively. No one else reached four figures in County matches, though C. T. M. (Tom) Pugh, an old Etonian amateur who had appeared in a few games in 1959, did so in all matches. David Smith, forced to shoulder a heavy burden because of the side's injury problems, bowled nearly 1,200 overs in the Championship and took 127 wickets; in all matches his tally was 143. Dennis A'Court, Brown's deputy, took some useful wickets, but Mortimore had a modest season by his standards, taking 60 wickets at 26, and Cook's bag fell to 63, average 20.55.

Despite these problems the side played well enough early on, recovering from reverses at the hands of Worcestershire and Yorkshire to put together a sequence of six wins in nine Championship matches, during which they defeated the tourists. Injuries took their toll then, and only two of the last 14 County matches were won. It was during this period that a certain amount of dressing room unease began to display itself. Certainly when Oxford University came to Bristol in late June, that is, in the middle of the County's winning streak, there was some muttering about Tom Graveney's captaincy. One or two of the players thought he was too negative and offered us their sympathy when we were asked to make 343 to win at 75 runs per hour in the last innings, after Gloucestershire had declared twice. My own feeling was that the pitch was very good, and that if Tom Graveney didn't fancy losing to a University side on the chase, that was entirely up to him, his batsmen having controlled the game so far. In any event the problems were surely not so serious that they should lead to Tom Graveney's departure from the County for which he had batted with enormous distinction for 13 seasons, yet this is what did happen.

There seems little doubt that some curious dealings went on around this time, for which Gloucestershire's committee must shoulder its fair share of the blame. Tom Pugh was recommended to Sir Percy Lister, then the Club's vice-chairman, by P. G. H. Fender, formerly captain of Surrey and an England player, from London club cricket in 1958. He joined Gloucestershire in 1959 on the basis that he would play first team cricket and, at some stage, captain the side. This was the very year that Tom Graveney had been appointed to the captaincy, though the undertaking given to Pugh only came to Graveney's notice a year later. Following one or two problems within the side during 1960, which had by various means come to the notice of the committee, Tom Graveney was asked to stand down as captain for 1961 in favour of Pugh. Now Graveney had, in 1959, resisted the playing of Pugh in the side, for he knew nothing of Pugh's ability and could see no point in dropping a professional, like Nicholls or Derek Hawkins, in favour of him. Tom Pugh played only five Championship games in 1959, but the severity of the County's injury crisis the following season meant that he played 23 of the 28 Championship matches, and did not acquit himself too badly.

The request for Graveney's resignation was tied in with a heavy loss on the season. Graveney, having agreed initially to the proposal, on second thoughts did not see why he should carry the can for Gloucestershire's deteriorating financial position, and wrote to that effect to the Club chairman, Sir William Grant.

From this point, inevitably, the situation worsened. Sir William Grant and his vice-chairman could not understand why an employee of the Club simply should not do as had been kindly suggested to him. Graveney at all times said he would play for Gloucestershire under anybody, but refused to have his relinquishing of the captaincy linked either to the County's playing record under him—second, and then eighth in a season when injuries had crippled the side's effectiveness—or to their financial loss over his two seasons of captaincy, which he, quite understandably, considered to have had very little to do with him personally. Tom Pugh, having been promised something he wanted, was reluctant to relinquish it, having reorganised his life on the basis of that offer; no compromise was possible, and Tom Graveney resigned from the Club shortly before Christmas 1960.

There seems now little doubt that the County committee, having told Graveney personally that they would not oppose his joining another county, reneged in their dealings with MCC so that Graveney was forced out of county cricket for the 1961 season while he was qualifying for his new county, Worcestershire. It is interesting from this point in time, long after the George Eastham case in football and subsequent legislation over restraint of trade, to contemplate the stick that Tom Graveney took. It is pretty clear that the senior officers of the Club had not played straight with him, not only in the tangled dealing of the period after the end of the 1960 season, but also in promises made to Tom Pugh, a totally innocent party be it stressed, which they had made without the knowledge of their appointed captain.

Pressure was put on Graveney to remain with the County, on the basis that he had had a benefit of £5,000 in 1958, and therefore owed the County his loyalty for the rest of his career. There are two points to be made here; firstly, that loyalty is not a one-way commodity, and secondly, that a benefit is given as a recognition of services *already rendered*, and does not guarantee blind commitment in the future. That most respected of judges, E. W. Swanton, commented acidly on Graveney's stance at the time, though I feel sure that with fuller knowledge his sentiments might not have been the same.

In the event Tom Graveney's move to Worcestershire revived his Test career. It seems that after this upheaval the iron entered his soul, and, without losing his fluency of strokeplay, he became a much more difficult player to dismiss, his performances over several seasons on distinctly sporting wickets at Worcester being unapproached by any other player, whether team-mate or opponent.

In his career for the County Tom Graveney had made almost 20,000 runs, average 43, and hit 50 centuries. In the field he was initially an outfielder, but from 1953 on he was increasingly seen at slip. He took 227 catches for the County. His 48 Test matches had brought him 2,590 runs at an average of 39 with four centuries, the highest his 258 against the West Indies at Trent Bridge in 1957. He was a stroke-maker of great charm who also possessed the will and the technique to chisel out runs on untrustworthy surfaces and in situations of extreme danger to his side. In his ten seasons with Worcestershire he was virtually to double his tally of Test match runs, and improve his average from 39 to 44, making a further nine centuries. His final total of runs was 47,793, average 44.91, with 122 centuries. It seems sad that mismanagement, pure and simple, should have caused the County to lose such a rich talent.

Meanwhile, life went on at Gloucestershire and there was keen interest in how Tom Pugh would shape up to the task. Pugh, a personable young man of 24, was in fact a useful batsman and an extremely tough competitor, as befitted one of the best racquets players in the world. Unfortunately, his abilities were to be only partially tested, for he suffered a broken jaw when he ducked into a full toss from Northamptonshire's fast bowler David Larter at Peterborough in mid-May and did not play again until the end of July. Bearing in mind that Tony Brown missed the first 13 matches, that Allen missed seven because of Test calls and that Milton, Young and Cook missed 22 matches between them, the County did well to climb to fifth position in the table, with 11 wins and 11 losses in their 28 County matches.

The greatest advances were made by Ron Nicholls and David Allen. The former, moved up to open the innings when Young was injured, responded by having comfortably his best season to date. The discipline of going in first curbed a certain impetuosity in his nature but he remained a most attractive player. He scored 1,602 runs in the Championship, averaging almost 33, and hit four centuries. Allen, troubled with a sore spinning finger in 1961, remained fully fit this year and in only 613 Championship overs took 96 wickets at 16.43. He also scored 730 runs in County matches, and achieved the 'double' in all cricket for the only time in his career.

Milton, a shrewd acting captain, had a satisfactory year with the bat and made centuries in each innings against Sussex at Eastbourne, 150 and 100 not out in a game the County won convincingly. David Carpenter and Derek Hawkins each passed 1,000 runs for the first time, albeit at moderate averages, and John Mortimore, with 1,148 Championship runs, batted as reliably as most. Of the bowlers Smith again took 100 Championship wickets, though at increased cost, and Brown and Cook took wickets regularly and economically when fit. Dennis A'Court, however, standing in for Brown, was rather expensive as was Mortimore, who at this time was playing a definite second fiddle as an off-spinner to David Allen, though that situation, at County level at least, was to alter in the coming seasons.

It is comparatively rare for a side to field two successful off-spinners at the same time, though it has been done, as with Don Shepherd and Jim McConnon at Glamorgan. Gloucestershire managed happily enough with their two, though their position was complicated by the presence of a third high-class spinner in the left-armer Cook, the problem being that when the pitch was taking spin, there were only two ends and three bowlers fighting to get on.

The reason why it was feasible to play both Allen and Mortimore was that they were such different types of bowler. Allen was a fierce spinner of the ball, with a fine, rocking action that helped the occasional ball to drift away from the right-hander, and he was also, when at his best, extremely accurate, which made him something of an executioner on helpful pitches and very hard to get away on flat ones. Mortimore, who spun the ball nothing like as much, had learnt an infinite variety of subtle alterations of flight and pitch and he bowled a well-concealed slow outswinger, off the index finger, in a way that Titmus and Illingworth did but Allen did not. Mortimore would plot a whole series of deliveries against a particular batsman— and nobody studied batsmen's methods and peculiarities more closely than he did—designed to get him playing in such a way that he would be vulnerable to the final ball of the sequence. There were arguments among county players as to which was the better bowler, a narrow majority awarding the palm to Mortimore. Yet Sir Garfield Sobers considered Allen the best off-spinner he ever played against, and his was the view shared by the England selectors, who picked Allen in 39 Tests and Mortimore in nine. Suffice it to say that they were both very fine bowlers, though Allen in his middle and later years seemed to find it increasingly difficult to reproduce his Test match form in the more humdrum arenas of the County circuit.

The second and final year of Tom Pugh's captaincy, 1962, brought results identical to those of the previous season, 11 Championship wins against 11 losses, a late surge of six wins in the last eight games enabling the County to climb one place to fourth. There was again some wretched luck with injuries. David Smith missed 11 matches, as did David Allen through a combination of Test calls and injury, and Cook through injury alone. Smith's deputy A'Court was also out of action for long periods, a circumstance which thrust a heavy burden on to the shoulders of Tony Brown. This he met manfully, taking 110 wickets in all matches, but the loss to the County of Smith for so long can be measured by his 66 wickets at 21 in only 17 games, the same number played as Cook who headed the averages, both County and national, with 56 wickets at 17.03. Mortimore returned to form with 77 wickets at 20 in the Championship, Allen's 66 costing nearly 23. Mortimore, indeed was close to the 'double', with 93 wickets and 1,313 runs in all matches. A. R. Windows, the Cambridge blue, bowled usefully after the university term. He brought with him a South African colleague from the Cambridge side, R. C. (Ray) White, Johannesburg born, who played one electrifying innings of 102 not out against Nottinghamshire at Cheltenham. Made in only 68 minutes, this was the fastest century of the season.

The batting was much more solid than in the previous year, Milton hitting four centuries, two of them in the same match against Kent at Bristol. Nicholls was the heaviest scorer, with nearly 1,700 in the Championship, including three centuries, and over 2,000 runs in all cricket. Young, too, had a goodish season, he and Nicholls setting a Gloucestershire first-wicket record by putting on 395 against the somewhat toothless Oxford University attack in The Parks, Young making 198 and Nicholls 217.

Such was the County's form during the last month of the season that, but for their long injury list, it seemed they might have mounted a serious challenge to Yorkshire, Worcestershire and Warwickshire. From early August, when they defeated Somerset by two wickets in a fourth innings run chase, thanks to Tony Brown's 71 in an hour, they lost only two matches. The first, at Clacton, was decided by Essex keeper Brian Taylor's violent 105 in 110 minutes, in the fourth innings of a game the County had controlled for two days. Without Smith, Cook and A'Court they could not stem Taylor's assault. The second, at Worcester, saw the County, almost at full strength now, beaten by 154 runs, Len Coldwell being their chief tormentor with seven for 33 in their first innings of 87 all out and five for 63 in their second of 239. The rest were victories, all except the last, against Sussex at Hove, clear-cut ones.

Lancashire were bowled out for 90 and 64 at Cheltenham and beaten by an innings and 73, Mortimore having the startling match figures of 24.3 overs, 15 maidens, 22 runs, 8 wickets. Also at Cheltenham, Nottinghamshire were beaten by 184 runs, White hitting four sixes and 13 fours in his rapid unbeaten 102, Smith having match figures of nine for 98 and Cook seven for 39. Then followed an astonishing match against Glamorgan at Margam, near Port Talbot, in which neither side topped 100 in either innings, Gloucestershire being bowled out for 88 and 92 and Glamorgan for 62 and 49. The surface was such that the ball turned acutely from the start, either scuttling along the ground after pitching or leaping up almost vertically. In Gloucestershire's first innings Don Shepherd's figures were 18-7-19-5: in Glamorgan's first Cook had 17-8-15-4 and Allen 17-6-31-5, the latter loosish bowling in the context of this match! When the County had another go Young made 24, comfortably the highest individual score of the game, Shepherd had 30.5-14-32-6 and Walker 22-11-24-3. Glamorgan, now needing 119 for victory, which might as well have been 519, did not get half-way against Mortimore (26.4-19-10-5), Cook (21-14-18-3) and Allen (19-12-14-2).

It was during this game that Tom Pugh, padded up and ready to go in number four in the Gloucestershire second innings, became irritated at the funeral rate of scoring and said to Sam Cook, whom Pugh alone addressed by his given name: 'This is damn silly, Cecil. I'm going in to knock these chaps off their length.' Sam nodded and continued to watch play from the dressing room window, which, since this was a horizontal aperture placed high in the wall, necessitated standing on a bench. A wicket fell and Pugh went out to bat and did as he had promised, aiming a wide variety of violent blows at the Glamorgan bowling. Fifteen minutes later he was back in the dressing room, bathed in sweat, having been 'bowled Shepherd, 3'. Sam, still standing on the bench and peering impassively out of the window, said innocently: 'They don't seem to be having any trouble with that swarm of bees now, Skipper.' 'What swarm of bees, Cecil?' enquired Pugh. 'Why, that one you were trying to swat out there just now', said Sam.

Following this bizarre contest, Kent were beaten at Bristol by five wickets as Gloucestershire, set to make 247 for victory at almost 90 an hour, succeeded when Milton struck the winning run off the last ball. He finished on 102 not out, having come to the wicket in the first innings with the score 4 for one and batted through for 110 not out. In the last match Sussex, needing 322 in $4\frac{1}{4}$ hours, got to within seven runs thanks to Alan Oakman's fine century but Tony Brown with five for 84 to go with his first innings five for 46, saw the County home.

From the results of these two seasons it was clear that Gloucestershire had enough talented cricketers to put them, at the worst, among the top half-dozen sides in the Championship. It was also clear that Tom Pugh, though by now well-liked by the players, was not going to make it as a first-class cricketer. His 51 innings in the 1962 Championship had yielded only 741 runs, average 15.76, an inadequate return for a man playing purely as a batsman. The side would be manifestly strengthened if he did not play, though inevitably his sense of humour and keen competitive edge would be missed.

Now Tom Pugh's appointment had reflected the attitude of the higher echelons of the County's management towards amateur players as captains. The appointment of Sir Derrick Bailey to succeed Basil Allen in 1951 reflected their wish to keep leadership away from professionals. Sir Derrick was not a particularly good player, nor did he handle his bowlers with much sensitivity, but it took a mutiny, or the threat of one, to have him replaced. Then professionals Jack Crapp and George Emmett had the job, but within a couple of years the

Cambridge blue Bill Knightley-Smith had joined from Middlesex, the expectation clearly being that as soon as possible he would become captain as well as assistant secretary, a combination of duties which had been offered to, and turned down by, Desmond Eagar, Donald Carr (approached in 1952) and Raman Subba Row, who preferred Northamptonshire, which County he joined at the same time as Knightley-Smith came to Gloucestershire.

In the event Knightley-Smith did not make enough runs, so George Emmett was succeeded by Tom Graveney, which meant three professional captains in a row, but only because there was really no alternative. When Yorkshire broke Surrey's virtual monopoly of the Championship title in 1959, under the captaincy of the amateur Ronnie Burnet, who was no more than a decent club cricketer, other counties felt inspired to take the same course, the appointments of Tom Pugh and of Joe Blackledge at Lancashire being obvious examples. However, in sides which did not possess Yorkshire's all-round strength, such virtual passengers were a luxury that could be ill-afforded.

It was curious then that for 1963, having dispensed in summary fashion with Tom Pugh, the Gloucestershire committee should appoint Ken Graveney as captain. He was now 38 years of age and had not played first-class cricket since persistent back trouble forced his retirement in 1951. He had made himself into a formidable golfer, at which sport he was to represent Gloucestershire on many occasions, still played in local club cricket, and in 1962 had captained the Second XI, but by now his qualifications as a player were really no better than Tom Pugh's had been. Ken Graveney had, however, been carving out a highly successful career in industrial catering. His employers would release him for the summer and, though this was the first year in which the difference between amateur and professional was abolished, and all cricketers could be paid, Ken Graveney would not require payment, an important consideration to a club whose finances were as limited as Gloucestershire's. There were obviously hopes that Ken Graveney's forceful personality might squeeze more out of the players than Tom Pugh had managed to extract, but with so many players below their 1962 form there was no way that this could happen, and the County slipped from fourth position to eighth.

Milton made four Championship centuries and headed the batting, and Young and Mortimore both batted effectively, Young scoring a wonderful 127 against the West Indies at Bristol, of which more anon. Ray White played some forceful innings in July and August, but Nicholls fell away, making over 500 runs fewer in Championship games. Mortimore led the bowlers, taking 93 wickets at 20 each in the Championship and achieving the 'double' in all matches. He was again rather more effective than Allen, whose 57 wickets cost 23 apiece. Cook, now taking something of a back seat, took only 45 wickets, at 21, while the main seamers Tony Brown and David Smith did well enough, the former taking 86 wickets in the Championship and the latter 64, despite missing the last seven matches through injury.

The match against the West Indies produced intense excitement. The tourists batted first, and were whistled out on a green pitch for 89, David Smith doing most of the damage with five for 25. Gloucestershire fared even worse, the fearsome Charlie Griffith taking eight for 23 to gain his side a lead of 29. Despite more fine bowling from Smith, who took six for 67, the West Indies made 250 at their second attempt, leaving the County an unlikely 280 for victory. That they got no more than 214 was no fault of Martin Young, first in and last out for 127, possibly the finest innings of his career. Apart from him only Carpenter, Meyer and Mortimore reached double figures against more hostile bowling from Griffith, who took five for 35.

The first of the one-day competitions, originally called the 'First-class Counties Knock-out Competition' but in the next season termed the 'Gillette Cup' in reference to its sponsors, was finally launched in 1963, the purpose being to raise much needed finance for a game which, because of social changes that had taken place, was being played before fewer and fewer paying customers. Every county had problems with money, even if they were not so acute as Gloucestershire's, where the annual loss was running at around £10,000 by the middle 1960s. Against such a background fund-raising for the Club by means not directly related to cricket became increasingly important but neither these activities, nor the sale of assets, like that of three acres at the far end of the ground from the pavilion to the Bristol Education Authority for the sum of £30,000, could keep the books balanced for long. The Club was very grateful during this decade for the contribution of the supporters club, which averaged around £7,000 per year and was used principally to maintain and improve facilities at the County Ground.

Gloucestershire did not adapt swiftly to the requirements of knock-out cricket; indeed they were not to win a Gillette Cup match against a first-class county until the sixth season of the competition, so their financial gains from its inception were marginal. Meanwhile there were further traumas on the Championship scene in 1964, with the County occupying bottom place for the first time since 1914.

Again there was wretched luck with injuries. Milton, an even more important player since the departure of Tom Graveney, played only six Championship games, breaking his right arm in the opening match against Oxford University in The Parks, and, returning towards the end of July, becoming once more incapacitated half-way through

The 1964 side. Standing (l to r): F. Dudridge (scorer), B. J.
Meyer, D. J. Brown, R. J. Etheridge, A. S. Brown, D. A.
Allen, D. R. Smith, H. Jarman. Seated: R. B. Nicholls,
J. B. Mortimore, J. K. Graveney, C. Cook, D. M. Young.
(NCCC)

August. Ron Nicholls had a good year, making almost 1,600 runs in the Championship and over 1,900 in all, and Martin Young, though by now less prolific than in his prime, once more passed 1,000 in county games before emigrating to South Africa, where he had been coaching during the English winter for 15 years. Terry Riley, specially registered from Warwickshire, made little impact, and Cheltenham-born David Brown faded after a promising start. Tony Brown completed 1,000 runs in all matches, but was rather exposed batting as high as number four, which he did for most of the season, and he averaged below 20. The Cambridge blue, White, had a poor time.

Mortimore, who again completed the 'double', was the foremost bowler with 91 Championship wickets at 20 each. David Smith had a useful season but Brown and Allen were expensive, both paying almost 28 runs per wicket. Allen, who had his best season with the bat, making 1,165 runs in all, played once for England against Australia, as did Mortimore, but England's first choice was now Middlesex's Fred Titmus, who played in all five. Allen was, however, to earn selection for the England tour of South Africa in the winter, and he topped the

Test averages out there. Martin Ashenden, signed from Northamptonshire in an attempt to bolster up the pace department, achieved little and Sam Cook, used less and less, retired at the end of the season to become a first-class umpire. Tony Windows performed well with both bat and ball after the University term.

The 1964 season was, in all conscience, a dismal one. Gloucestershire did not win a Championship match till mid-July and managed only two more subsequently. The last match, against Yorkshire at Bristol, must have seemed like the final straw, for after the visitors had made 425 for seven on the first day (Boycott 177, Close 82, Illingworth 70 not out) rain freshened the wicket on the second morning and the County were bowled out for 47 (Allen top scorer with 20, Nicholls next with 7) and 84, with only Ken Graveney, Meyer, Mike Bissex and Mortimore reaching double figures.

Ken Graveney's return to business meant that the captaincy devolved upon John Mortimore for the next three seasons. He was to bring to the job all his deep thought and technical knowledge and, if the County appeared in no better health when he relinquished the leadership, at least there was by then some new blood in the side which would help Gloucestershire towards some notable triumphs in the coming seasons.

THE ARRIVAL OF PROCTER

IN THE CONTEXT OF THE PREVIOUS YEAR, 1965 was a promising one. There were seven Championship wins against eight defeats, younger players were introduced and showed genuine promise, while the experienced ones did well enough generally. Tenth position in the table was certainly a welcome change from the wooden spoon. Of the younger players Michael Bissex, born in Bath, had played a number of games in 1964 as a 18-year-old without making any impression. In 1965 he made considerable strides. Initially he batted as low as number nine, and at that stage was being played more for his slow left-arm bowling than his right-hand batting. However, innings of 48 against Hampshire at Bristol at the end of May, and of 30 and 12 not out against Glamorgan early the following month clearly demonstrated his potential and he moved up to number five where he continued to score pretty regularly. His Championship figures of 850 runs, average 25, are not on the face of it spectacular, but in what was very much a bowler's year—the first nine bowlers in the national averages paid less than 16 runs apiece for their wickets and each took over 80—they represented excellent batting for an inexperienced youngster.

Another young man to make an impact was Cheltenham-born David Brown who, like Bissex, had played the previous year but without much success. Brown, now 23, made nearly 800 runs in the Championship, average 23.33, and hit his maiden century. This was an attractive 142, made against Glamorgan at Bristol after the County had followed on 172 runs behind. Brown, coming in number four, first helped Ron Nicholls to put on 52 and then, joined by his namesake Tony, who made 109 not out, put on 186 to ensure that the match was saved. David Shepherd, a rotund 24-year-old right-hander recruited from Devon, made a startling debut with a rapid 108 against Oxford University in The Parks. He played in only seven Championship matches but a solid 51 at Old Trafford, which held the lower order together in the face of some fine bowling from Brian Statham, showed his undoubted qualities.

S. E. (Sid) Russell, who after starting his Middlesex career in promising fashion had found himself unable to command a regular place, joined Gloucestershire at the start of the season and made a very useful contribution, scoring 1,124 Championship runs at an average of just below 25 and making an unbeaten century against Hampshire at Bristol in May. Mortimore had a poor year with the bat, by his own standards, but the all-rounders Tony Brown and Tony Windows, the latter now playing full time, made useful runs. A great deal depended on Arthur Milton and Ron Nicholls, and, though neither had a vintage season they did well enough, Milton making 1,342 Championship runs and Nicholls 1,218.

The bowling looked pretty healthy, with Windows' medium-paced outswing now regularly available to take some of the load off David Smith and Tony Brown. Both consequently had good seasons, Smith capturing 100 wickets in all matches and averaging below 18 and Brown taking 94 at 23.9. Allen and Mortimore discharged the spinners' duties effectively, and Bissex's left arm-spin showed promise. Sadly though, if ever there was a false dawn, it was the 1965 season.

Next year saw the County slide to 15th in the table, though their six wins were only one less than the previous year, but certainly cracks were appearing in the masonry. Gloucestershire's misfortunes with injuries continued, with David Smith missing the first two months through a cartilage operation, but this sort of thing is common to all counties, Gloucestershire's problems being that they did not have the depth of talent to provide themselves with adequate replacements. They suffered principally in 1966 through the inadequacy of their middle-order batting. Nicholls dropped down after a while in an attempt to bolster it but this left a void in terms of Milton's opening partner, which was not filled until Bissex moved up near the end of the season.

Once more only two players (Milton and Nicholls again) passed 1,000 in the Championship, Milton's 1,526 runs, at an average above 30 representing a noble effort in view of the lack of support available to him. Nicholls, too, with 1,124 runs at just below 25, did pretty well in view of his unsettled position in the batting order. No one else, however, could return a batting average above 22. Bissex and David Brown made around 900 runs, which, though in view of their inexperience not an unreasonable tally, meant that there was little likelihood of commanding scores being made. Sid Russell fell away badly just when a prosperous season was needed from him, averaging below 18 for his 592 Championship runs and Michael Mence, an all-rounder signed from Warwickshire, shaped well enough without producing too much in the way of concrete achievement. The difference that a Tom Graveney at number four would have made is incalculable, but unfortunately he was creaming it through the covers up the road at Worcester, or batting with his customary elegance and resolution for England against the West Indies.

Gloucestershire's bowlers, all things considered, did not do badly. When David Smith returned to the side in July he showed just what they had been missing by taking 57 wickets at 16 apiece in only 13 Championship matches. Allen had his best county season for some time with 78 wickets at below 21, and he earned a brief Test match recall. Mortimore had another satisfactory season with the ball, taking 69 Championship wickets at 23 each, but the rest of the bowling was not penetrative enough, even if there had been enough runs available to bowl at. Tony Brown was as persevering as ever but his 74 Championship wickets cost 30 runs each. Windows' swingers, though rarely collared, brought him 42 wickets at 32.5 each, while Mence's 17 cost 35.

The County's problems were plain for all to see: there was a general lack of class and effectiveness about the batting while the bowling, if good enough when all were fit, suffered from the lack of credible reserves. The hard work done over the past decade by David Smith and Tony Brown was beginning to show, the former having been forced to have a knee operation and the latter, though more robust physically, now showing every evidence of weariness. Moreover, lack of financial resources led to a largely amateur Second XI which was unlikely to provide cricketers of the required calibre to replace the injured or the out-of-form.

In these circumstances it was not surprising that Gloucestershire should sink further to 17th place in 1967, despite the wonderful batting of Arthur Milton, who at the age of 39 had the best season of his career. He scored 2,089 runs, more than anyone else in the country, hit seven centuries and, with a batting average of 46.42, came sixth in the national averages. Once again the batting depended almost entirely on him and Nicholls, the latter having a most consistent Championship season in which he scored 1,250 runs, and averaged only a fraction below 30 despite having a top score of only 73. Those two aside, it was the same story as in 1966, only more so. This time no one else topped 700 runs in the Championship, the nearest being David Shepherd with 684, average 17.5. Since he scored two centuries in that modest total, his poor form in his other innings can be easily imagined. David Brown, whose uncertainty against fast bowling had been diagnosed quickly by his opponents, had a similar average to Shepherd, and returned at the end of the season to club cricket in Cheltenham, where he continued to score heavily for many years. Just above those two in the County averages were Tony Brown, with 605 runs at 19.5, and David Allen, whose 521 runs, average 21, were sufficient to gain him third place behind Nicholls! Such was the poverty of the County's batting, despite Milton's heavy scoring and Nicholls' dependable support.

The bowlers, generally, fared not much better. Both Mortimore and Allen had reasonable years, with 77 and 66 Championship wickets and averages of 23 and 24 respectively, while Bissex took 46 at similar cost, but Tony Brown, who missed six matches through injury, captured only 39 at 34 and David Smith, out of action for 12 games, had 35 at similar average. It was as well that Jack Davey, a tall fast-medium left-armer from Tavistock in Devonshire, made an early impact, his 59 Championship wickets at under 27 each representing a very satisfactory start from a 23-year-old having his first taste of big cricket. Jack Davey, humorous, dependable and a marvellous 'trier', was not wholly to fulfil that promising start, for injuries and strains troubled him constantly, but his final bag of 411 wickets at 28 apiece meant a great deal to Gloucestershire in the coming seasons, and the County never had a more loyal or persevering servant.

The winter of 1967–68 represented another key time in the history of English cricket, for it was decided by MCC that from 29 November 1967 one overseas cricketer per county could be immediately registered. Overseas players had been a regular feature of English cricket since the early years of the century and before, though normally, as with W. E. Midwinter, some sort of dual qualification assisted in their entry into County cricket. However, the Australian Albert Trott had joined Middlesex in the 1890s and had had to qualify by residence, as had later imports like E. A. McDonald of Tasmania, Victoria, Lancashire and Australia. In the immediate years after the Second World War, when Australian cricket was so particularly strong, many fine cricketers despaired of gaining regular Test recognition there and came to England to seek their playing fortunes, initially in League cricket, but after appropriate residence, with counties. Among them were Bruce Dooland of Nottinghamshire, who among players I have talked to is regarded as a leg-spinner without peer in the post-war game, Bill Alley and Colin McCool of Somerset, George Tribe, Jack Manning and Jock Livingston at Northamptonshire, Jack Pettiford at Kent and Ken Grieves at Lancashire, with men also coming from other nations, like Gamini Goonesena at Nottinghamshire, Yawar Saeed at Somerset and the superb Roy Marshall at Hampshire. All had to qualify by two years' unbroken residence.

Gloucestershire pressed hard for a relaxation of rules concerning residential qualification, for they had found in 1965 two very good reasons for doing so: Michael Procter, born in Durban on 15 September 1946, and Barry Richards, who was two months older, had both toured England in 1963 with the South African schoolboys side which dealt severely with the public schools sides they met. Gloucestershire's coach Graham Wiltshire, a fast-medium bowler who had made 19 appearances for the County between 1953 and 1960, had noted the performances put up by Procter and Richards over the tour and when David Allen visited South Africa with Mike Smith's England side in 1964–65 he was asked to contact the parents of both boys, and they were duly invited to Gloucestershire for the following summer. There they played local club cricket, Second XI cricket and appeared in one first-class match, against their own countrymen who were touring under the captaincy of Peter van der Merwe. Only one day's play was possible in this match owing to rain but during it Richards, batting number four, made 59 and Procter, from number six, 69, and they put on 116 together in just over 90 minutes. Neither had yet turned 19 years of age. Their performances in Gloucestershire's second team were such that the side were runners-up in the Second XI Championship. Both averaged over 30 with the bat and below 14 with the ball, Richards' off-spinners capturing 29 wickets, and Procter, then bowling little above medium-pace claiming 53.

With their hands on two such talents it was not surprising that the County sought a relaxation of the qualification rules, under which players who returned home during the English winter to take part in their own domestic season could never qualify for a county. The MCC's position on this was defensible, for they were in principle against the concept of overseas players floating in and out of the English game. If cricketers like Roy Marshall, Bill Alley and Ken Grieves wished to make their lives here, that was a different matter, as too was the situation of those like Bruce Dooland and George Tribe, who came for a shorter period, returning home after several years. Clearly, the two years' qualification requirement eliminated the fly-by-nights, but did not discourage those with something to offer the English game. However, with cricket's financial problems still acute it was felt that the injection of overseas superstars into English cricket might galvanise the game, so firstly the term 'unbroken' in the qualification rules was to refer only to the English cricket season, while in November 1967 legislation was passed permitting immediate registration of one overseas player.

In these circumstances the County, which had hoped to sign both Procter and Richards in the slightly longer term, were now, like everyone else, scrabbling about for a world star for the 1968 season. Initially they chased Garfield Sobers, the world's finest cricketer, but the competition was too fierce, and they settled for Procter, whose Test career had started successfully in 1966–67 at Durban, where South Africa beat Australia by eight wickets in the third Test, Procter taking three for 27 and four for 71. He then picked up another six in the next Test at Johannesburg. Richards moved to Hampshire, where his consistent scoring and the purity of his strokeplay confirmed his greatness: he was for almost a decade arguably the best batsman in the world.

Gloucestershire could not, in fact, have made a better choice for their overseas player. Between 1968 and 1981 Mike Procter was to score over 14,000 runs for Gloucestershire, with 32 centuries, take over

800 wickets and complete over 200 catches, most of them at slip. He was an attacking strokeplayer of the highest quality, the greatest glory of his play being his driving in the arc between cover point and the bowler, in which area I have never seen the ball hit so consistently hard, whether in the air or along the ground. His bowling was, at first, tearaway fast, with an odd chest-on delivery, the pace coming from a swift and athletic approach and a great heave of a powerful right shoulder at the end of a whirling double-overarm action. It almost appeared as if he bowled off the wrong foot, but photographs prove that he delivered the ball very early, almost as his front foot landed, whereas most bowlers plant the front foot before the final bowling action commences. Procter's right foot therefore had landed almost as the ball left his hand, which made it appear that the right foot was the one he bowled off. This unorthodoxy caused great strain, even on a physique so powerful and athletic as Procter's, so that later in his career he learnt to move the ball about off the seam at just over medium pace, reserving his flat-out burst for the new ball, or for the not-infrequent occasions when it was 'death or glory'.

Procter's action imparted a lot of inswing which was aided in his early years by his delivery from the extreme edge of the return crease. He was always a deep thinker about the game, however, and became disturbed by his inability to gain lbw decisions. He therefore came in closer to the stumps, from which position he still swung the ball in but could also make it 'hold up' off the seam, i.e. straighten or even move a little from leg to off. This is the cricketer's 'death ball' when bowled at Procter's top pace, and it could find the outside edge or hit the off stump of the best players in the world. Though not a Wes Hall or a young Fred Trueman in pace, he was very sharp, and had, like the Australian Jeff Thomson, who was also a very strong man, the ability to make the ball 'kick' from well inside the batsman's half of the pitch. The bouncer which pitches in the bowler's half and whistles over the batsman's head looks very spectacular, and brings 'oohs' and 'aahs' from spectators, but is comparatively harmless. The ball which lifts from not far short of a length and finds the glove or the bat's shoulder is the one that takes wickets.

More than all this, though, was Procter's dedication to the cause. Whichever team he played for had 110 per cent of his endeavour. He was a great cricketer, between the decline of Sobers and the maturity of Imran Khan certainly the best all-rounder in the world (he could even bowl off-spin, and won matches for the County with it) and he was later, after Tony Brown's retirement, an inspirational captain.

In 1968 John Mortimore had handed over the captaincy to Arthur Milton and there were high hopes that, with Procter's arrival, the County might emerge from its doldrums. Ironically, however, only two Championship matches were won, with eight lost, the final position of 16th being only a marginal improvement on 1967. This did not entirely reflect the quality of the cricket played, for rain deprived the side of two virtually certain wins, against Sussex and Surrey at Cheltenham, the additional points from which would have secured 12th place at the worst. Essex would surely have lost at Bristol had the injured Procter been there to blast out the visitors' tail, and rain nullified strong positions earned against Northamptonshire at Gloucester, Somerset at Bristol and Glamorgan at Cardiff.

The feature of the season was Procter's all-round play. He was within measurable distance of the 'double' but, suffering from wear and tear of his right thigh, did not bowl in the Championship after 26 July. By then he had taken 67 wickets at 16 apiece. He played on for a match or two as a batsman, and bowled in the unsuccessful Gillette Cup semi-final against Sussex at Hove on 7 August but returned home immediately after it, by which time he had made 1,167 runs, average 30. He had scored three centuries, one of them, 134 against Middlesex at Bristol, occupying only two hours in all and containing 24 fours. Opposed by that wiliest of off-spinners, Fred Titmus, Procter simply

'Proccy' in full flight—one of the great sights in cricket. (GCCC)

141

murdered him, the manner in which he used his feet to get inside the ball and drive it through or over the covers being marvellous to see.

This was my own first season with Gloucestershire. I have referred earlier to the help given me by George Emmett, and after my first 16 innings had brought only 224 runs, more assistance was needed, and was given by my team-mates, principally Milton and John Mortimore, on matters of technique and attitude. A move up to open the innings, which I did with Ron Nicholls, Milton himself, and Mike Bissex at various times, also helped, and I ended up with over 2,000 runs, 1,875 of them in the Championship. Milton and Nicholls scored over 1,300 runs in all matches and with David Shepherd making nearly 800 in the Championship and passing 1,000 in all matches for the first time the batting was, if not completely dependable, certainly capable of running up big scores when it 'clicked'.

Procter apart, Mortimore was the leading bowler with 68 Championship wickets, Brown and Smith taking around 50 each and Jack Davey 36, though at rather high cost. Barrie Meyer continued to keep wicket with the utmost reliability, securing 60 victims.

The high spot of the season was the success in the Gillete Cup, which had, in all conscience, been a long time in coming. As has been noted, the County had not defeated first-class opposition in the competition since its inception in 1963. In 1968, a first-round bye ensured progress into the second round, but when it was known that our opponents would be Kent, the Cup-holders, at Bristol, confidence was not high. Hearts lifted somewhat when David Smith (three for 15) and Tony Brown (four for 17) winkled Kent out for 110 on a slow, green pitch. Even then victory was by no means certain for in Norman Graham, John Dye, John Shepherd, Asif Iqbal, Derek Underwood and Alan Dixon Kent had an attack tailor-made for the conditions. Gloucestershire edged their score along, losing wickets every now and again, but with the score 109 for six and five overs left surely they were home and dry? But no; amid scenes of frightful tension among the watching Gloucestershire team Graham had David Shepherd caught behind, and then Asif Iqbal dismissed both Meyer and Smith for ducks. Three overs left, 109 for nine and Jack Davey, who was never quite sure which end of the bat to hold, at the wicket with David Allen. Allen, fortunately, was facing and pushed Dixon's second ball calmly past cover for two to win the match.

In the next round Gloucestershire had to play Nottinghamshire at Trent Bridge. Nottinghamshire had had a poor time in previous seasons, finishing bottom of the Championship in 1965 and 1966 and 15th in 1967, but the arrival of Gary Sobers had had an electrifying effect and they were now a formidable side, as their fourth place in the 1968 Championship showed. It was a hot sunlit day, with a big crowd,

MICHAEL JOHN PROCTER

Mike Procter, born in Durban on 15 August 1946, was one of the great all-rounders. He was a batsman in the classical mould, entirely orthodox, powerful and almost invariably aggressive. The chief glory of his play was his driving straight and to the off side, though there was no stroke he could not play. He made 47 centuries, 32 of them for Gloucestershire. In 1970–71, when playing for Rhodesia, he scored six centuries in successive innings, a record he holds in the illustrious company of C. B. Fry and Sir Donald Bradman.

As a bowler he was initially a tearaway quickie, releasing the ball from the edge of the crease and almost off the wrong foot, a method which imparted a lot of inswing. Gradually, however, he moved closer to the stumps, thereby giving himself a better chance of winning leg-before decisions, and developed the ability to move the occasional ball away off the pitch. In the interests of keeping fit—his odd action placed a lot of strain on his right knee, giving problems which eventually caused

Mike Procter hits to leg with effortless power. (GCCC)

his retirement at the early age of 34—his flat-out bursts became less frequent, though to the end of his career he remained capable of spells of great pace and hostility. He could be very effective at medium-pace, in which role he often swung the ball prodigiously, and he also bowled flighted off-spin with a success he found hugely amusing. Indeed, the best performance of his career, nine for 71 for Rhodesia against Transvaal at Bulawayo, was achieved with off-spin.

His career figures of 21,000 runs, average 37, and 1,300 wickets, average 19, are the barest measure of his skill, for they say nothing of the weight and beauty of his stroke-play or of the marvellous athleticism of his fast bowling in the days of his prime.

crowd, and the County started as well as they could have wished, Arthur Milton and your humble servant putting on 164 for the first wicket on a perfect pitch. Later Procter scored 53 in 30 minutes and the County seemed favourites, having scored 296 for eight. Things looked better still with Nottinghamshire 78 for three but then Sobers and Mike Smedley put on 114 in 21 overs with some brilliant hitting, and Gloucestershire's winning margin was only 25 runs.

The semi-final against Sussex at Hove was slightly farcical. Shortly after lunch on the first day Sussex were 142 for five. Heavy rain then set in and did not cease till about 8.30 on the morning of the third day. Gloucestershire were astonished to find that play was due to start on time, on the third morning, despite the water-logged condition of much of the ground. With fielding hazardous and the ball wet, Sussex scrambled another 77 runs in 20 overs. Sussex then fielded in rather less unpleasant circumstances, the ball by now at least remaining dry though the fielders still struggled to keep their feet in some parts of the ground. The County were not too badly placed at 106 for two but faltered after David Shepherd had been run out and lost by 48 runs.

This run of success was nevertheless a bonus and helped to maintain the good spirit which had been established from the early days of the season. This can be illustrated by the match against Yorkshire at Bristol at the end of May in which, after the visitors had established a first-innings lead of 103, Gloucestershire were 80 for six at the close of normal time on the second day, when Brian Close claimed the extra half-hour. No wicket fell then, however, and on the third day David Allen, 51, John Mortimore, 45 not out and Barrie Meyer, 36, completed a rearguard action which left Yorkshire to make 136 in two hours for victory. Procter, with five for 24 cut them down to 47 for seven and only Illingworth's unbeaten 45 saved them from defeat, he and Chris Old playing out the last 15 balls as they finished at 93 for nine. It is rare for such fightbacks to be produced by other than sides which are pulling very much together.

It may be appropriate to talk a little about Arthur Milton's batting, for I had had the opportunity to study it at close quarters in several productive opening stands during 1968, notably a Gloucestershire Championship record of 315 against Sussex at Hove in July. I was first struck by his certainty about the position of his stumps in relation to the ball's path, for he would confidently leave alone deliveries which were only missing by an inch or so. Then two things in combination struck me, namely his ability to score off defensive strokes and his instant recognition of a risk-free run, however apparently short it might appear. He did, in fact, place his defensive shots quite carefully, which, if his partner was prepared to do the same, and trust Milton's judgement of a run, which was impeccable, opened up another avenue of scoring runs, and one which caused bowlers enormous irritation. There is nothing worse for a bowler than to force the batsman to block six balls in an over and still concede three or four runs in it. Milton, incidentally, never called 'Yes'. If he had hit the ball, an enquiring look up the pitch to his partner indicated that he thought there was a run (and there always was). He did not expect his partner to call 'Yes' either. If his partner started, and Milton thought there was a run, he flew in, and he was still very quick, even when over 40. He insisted, though, that a 'no' call should be early and final, having seen many disasters result from shilly-shallying between batsmen.

His attacking strokes were beautifully produced and timed. His preference for playing off the back foot meant that he liked quick wickets with bounce in them, for these gave him the greatest value for his deft cutting and on-side placements, strokes which become more profitable as the pace of the ball on to the bat increases. However, he played every stroke, and his driving, though not normally particularly powerful, was firm and well-placed enough to give him full value for the stroke. Once, in a match against Surrey at Bristol, in which he made 100 in the first innings and, well set in the second, was tapping the ball here and there for ones and twos, it was suggested by his partner that Milton was becoming too weak to hit the ball off the square, and that he should consider eating a greater quantity of raw meat. He looked slightly irritated and next ball advanced to the Surrey off-spinner Pat Pocock and heaved him high over wide long-on, a hit of well over 100 yards. His point made, he continued to stroke the ball about in his earlier contemplative fashion.

At the end of the season Milton gave up the captaincy, which passed to Tony Brown. Milton felt that he had come too late to captaincy, at the age of 40. He had in his earlier years frequently acted as deputy captain, but this is never so arduous as holding the office *in toto*, which involves the greater responsibility of longer-term selection, assessment of the quality of recruits and younger players and the maintenance of harmony and effort among a group of men whose individual ambitions and desires frequently conflict with each other's. He continued to serve the County faithfully until his final retirement at the end of 1974—he actually retired at the end of 1970 but was recalled the following season owing to an injury crisis, and played valuably thereafter.

A TROPHY AT LAST

A NEW DEPARTURE FOR ENGLISH CRICKET in 1969 was the Sunday League, a 40-over competition played on Sunday afternoons and sponsored for the first 18 seasons by John Player, and subsequently by Refuge Assurance. The large crowds that had attended the Rothmans Cavaliers matches, also played on Sundays, in the early 1960s, together with the interest shown by television companies in broadcasting those matches 'live', indicated a fruitful field for the gathering of revenue. So, indeed, it has proved, but it must be doubtful whether the limitation of bowlers' run-ups to 15 yards—a consequence of the need to accommodate tight television schedules by preventing matches from taking too long to finish—the general absence of fielders in the close-catching positions and the consequent emphasis on purely defensive bowling which the 40-over game encourages have brought any benefit to the game apart from the financial one.

Gloucestershire's season was a very successful one in playing terms, second place in the Championship being secured and a respectable sixth being attained in the John Player League. The batting had been strengthened by the arrival of the experienced and resourceful left-hander Geoffrey Pullar from Lancashire. Though Pullar's Test career, which brought him nearly 2,000 runs at an average of 41, had ended with the 1962–63 England tour of Australia he was still a fine player of the moving or turning ball. Unfortunately he was to miss ten Championship matches, a significant number now that there were only 24 of them. David Shepherd, who with Pullar, was the most consistent batsman that year, played only 11. These two averaged over 34 in the Championship and Ron Nicholls and Arthur Milton both passed 1,000 runs and averaged above 30. My own Championship total was down by 700 runs and my average by 12, and with Procter also having a poor time with the bat—his top Championship score was 52 and his average only 16—the County was too often struggling for runs. The bowling, however, was a different matter. Procter had a marvellous season, taking 108 Championship wickets at 15 apiece. Tony Brown had 42 at 21 and David Smith 77 at 23, so that the seam department certainly could not be faulted. The spinners, too, rarely failed to bowl sides out when conditions favour them, Mortimore and Allen sharing 120 wickets at an economical cost. It was this ability to bowl sides out that underpinned a run of success which gave the County a 50-point lead in the Championship mid-way through July. Glamorgan, though, the eventual Champions, had two matches in hand at this juncture, and under the points system then in use, that 50-

point lead could be virtually wiped out if the two games in hand were comfortably won. At that time there was no theoretical maximum to the number of points a side could score in the Championship. The points were awarded as follows: ten for a win, plus a point for each two wickets taken by the fielding side in the first 85 overs of the first innings—a maximum of five—and one point for each 25 runs scored above 150 by the batting side in the first 85 overs. Thus a first innings score of 275 at 85 overs, a reasonably modest total, would earn five points, and 400 could earn ten: where one side completely outplayed the other points totals of 22 and 23 were not uncommon, so a 50-point lead was no reason for complacency.

The season began inauspiciously with Championship draws against Hampshire, Warwickshire and Somerset. In the first, at Southampton, a match reduced to two days owing to rain, Hampshire were 116 for seven, needing 192 to win and hanging on grimly when the end came. The second, at Edgbaston, was abandoned at 4.50 on the final day in an even state, with victory for both sides possible: on the third there was only enough time for the County to declare at 159 for seven, Somerset replying with 82 for six. Then Essex were beaten comfortably at Bristol, but the next match, against Surrey at Bristol, was also drawn on a very good pitch. Then, in the Gillette Cup match at Hove, which Sussex won by eight wickets after Gloucestershire had been put in and bowled out on a green pitch for 87, Tony Brown suffered a strain and did not play for a month, David Allen taking over the captaincy. At that stage the County had played five Championship games, three being rain-wrecked draws, one being also drawn without weather interference, and one victory being recorded.

Allen's first match as captain saw Gloucestershire beaten by 224 runs at the Oval, where they collapsed to 92 all out in the fourth innings against Intikhab Alam. Leicestershire were beaten in a desperately close finish at Leicester, Jack Davey bowling McKenzie with the last ball of the penultimate over when Leicestershire needed only six more runs to win. Then to Middlesbrough, when the pitch 'went' around lunch time on the first day and Yorkshire won in two days by an innings and 53 runs. The ups and downs continued as Hampshire were hammered by 202 runs at Bristol, with Mortimore (five for 13) and Allen (four for 16) dismissing them for 62 in their second innings. Mike Procter (11 for 117 in the match) and John Mortimore (a violent 124 not out in the first innings) set up a nine-wicket win at Northamptonshire and then Sussex were beaten by an innings on a turner at Lydney, Allen taking eight for 34 in their second innings.

Tony Brown was now fit again, and led the side to a three-wicket win at Worcester and then another innings victory, over Derbyshire at Gloucester, after which Brian Close's challenge to score 151 in 105

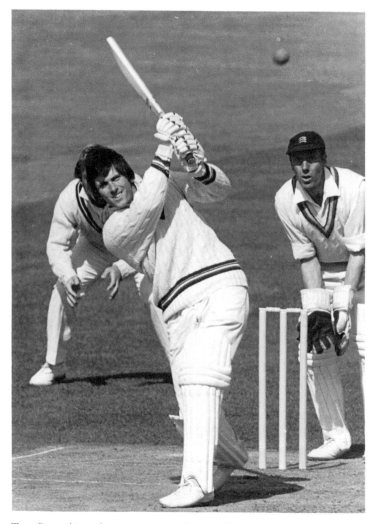

Tony Brown hits to leg in aggressive style. (Patrick Eagar)

minutes to beat Yorkshire, also at Gloucester, was accepted, Mike Procter's unbeaten 51 ensuring victory by five wickets. Then came the first of the two fatal encounters with Glamorgan, this one at Sophia Gardens when, again, brittle batting in both innings—no Gloucestershire man reached 50 in the match—made things easy for the Welshmen, who won by 208 runs. A draw followed against Lancashire at Bristol where, in the next match against Nottinghamshire, which was Tony Brown's benefit game, only $4\frac{3}{4}$ hours play was possible. Kent then had the best of the draw at Canterbury but in the first match of the Cheltenham Festival Worcestershire struggled against Procter, Brown, Mortimore and Allen and were bowled out for 98 and 103, going down by an innings and 57, Pullar playing a masterly innings for Gloucestershire on a turning pitch.

This good result was more than nullified when Glamorgan won the next match, again by an innings, as the County, by now without both Shepherd and Pullar, were bowled out for 75 and 160. That, really, was Gloucestershire's last chance of catching Glamorgan, who went on to carry off the title by the comfortable margin of 31 points. Nor could there be any complaint about this, in terms of weather, injuries or anything else, for on the two occasions the sides had been opposed Glamorgan's superiority had been overwhelming. The John Player League performance in 1969 was curious. No one really batted particularly well, the most effective, albeit with limited opportunities, being Roy Wycliffe Phillips, a West Indian right-hander almost totally committed to attack, who had qualified by residence. The rest of us either blocked or hit it straight up in the air. Only two 50s were scored in the competition, one by Phillips and one by Pullar, and the County's highest score was 173 for six at Northampton, which the home side passed with six wickets and eight balls to spare. Yet through good bowling and Tony Brown's imaginative field settings—I do not remember a seamer bowling that year without at least two close catchers—eight games were won, and in three of those Gloucestershire batted first and made 150 or fewer! The 40-over game has surely changed mightily, with sides now chasing—and getting—scores of 230 plus with some regularity.

The County's centenary was celebrated in 1970, but it was not to be at all a successful year on the playing side. Indeed, from second position in the 1969 Championship there was an abrupt and catastrophic plunge to 17th. Three of the first five Championship matches were won and another strong challenge for the title again seemed likely but there were to be no further wins in the competition. Not everything that year went Gloucestershire's way. Procter, a vital figure, was engaged in the matches between the Rest of the World and England and so took part in only 15 Championship matches out of 24, and in those he did not command the 'nip' and fire of the previous season, though he was much more successful with the bat than in 1969. The batting, despite the fact that Pullar's arthritic knee caused his retirement from the game after only six months, and that a broken arm restricted Milton to 14 games, was reasonably adequate, for Mike Bissex had a fine season, making over 1,300 runs and averaging almost 38. Nicholls was thoroughly dependable, Shepherd made over 1,000 Championship runs and Brown was not far away.

Unfortunately only Procter of the bowlers took his wickets at below 21 each. Mortimore broke his collarbone in pre-season training and missed the first six matches which partially accounts for his high bowling average of almost 29, which was still one point better than David Allen's. Smith worked hard but his 66 wickets cost 33 each and he retired at the end of the season. Until Procter's arrival he spearheaded the County's attack most effectively as his bag of 1,159 wickets in 15 far from injury-free seasons bears witness.

In the Gillette Cup Lancashire, the County's bogey side for so long, won a tight match at Bristol by 27 runs, despite Nicholls' fine 76. In the John Player League seven matches were won and there were two 'no results', which meant a drop to a still respectable eight place.

That Gloucestershire were a much better side than their 1970 form indicated was demonstrated the following season. Despite a barren start, in which there were seven draws (in one of which, against Glamorgan at Bristol, not a ball was bowled owing to rain) and one defeat in the first eight Championship games, the County then played such positive cricket that of the next 16 games seven were won and three lost. At one time it seemed that the County might make a real

The 1970 side at the Oval. Standing (l to r): D. R. Shepherd, J. Davey, M. J. Procter, D. M. Green, M. Bissex, D. A. Allen, B. J. Meyer. Seated: R. B. Nicholls, J. B. Mortimore, A. S. Brown, C. A. Milton, D. R. Smith. (NCCC)

challenge for the title, but the Cheltenham Festival dashed these hopes, for all three matches were badly affected by rain and ended as draws. In the John Player League a record of only five wins meant a drop to 16th but there was compensation in reaching the semi-final of the Gillette Cup for the second time.

Gloucestershire had been strengthened by the signing during the close season of Roger Knight, a tall powerful left-handed batsman and useful medium-paced right-arm bowler. Educated at Dulwich, Knight had won four cricket blues at Cambridge University between 1967 and 1970. He had some appearances for Surrey but saw greater opportunity at Gloucestershire for whom he was to play with distinction until 1975 when his appointment to a teaching post at Eastbourne caused him to throw in his lot with Sussex. Later he returned to the Oval, where he became captain of his original club. Knight made an important contribution that season with over 1,200 Championship runs, but the star batsman was undoubtedly Mike Procter who scored 1,762 runs and averaged 47.62, hitting seven centuries, of which perhaps the most notable was a wonderful innings at Sheffield which won the match for Gloucestershire after they had been asked to make 201 in 135 minutes in the fourth innings. They rapidly declined to 11 for three but Procter, who hit three sixes and 17 fours, made 111 in even time off an attack which included Chris Old, Tony Nicholson, Richard Hutton and Geoff Cope to set up a four-wicket win.

The greatest problem on the batting front was to find an opening partner for Ron Nicholls, who was again most reliable. John Sullivan, a Bristolian from local club Long Ashton, had an extended trial which was ultimately unsuccessful. Tony Brown batted at number two briefly, but in the end it was decided to recall the 43-year-old Milton, who had indicated when he retired in 1970 that he would be available in emergencies. Milton batted as well as ever and, though twice briefly out of action with injury, averaged over 41 in scoring 700 runs. Of the other batsmen Shepherd fell away slightly and Bissex badly, the latter's aggregate and average being less than half of those of his excellent season in 1971.

Procter had a good season with the ball, improving both in number of wickets and average. Davey, given more opportunity following Smith's retirement, responded well and earned his county cap. Mortimore took 85 Championship wickets, his chief support now coming from the slow left-arm Bissex, who took 55. This meant fewer chances for Allen, who appeared in only ten matches.

The Gillette Cup run provided the greatest drama of the season. In the first match, at Hove, the Sussex hurdle was at last cleared. Solid early batting followed by a brilliant 107 from Mike Procter set up a total of 252 for seven which Sussex never looked like matching against tight bowling. They were bundled out for 129 in only 42.3 overs, Procter taking three for 20 and gaining the Man of the Match award. The next match, in the third round against Surrey at Bristol, was snatched from the fire when all seemed lost. Despite an opening partnership of 99 and the excellent batting of Nicholls, who made 77, Gloucestershire could total only a disappointing 214. This did not seem anything like enough when Surrey were 155 for two with Mickey Stewart and Younis Ahmed both going like trains. Then Jack Davey dismissed Younis and Stuart Storey in quick succession and Knight, who had had an unsuccessful bowl earlier, returned to have Stewart caught behind and then got rid of Roope, Long, Pocock and Jackman in ten balls while conceding only a single. Procter had Willis caught at slip and Gloucestershire had won an astonishing victory by 15 runs.

The semi-final against Lancashire at Old Trafford, played before a crowd officially returned at 23,520, was one of the most exciting in the competition's history. Gloucestershire, thanks principally to Nicholls, 53, and Procter, 65, made 229 for six, a total which certainly gave them a chance of victory and this looked a distinct possibility as Lancashire declined to 165 for six. It should be mentioned here that, partly because of an hour's play being lost to rain around lunch time, and partly due to delays occasioned by the vast crowd spilling over in front of the sight-screens early on—only eight overs could be bowled in the first hour for this reason—the last stages of the game were played in extremely poor light. This might be thought to be an advantage to the fielding side but this was not entirely the case. The sight-screens at Old Trafford are excellent, so that when the light was at its worst bowler, batsman and wicket-keeper had some chance of seeing the ball whereas fielders, peering into the darkness of the crowd, had no chance whatever if the ball went slightly in the air.

In these circumstances Jack Bond and Jack Simmons raised the score to 203, at which point John Mortimore, who had earlier struck two tremendous blows for his side by bowling Clive Lloyd and causing Farokh Engineer to hit his wicket, bowled Simmons also. This meant 27 were then needed from six overs, with three wickets remaining. No game could have been more nicely posed, it seemed. Then David Hughes, in one historic over from Mortimore, struck 24 runs, two driven sixes, two fours and two twos, to settle the issue. Incidentally, I cannot believe that there has been, in modern times anyway, a longer fielding session than the final one in that match. Tea was taken between innings, with the result that Gloucestershire were in the field from 4.30 until the match ended a minute or two before 9 pm!

After some promising performances in 1971 Gloucestershire were strengthened by the appearance in 1972 of two very distinguished Pakistan Test players in Zaheer Abbas and Sadiq Mohammad, of the great cricketing family, whose elder brother, Mushtaq, had been playing with great success for Northamptonshire since 1966. Sadiq had come to England in 1967 when Gloucestershire had given him a trial but, with their main interest being in signing first Garfield Sobers, and then Mike Procter under the new 'immediate registration' rules, he had not been taken on. In fact no other county showed any interest in him, and he therefore turned to League cricket. In 1970 Tony Brown played with him for D. H. Robbins' XI at Eastbourne and was sufficiently impressed to suggest a further trial. Sadiq was offered a contract and served his two-year qualifying period. Meanwhile, there had been another change to the qualification rule, in 1971, when it was decided that an overseas cricketer would be eligible to play for a county after five years residence in Britain. This meant that Sadiq would be qualified anyway by May 1972 and with counties now permitted to have two overseas players, the County hastened to contract Zaheer, who had electrified the cricket world with his monumental innings of 274 against England at the Oval the previous year. Zaheer, in fact, was not permitted to play until one year after the conclusion of Pakistan's tour, a curious piece of legislation, which meant that he did not turn out for Gloucestershire until mid-July 1972. In the event neither was to do anything particularly startling in their first season, but the final contribution of each was to be very great.

Zaheer, tall, slender, bespectacled, with a high backlift and a wide range of strokes, was to be the key Gloucestershire batsman over the next decade. In only 206 matches for the County he was to score over 16,000 runs at an average close to 50, and hit 49 centuries—in all first-class cricket he made 108 centuries, 12 of them in Test matches. His batsmanship, silken, graceful, deft, was as attractive to watch as anyone could have wished. Beneath that outward bloom, however, there was a fine technique and a will to dominate bowlers that was belied by Zaheer's gentle and shy persona. He was, in fact, quite merciless when on top and bowlers found him dreadfully difficult to contain, firstly on account of the range and surprising power of his strokes and secondly because there were very few balls he could not score off. None of his contemporaries, except perhaps Vivian Richards, has scored with such ease and regularity off the straight, good-length ball.

His compatriot, Sadiq, was entirely different in appearance and method. Short and dapper, Sadiq had all the left-hander's traditional fluency off his legs, and he also cut and drove powerfully for a small man. He could, too, play the 'run-thief', dabbing and pushing the ball here and there and generally upsetting bowlers and fielders. He was

Zaheer Abbas eases one gracefully past square-leg. (Patrick Eagar)

always a brave and resilient player of fast bowling, possessing that quality of self-belief which is so important to games players. His early struggles for recognition have been noted and he must have been aware of the contrast between his own stuttering early career and those of his brothers Hanif, a Test cricketer at 18, and Mushtaq, who first played for Pakistan only three months after his 15th birthday. Sadiq's perseverance in the face of early setbacks paid off handsomely for Gloucestershire, for whom he made over 12,000 runs, averaging nearly 37, scored 25 centuries and also took 138 wickets with quickish leg-spinners.

Gloucestershire finished third in the Championship in 1972 and reached the semi-finals of the new Benson and Hedges Cup, the preliminary rounds of which were then and for some time afterwards established on a geographical basis, the County qualifying for the knock-out stage by coming second to Glamorgan in the West section. They then beat Middlesex comfortably in their quarter-final but were outplayed by Yorkshire in the semi-final. Against these successes, Gloucestershire were 16th in the Sunday League with only three victories, and were beaten by Kent at the first hurdle of the Gillette Cup.

The weakness lay in the erratic nature of the batting, the strength in the skill and variety of the attack, which earned them 77 Championship bonus points, a tally equalled only by Northamptonshire, despite a heel injury which severely affected Mike Procter in the later stages of the season and limited his Championship overs to 424. Only Procter and Knight passed 1,000 runs in the Championship, but Milton, called on again for 14 matches, again did well, while the aggressive Shepherd had his moments. Unfortunately Ron Nicholls had a lean year and with Sadiq averaging barely 20 the run-getting was too unreliable.

The bowling was a different matter, four men taking their wickets at below 21 runs each at good striking rates. Procter, before his heel began to trouble him, had taken 52 wickets at 13 each, and still finished with 58 at 16.44. Tony Brown had 48 at below 20, Mortimore took 68 at 20.52 and Sadiq 33 at similar cost. The hard-working Davey also had a satisfactory season, taking 46 at 26. Performances of high quality by their bowlers sparked off a fine run between 7 June and 11 August when, in 11 matches, the County had six wins and five draws and looked well-placed to carry off the title, but with Procter forced to play purely as a batsman and then missing the last two matches entirely, their challenge fell away. Victory over Glamorgan at Bristol in their last match would have brought second place, but the Welshmen, in trouble at 76 for six having been set to make 185 to win, held on for a draw.

First appearances were made by a number of players. Barrie Meyer's fine career having ended at the end of 1971—he was later to become a respected Test match umpire—the County recruited Roy Swetman, formerly of Surrey, Nottinghamshire and England, to take over the wicket-keeping duties. Swetman, then 38, was still very fit and had a successful season, with 42 catches and six stumpings. Two 19-year-olds, James Foat and David Graveney, son of Ken and nephew of Tom, also played for the first time. Foat, a strokeplaying batsman and fine ground fielder was to have a comparatively short career but Graveney, a steady and thoughtful slow left-armer, was later to captain the side for eight seasons and played into the 1990s. That year Foat made an inauspicious beginning, averaging under ten in his eight innings but Graveney, like Foat a product of Millfield School, started more happily, taking 14 wickets in his five matches.

David Graveney made his debut in controversial circumstances in David Allen's benefit match at Cheltenham against Lancashire. Allen had played only seven matches that season and his six wickets had cost 41 apiece. With Gloucestershire chasing hard for the Championship it was decided to play the untried Graveney to the exclusion of Allen. Gloucestershire hung on for a draw in this match, Graveney's figures in Lancashire's one innings of 354 for six declared being 20-3-61-0, but in the next match, in which Derbyshire were beaten by five wickets, he justified his selection by taking five for 63 in the second innings. He then had match figures of six for 89 in the third match of the Festival, which Middlesex won by six wickets. This season was Allen's last, the

20th of a career of considerable distinction which brought him 882 wickets for the County. Mention should finally be made of one of the great one-day performances of all time, produced by Mike Procter at Taunton on 3 June 1972 in a Benson and Hedges qualifying match against Somerset. He came to the wicket with Gloucestershire 37 for two and proceeded to make 154 not out, with eight sixes and 20 fours, in 130 minutes, out of 215 scored while he was at the wicket. As if that were not enough, he then took five for 26 in 9.2 overs.

In 1973 the promise shown in the previous season was fulfilled with victory in the Gillette Cup Final against Sussex at Lord's, the first major prize the County had carried off since 1877 when they won the Championship. All in all, Tony Brown's side had an excellent all-round season. They finished fifth in the Championship and might have done better still but for injuries to Mike Procter which prevented him from bowling more than 238 overs in the competition, and they climbed to sixth in the Sunday League. The only blot on their record was their failure to qualify for the Benson and Hedges quarter-finals, disappointing batting leading to defeats at the hands of Hampshire and Glamorgan.

Generally though, the batting was sounder than it had been for some years. Procter again led the way, with 1,351 Championship runs, average 64, and six centuries. The power and purity of his off-side stroke-play was such that older spectators were moved to make comparisons with the immortal Walter Hammond. Sadiq had an excellent season, comfortably exceeding 1,200 runs, hitting three Championship centuries and an unbeaten 184 against New Zealand at

Tony Brown steals a quick single in the Gillette Cup Final against Sussex in 1973. (Patrick Eagar)

Gillette Cup winners, 1973. L to r: Andy Stovold, Jack Davey, Mike Procter, Sadiq Mohammed, Roger Knight, Tony Brown, David Shepherd, Jim Foat, Zaheer Abbas, David Graveney. (Patrick Eagar)

Bristol, and averaging over 40. Roger Knight also had a good season and with Zaheer finding his form later on and Tony Brown getting runs regularly it did not matter too much that David Shepherd and Ron Nicholls were below par. Brighton-born Andrew Stovold made a good impression in his seven Championship games but the Cornishman Malcolm Dunstan, from Redruth, was less successful.

Though Procter took only 26 wickets the bowling was still

adequate, with Tony Brown, Jack Davey and John Mortimore all having their share of success and Sadiq, Knight and Graveney giving useful support. The County never really challenged for the Championship, indeed their comparatively high placing was achieved by a late run of success, five of their six Championship wins coming in their last seven matches. It was during this run that Somerset were beaten at Bristol by an innings and 164 runs. Gloucestershire won the toss and made 357 (Zaheer 103, Knight 122, Stovold 74) on a heavily marled pitch, which took spin to such an extent that Somerset were bowled out for 91 and 102 on the second day, Mortimore's match figures being ten for 55 and Graveney's nine for 86. Somerset skipper Brian Close repeated Jack Meyer's remarks about Weston-super-Mare beach and said a good many other things as well. In the end fifth in the Championship was not too poor a result.

The high spot of course, was the Gillette Cup and certainly there were plenty of dramas on the way to that triumph at Lord's, and not a few during it. In the first round, against bogey-side Glamorgan at Cardiff on 30 June, the County, who were without the injured Procter, could not have been too confident but in the end the Welshmen were overcome without great difficulty. Sadiq's solid 42, followed by punishing innings of 72 from Knight and 43 from Zaheer took Gloucestershire to 196 for three, and though they lost their last five wickets for 25 runs in 15 overs they still totalled 230. Despite 61 from Alan Jones and 51 from Tony Lewis, Glamorgan never really got on terms and finished 38 runs short.

In the second round, Gloucestershire were drawn to play Surrey at Bristol, and, as in the match two years before, there were palpitations galore before the County won through. Put into bat by Surrey skipper John Edrich, they were 24 for five after 11 overs, Sadiq being the only man to have reached double figures before being caught at slip off Robin Jackman. Geoff Arnold was the main destroyer, having had Nicholls caught at short-leg for one, bowled Knight for four and had Zaheer and Procter both taken at slip, the latter for a stunning duck. At that point Arnold had four for 12 off six overs. Unaccountably, Edrich gave Arnold only two more overs in that opening spell, and Shepherd and Tony Brown took the score to 60 before the sixth wicket fell. Once again all seemed lost, but Shepherd, batting with marvellous concentration, found an inspired partner in young Graveney who held on with him while 107 runs were added, Graveney's important contribution being 44. Shepherd carried his bat out for 72, an innings of such value to his side that, if he had never reached double figures before or since, his honoured place in the County's history would have been secure.

Even so, 169 was a far from formidable target in a 60-over match on

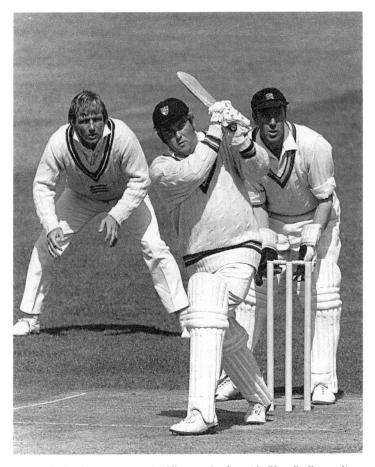

David Shepherd batting against Middlesex at Lord's, with Clive Radley at slip and John Murray keeping wicket. (Patrick Eagar)

a wicket from which the early-morning juice had long departed. Surrey looked fallible at the start and were at one point 52 for three, but at 112 for four with young Younis Ahmed and Storey looking comfortable the match seemed theirs for the taking. Then Younis was needlessly run out, Procter caught and bowled Storey and the innings fell away, Surrey finishing 19 runs short.

The third round match, against Essex at Chelmsford, was altogether more comfortable. Gloucestershire, having been put in by Brian Taylor, made a very useful 236 for nine thanks principally to Sadiq (56), Knight (60) and Zaheer (45). Knight, Brown and Davey cut down the first eight Essex batsmen for only 130 and though Stuart Turner and Ray East mounted a defiant rearguard action, the result

GILLETTE CUP FINAL
GLOUCESTERSHIRE *v* SUSSEX

Played at Lord's, 1 September 1973

GLOUCESTERSHIRE

Sadiq Mohammad	lbw b Buss	9
R. D. V. Knight	b Snow	2
Zaheer Abbas	b Buss	9
M. J. Procter	c Morley b Buss	94
D. R. Shepherd	c Griffith b Marshall	11
†A. W. Stovold	c Griffith b Snow	10
*A. S. Brown	not out	77
J. C. Foat	b Snow	7
D. A. Graveney	run out	6
Extras	b 4, lb 10, nb 9	23
Total	(8 wkts, 60 overs)	248

1-5, 2-22, 3-27, 4-74, 5-106, 6-180, 7-229, 8-248

J. B. Mortimore and J. Davey did not bat.

BOWLING	O	M	R	W
Snow	12	4	31	3
Greig	12	1	53	0
Buss	12	5	46	3
Marshall	12	3	29	1
Spencer	12	0	66	0

SUSSEX

G. A. Greenidge	b Knight	76
J. D. Morley	c Zaheer Abbas b Brown	31
R. M. Prideaux	b Davey	28
P. J. Graves	not out	36
*A. W. Greig	run out	0
M. A. Buss	c Graveney b Knight	5
†M. G. Griffith	b Knight	3
M. J. J. Faber	run out	9
J. A. Snow	b Procter	4
J. Spencer	b Knight	2
R. P. T. Marshall	b Procter	0
Extras	b 5, lb 9	14
Total	(56.5 overs)	208

1-52, 2-121, 3-155, 4-156, 5-173, 6-180, 7-195, 8-204, 9-207

BOWLING	O	M	R	W
Procter	10.5	1	27	2
Davey	10	1	37	1
Mortimer	12	3	32	0
Brown	12	1	33	1
Graveney	2	0	18	0
Knight	10	0	47	4

Umpires: A. E. Fagg and T. W. Spencer

was never in doubt. Essex finished 30 runs short, Jack Davey taking four for 35 and Roger Knight three for 40 to earn a second Man of the Match award to go with the one he had won at Cardiff.

The semi-final, at Worcester, was another desperately close game which Worcestershire, had they held their catches, would surely have won—though after that astonishing recovery against Surrey, who can say that anything in cricket is sure? Gloucestershire again batted first and, losing Nicholls and Knight cheaply, were immediately in trouble. Procter was dropped off the first ball he received, as was Sadiq shortly afterwards. Had these two chances been accepted, Gloucestershire would have been 36 for four. Then, to add to Worcestershire's woes, Procter was dropped again, on 18. Sadiq went on to make 36 and Procter a brilliant 101 which, with useful contributions from Zaheer, Shepherd and Stovold (the latter having recently displaced Swetman as wicket-keeper owing to his superior batting) carried Gloucestershire to 243 for eight. This did not appear too formidable a target as Glenn Turner (109) and Ron Headley (56) put on 123 for Worcestershire's first wicket before Davey dismissed Headley. D'Oliveira, Imran Khan and Yardley were dismissed fairly cheaply but Worcestershire, with Turner well set, six wickets in hand and 41 wanted from the last six overs, looked favourites. Then Procter returned to dismiss Turner, Gifford and Cass, but Ormrod and Inchmore, running hectically between the wickets, got their side to a situation where a six off the last ball would win the match. Jack Davey,

---

Gloucestershire won by 40 runs. Inspired by the captain Tony Brown, whom Alec Bedser named the Man of the Match and the all-round brilliance of Procter, Gloucestershire deserved their first major success since 1877, when they last won the County Championship. Sussex, appearing in their fifth Gillette Cup final, a record, put up a gallant performance before a restricted crowd of 21,300 who paid £56,000. In a remarkable sequence of these finals since 1963, the side batting first has won in alternate years, and Sussex could consider themselves unfortunate in losing the toss as the light deteriorated and was quite bad in the later stages of their innings.

Moreover, Sussex were without one of their key men, Tony Buss, injured, although his deputy, Marshall, a young, quick, red-haired, left-arm bowler, performed most creditably. Gloucestershire had their anxious moments, their worst period being at the beginning when they lost their first three wickets for 27. Procter came to the rescue and he received staunch support from Shepherd and Stovold. Procter promptly struck two short balls from Michael Buss for 6 but at 106 for five Gloucestershire could not have been happy.

This was a critical stage; Brown took charge at one end while Procter, steady and sure in defence, drove and hooked at every opportunity until after batting two and a half hours, he was held at deep square leg for 94. The stand produced 74 and on Procter's departure Brown took up the assault. He hit 46 out of 68 in the last eight overs, pasing his fifty when he helped himself to 14 from Spencer in the 56th over. The agile Foat, aged 20, ran like a gazelle while getting seven in a stand of 49, and finally Brown pulled Greig twice for 6, the first into the grandstand balcony.

Greenidge and Morley were not awed by Gloucestershire's formidable total of 248 and gave Sussex a sound start of 52. The side reached 155 for two in 44 overs against a varied attack in which Mortimore played an important part by bowling his 12 overs off the reel for only 32 runs. Prideaux played some grand strokes, but when Procter came back for his second spell in inferior light the issue swung clearly in Gloucestershire's favour.

The Sussex captain tried to steal a leg-bye off the last ball of the over, but the tall and agile Foat swooped in from cover and ran him out before he could get back. Graves continued to bat splendidly, but Knight and Procter were too much for the tail and Gloucestershire in the end won comfortably.

taking great care not to no-ball, fired in a quick, straight one which Ormrod could only pull for a single and Gloucestershire were through to their first Lord's final, against Sussex.

The traumas in the final occurred in its early stages when the County, having chosen to bat, were soon 27 for three in face of the speed of John Snow and the slow-medium left-arm swing of Michael Buss, who had had Sadiq leg before and bowled Zaheer. Procter's reponse was immediate. He pulled two short balls from Buss into the Father Time stand for six but neither Shepherd nor Stovold settled and Gloucestershire were still in trouble at 106 for five. Then Tony Brown entered to play a decisive innings of 77 not out. First he played second fiddle to Procter, who was out for 94 with the score 180 for six; then, in the last eight overs of the innings, he scored 46 out of 68, twice pulling Tony Greig for 6. Jim Foat fairly flew between the wickets and played an invaluable part, even though he made only seven out of a partnership of 49, and Gloucestershire totalled 248 for eight.

Sussex, thanks to Geoffrey Greenidge (76), Jerry Morley (32), Roger Prideaux (28) and Peter Graves (36 not out) were 155 for two after 44 overs and in with a very good chance, but after Davey bowled Prideaux and Foat threw out Greig superbly for a duck the innings fell away before Knight (four for 47) and Procter (two for 27) and the County triumphed in convincing fashion by 40 runs. Despite the great part played by Mike Procter, Alec Bedser had no hesitation in giving the Man of the Match award to Tony Brown for his batting, economic bowling and excellent captaincy.

The next two seasons were to be deeply disappointing ones following the delirium of that success at Lord's. In 1974 the County suffered through the absence of Zaheer and Sadiq, who were touring with the Pakistan side and hence could appear in only four Championship games each. Though Procter again batted well his knee continued to trouble him and he was to undergo an operation in the winter of 1974–75. Knight had a fine season, hitting four Championship centuries and averaging 42, but he was the only batsman to pass 1,000 runs in the Championship, Procter making 950 and no one else topping 700. There was, though, a distinct advance from Stovold, who scored his first Championship century, 102 against Derbyshire at Cheltenham.

No bowler that season took 40 Championship wickets, Procter and Graveney having 39 each at modest cost but the rest being expensive. Mortimore, his mind perhaps more on the accountancy career for which he had been studying out of season with commendable single-mindedness, had a particularly poor time, his 29 wickets costing 45 each. His splendid career officially closed in September, as did that of Ron Nicholls, though both returned to the colours during the following season's injury crisis. Unsurprisingly the Championship position slipped to 14th and one-day ventures were unsuccessful.

The 1974 season was, however, a year of first appearances. The 18-year-old Alistair Hignell, who was later to get Cambridge blues for cricket and rugby and skipper both sides against Oxford, became qualified and played eight games without making any impact except with his fielding. Though Hignell was born in Cambridge he had Gloucestershire roots, his father having played one match for the County. Another debutant was Andrew Brassington, from Bagnall in Staffordshire, whose highly promising career as a wicket-keeper was to be cut short by a badly injured Achilles tendon, while Philip Thorn, Bristol-born slow left-armer and left-hand bat, also played in four matches. Julian Shackleton, son of Derek of Hampshire and England and, like Graveney and Foat a product of Millfield School, played in six matches. He had appeared infrequently since as early as 1971. A medium-paced bowler like his father, with a good easy action, he took plenty of wickets in all cricket except first-class, where his accuracy was not quite strict enough, bearing in mind his modest pace, for him to avoid punishment on good pitches.

With injuries again a dominant factor in 1975 those youngsters, plus one or two more, got plenty of opportunity. This was another poor season, four Championship wins, the same number as in 1974, resulting in a drop to 16th place. Only one of the four Benson and Hedges qualifying matches was won, and the County slipped from 12th to 15th in the Sunday League. There was, however, a reasonable run in the Gillette Cup, Oxfordshire being beaten by 77 runs and much-fancied Leicestershire by 32 runs after Sadiq and Zaheer both made centuries to enable the County to score a massive 314 for four. In the semi-final at Old Trafford there was another fine match, Lancashire squeezing home by three wickets with only three balls to spare.

The biggest single blow to the County's hopes that year was the inability of Mike Procter to play in more than four Championship games. Following his winter knee operation he was unable to play until the second week in July. After those few appearances, in which he had bowled off-breaks, he dropped out again, returning for the Gillette Cup semi-final at Old Trafford on 20 August. During this match he tried to bowl quick to halt Lancashire's advance towards victory, broke down and did not play again. The plusses of the season were the confirmation of known talent rather than the discovery of new ones, which, with the retirements of Milton, Nicholls, Mortimore, Smith and Meyer over the past few seasons, and that of Brown imminent, was what was really needed. Zaheer and Sadiq had fine seasons, averaging 47 and 37 and scoring 1,426 and 1,268

Championship runs respectively. Knight passed his 1,000 in all matches and Shepherd made over 900 in the Championship. Stovold, who formed a promising opening partnership with Sadiq, made 925 runs in the Championship, a notable advance.

Davey, Brown and Graveney were the main bowlers in Procter's absence and all did fairly well, though suffering from the lack of a really quick and penetrative new ball operator. The Devonian John Childs, who threatened to reach the heights with Gloucestershire and later did so with Essex, also made his debut.

Of the young cricketers who appeared over these two seasons, when the side was really in a state of considerable flux, Stovold, Graveney, Hignell, Childs and Brassington were to come through but, sadly, Nick Cooper, Philip Thorn, John Dixon, Ian Crawford, Julian Shackleton, Nick Finan and even, for all that he played 91 matches, Jim Foat, were not to make it. At the end of the season Roger Knight left for Sussex which, in view of his important contributions during the lean years of 1974 and 1975, could only be regarded as a serious blow, and prospects for 1976 were not auspicious.

Before moving on, however, it is necessary to look in some detail at the financial difficulties the County had been experiencing. Gloucestershire had found, along with other counties, that the signing of overseas players, while having only a minor effect on gate receipts, had a quite startling one on expenditure. This, together with general inflation, and despite the increased revenue brought about by three types of one-day competition, had resulted in another financial crisis—imminent since the early 1970s but staved off by the forbearance of creditors and by the sale, in 1967, of a piece of land at the Ashley Down Road end of the ground.

The season of 1974 had produced a working loss of over £26,000 and heads were being shaken in despair over what the future might hold. However, in December 1974 contact with the Club was made by the Phoenix Assurance Company, in the process of moving to Bristol, who were looking for a sports and social centre to accommodate their staff, whose numbers would eventually exceed 1,000. It seemed to Phoenix that their needs and the County's financial problems might be solved at a stroke. A special general meeting was called in September 1975 to consider the 'proposed agreement with Phoenix Assurance'. Approval was given, after which the County's president, R. F. P. Holloway, chairman Frank Twiselton and vice-chairman Ken Graveney undertook the detailed negotiations with Phoenix. These resulted in the formation of the Gloucester and Phoenix Assurance Amenity Company. Under the agreement made, Phoenix paid £125,000 for the ground and granted the Amenity Company a 99-year lease. Gloucestershire used part of their windfall to pay off debts, which had accumulated to an amount exceeding £55,000, and then entered into a 50/50 partnership in the Amenity Company with Phoenix. The Gloucestershire CC Social Club was moved across to the Jessop Tavern, on the far side of the ground, the vacated accommodation being used by the Phoenix Social and Sports Club. Gloucestershire were to have use of the playing surface for all their home fixtures and retained their own accommodation— dressing-room, offices etc—within the pavilion.

Thus fortified by unaccustomed financial security Gloucestershire embarked on the 1976 season during which, despite the vast relief of rising to third in the Championship, their performances in other competitions were so erratic as to cause their long-suffering supporters almost to tear out their hair.

Once again the County could not reach the knock-out stages of the Benson and Hedges Cup. In the Gillette Cup they convincingly beat Worcestershire and Yorkshire, only to go down to humiliating defeat at Old Trafford (again!) where they were bowled out on a good pitch for 125 and lost by seven wickets. In the Sunday League they could win only four games from 16 and duly finished bottom.

The main feature of the season was the remarkable form of Zaheer Abbas, who for the first time for the County revealed the true extent of his talent. He made 2,431 runs in the Championship, hit 11 centuries and topped the national averages. Twice he scored a double hundred and a hundred in the same match, against Kent at Canterbury and against Surrey at the Oval, the latter ground the scene of so many of his triumphs. On both occasions he was unbeaten in both innings. The gracefulness of his stroke-play and the rapidity of his scoring were alike breathtaking. Such was Zaheer's form that Sadiq's splendid season was almost overshadowed. The Pakistani left-hander made over 1,600 in the Championship, average 47, and hit seven centuries in the competition, plus another against Oxford University. Procter, too, did remarkably well for a man whose career had seemed very much in the balance the previous year, for he scored over 1,000 runs and took 65 wickets in the Championship. Stovold reached his 1,000 for the first time and was capped at the same time as David Graveney. Another player to advance was Hignell, who averaged nearly 33 in the Championship and also took 119 off the West Indies' attack at Bristol.

Brian Brain, a highly respected seam bowler for many years with Worcestershire, joined at the start of the season and, though troubled constantly by a groin strain, bowled well enough to offset Jack Davey's poor season. Brown's 39 wickets at 22 headed the averages with Brain's 40 at 25 coming just before Graveney's 65 at just over 25. Childs advanced, taking 34 Championship wickets against 11 the previous year and greatly reducing their cost. Bowling was certainly the County's weaker suit that year, but a surprising number of match-winning performances came from the bowlers during the late run of six wins in seven matches which saw them surge up the table. Among these was Procter's six for 28 in Warwickshire's second innings at Edgbaston which opened the way for a seven-wicket win, Childs' match figures of eight for 71 at Cheltenham, where Essex lost by an innings, and Brain's ten for 122 in the match against Somerset at Bristol in late August, when another innings victory resulted.

The most remarkable game of the season, though, was against Somerset at Taunton at the end of May. Somerset, batting first on a green pitch, declared having made 333 for seven, a huge total in the conditions. Ian Botham's six for 25 saw Gloucestershire skittled for 79. They fared better following on, Zaheer making 141, but their total of 372 meant that Somerset needed only 119 for victory in $4\frac{1}{2}$ hours. With Brian Rose, who had made 104 in the first innings, again leading the way, Somerset needed only 22 more runs with seven wickets in hand. Then Procter, either throwing up slow off-spin or roaring in off a full run, often in the same over, so unsettled the batsman that his final spell of six for 13 earned Gloucestershire victory by eight runs.

In the end, though, it was Zaheer's year, and should not be allowed to pass without a fuller look at his wonderful batting against Kent at Canterbury in the second week of August. After Kent had been bowled out, principally by Graveney and Brown, for 251, Zaheer played an innings designed to ensure his side a substantial lead. Coming in at 3 for one, he made his unbeaten 230 in 6 hours 11

Andy Stovold, a stocky, aggressive opener. (Patrick Eagar)

minutes, a brisk but far from headlong rate of scoring, and hit no fewer than 37 fours. Gloucestershire declared 123 runs on but Kent made 369 at their second attempt, using up a lot of time in the process. Gloucestershire now needed 241 to win at a little more than five runs per over, a very stiff task which they achieved with 3.1 overs of the last 20 remaining, as Zaheer, well supported by Sadiq and Stovold, made 104 not out in 98 minutes with 12 fours, completely mastering Derek Underwood in the process.

During the winter Tony Brown, having captained his side to a nine-wicket win at Worcester in the last match of the season, gave up the captaincy after eight years in office and succeeded Grahame Parker as secretary-manager, Parker taking over responsibility for sponsorship and advertising. Brown could look back with some satisfaction to the achievements of the County during his tenure. Though the Championship, that elusive grail, had not been won there had been one second place finish and two thirds. Moreover, with the 1973 Gillette Cup win, the County had secured its first trophy since the days of W.G. He handed over to his successor, Mike Procter, a side which combined youth and experience in shrewd measure and on occasion, looked capable of challenging the best teams in the land.

Gloucestershire have cause to be grateful to Tony Brown. He was an all-round cricketer of high quality, a dangerous medium-fast swing bowler of great stamina, a fine close catcher and a batsman who, though too frequently betrayed by impetuosity, was always capable of playing a match-winning innings. He was one of only four Gloucestershire cricketers to take 1,000 wickets and score 10,000 runs, the others being W.G., Reg Sinfield and John Mortimore. These three all played for England and there are many good judges who consider that Brown was a little unfortunate not to have done so as well. His captaincy, though basically orthodox, was incisive and intelligent. He had no time at all for players who shirked their responsibilities, but offered every encouragement to those he felt were doing their very best, however unsuccessful a patch they might be going through.

MIKE PROCTER'S CAPTAINCY

THE FIRST YEAR OF MIKE PROCTER'S five as captain, 1977, was also by some way the most successful. Gloucestershire finished in third place in the County Championship, only five points behind Middlesex and Kent who shared the title, and could count themselves unlucky at that, for their matches against Northamptonshire at Gloucester and Yorkshire at Bristol were both abandoned without a ball being bowled. There was, though, compensation in their victory over Kent in the final of the Benson and Hedges Cup at Lord's. They went out of the Gillette Cup at an early stage, losing narrowly to Northamptonshire at Bristol, but might have finished higher than equal sixth in the Sunday League but for the weather, which caused no fewer than five of their 16 matches to be 'no results'. Procter's captaincy, at once determined and inventive, was widely admired.

Though Zaheer did not touch the heights of 1976 he had a very fine Championship season, averaging 56, scoring almost 1,600 runs and hitting five centuries. Against Sussex at Cheltenham he again made a double century and a century, 205 not out and 108 not out. Sadiq fell away, failing to reach 1,000 runs and averaging below 30, but Stovold's steady improvement continued. Shepherd and Hignell, after the university term, made useful runs and Procter also gave glimpses of his power, but Foat continued to disappoint. A good first impression was made by Philip Bainbridge, a 19-year-old batsman from Stoke-on-Trent.

Procter had a great season with the ball, taking 108 Championship wickets at 17.83 each. He and Brian Brain, who had 69 at 22.15, were day in and day out the most effective new ball combination in the land. Graveney and John Childs, with 105 wickets between them, played an important part and the only real weakness in the attack was the lack of a reliable third seamer. Injury restricted Davey to a single Championship match and though Shackleton, Finan and Martin Vernon, signed from Middlesex, were tried none looked the part. In retrospect, it might have been wise to call on Tony Brown, who at 41 was very fit and was still a registered player.

Periodic frailty in the batting and the lack of depth in bowling made the County a shade vulnerable and for so gifted a side they suffered some remarkably heavy defeats, Kent winning at Gloucester by an innings and 161 and Northamptonshire by 214 runs at Northampton, but when Gloucestershire were on top they were ruthless; of their nine Championship victories two were by an innings and three by a margin of eight wickets. Procter was at his best in the game against

Worcestershire at Cheltenham. He swung the ball into the bat on the first day to such an extent that he was forced to bowl round the wicket to have any chance of a leg-before decision. Bowling at a little over medium pace he took seven for 35 and Worcestershire were bowled out for 167. He followed up with 108 in the County's total of 338 and then, bowling off-spinners on a pitch made treacherous by rain, took six for 38 to clinch victory by an innings and 35.

During the Gloucestershire innings, which at one point had slumped to 112 for five, Procter, who had only a few runs on the board, mishit Worcestershire skipper Norman Gifford up towards deep mid-wicket. Now the visitors, for some reason, had no 12th man and with D'Oliveira injured, had borrowed Gloucestershire's, who was Jim Foat. Unfortunately Foat, who was on the deep mid-wicket fence, did not sight the ball against the red brick of the College gymnasium and, starting late, failed completely to reach what might have been a catch. As Procter thereafter began to thump the Worcestershire bowling all round the ground Gifford, a fiery competitor, began to mutter and grumble, implying that Foat had not really tried for the catch. Procter resented this slur on one of his players and said: 'Well, Norman, if you don't want our 12th man you don't have to have him.' Worcestershire therefore fielded with ten men for a while, though, happily, more cordial relations were soon restored.

Gloucestershire came to their last Championship match, at Bristol, against Hampshire, four points ahead of Middlesex and Kent and therefore slight favourites for the title. Scores of 115 by Procter and 94 by Barry Richards for the opposition were the features of the first innings, Gloucestershire making 223 and Hampshire 229 (Procter six for 68). After the County's second innings of 276 (Hignell 92, Procter 57) Hampshire needed 271 to win in 275 minutes. Unfortunately, Brain at mid-off dropped Gordon Greenidge when he was 30, and David Turner was also missed when eight. Their partnership put on 128 in 65 minutes. Greenidge made 94 in even time and Hampshire won by six wickets with 80 minutes to spare. With Kent and Middlesex both winning their final games, the County's hopes were dashed.

Hampshire, one way and another loomed large on Gloucestershire's horizon in 1977. They had beaten Gloucestershire by eight wickets in the qualifying stages of the Benson and Hedges Cup but both sides qualified for the quarter-final, with one defeat and three wins. There Hampshire disposed comfortably of Glamorgan at Swansea while Gloucestershire, thanks to the batting of Zaheer and Shepherd and the bowling of Procter and Graveney, beat Middlesex in a rather closer match. The semi-final between Hampshire and Gloucestershire at Southampton was a game full of high drama.

*Mike Taylor ct Stovold b. Procter, in the Benson and Hedges semi-final at
Southampton, 1977. (Patrick Eagar)*

Gloucestershire, who batted first on an excellent pitch, were given
the perfect start by Andy Stovold, 46, and Sadiq, 76, who put on 106
for the first wicket. Their innings then tailed away dismally against
Mottram and Mike Taylor and their total of 180 looked very modest
on such a good batting wicket. It was here that Procter's leadership
showed at its best—where almost any other captain would have tried
to 'keep it tight', get the opposition behind the needed scoring rate and
force errors that way, Procter opted for all-out attack. With his field
set 'Carmody' style, with seven close catchers, he flew in off his long
run, bowling as fast, in his own opinion, as he ever did in his life. With
the fifth ball of his fourth over he knocked back Gordon Greenidge's
stumps. With the first two balls of his fifth over, he had Barry
Richards and Trevor Jesty leg before and with the third he bowled
John Rice off his pads. That was four wickets in five balls, the last three
a hat-trick, and Hampshire's powerful top-order batting lay in ruins,
with their score at 18 for four. The effort Procter put in during this
opening spell was enormous and he was forced to rest with figures of
6-3-3-4. David Turner (49) and Nigel Cowley (59) took advantage of
the respite and by excellent cricket advanced Hampshire's score to 127.

Then came the breach Procter had been praying for as Brain bowled Turner and ten runs later Shackleton got through Cowley's defence. Procter returned to dismiss Taylor and wicket-keeper Stephenson, Brain had Murtagh caught behind, and, when the furious slogging of Andy Roberts threatened the County's hold, knocked back his stumps also. Procter's final figures of 11-5-13-6 are eloquent testimony to a brilliant performance, which without the support of his faithful lieutenant Brain, who had three for 28, might still not have been enough to tip the scales.

After that, the final against Kent at Lord's was almost anticlimatic. Gloucestershire batted first and their innings was launched by a dazzling 71 from Stovold. Zaheer weighed in with an elegant 70 and with Sadiq, Procter and Foat making useful contributions Gloucestershire totalled a satisfactory 237 for six. Brain and Procter soon reduced Kent to 5 for two and thereafter, despite Woolmer's fine innings and the brave hitting of John Shepherd, who made 55, Gloucestershire were never threatened and won by 64 runs, Brain returning final figures of 7.3-5-9-3.

Benson and Hedges Cup winners, 1977. Procter is chaired by David Shepherd and David Graveney; Zaheer Abbas is in the foreground, and behind him Julian Shackleton; on Graveney's left are Sadiq, Brain, Malcolm Dunstan and Ian Crawford. (GCCC)

BENSON & HEDGES CUP FINAL
GLOUCESTERSHIRE *v* KENT

Played at Lord's, 16 July 1977

GLOUCESTERSHIRE

Sadiq Mohammad	c Hills b Woolmer	25
†A. W. Stovold	c Underwood b Shepherd	71
Zaheer Abbas	c Underwood b Jarvis	70
*M. J. Procter	c Knott b Julien	25
J. C. Foat	not out	21
D. R. Shepherd	b Jarvis	9
D. A. Graveney	c Underwood b Julien	1
M. J. Vernon	not out	3
Extras	lb 7, w 2, nb 4	13
Total	(6 wkts, 55 overs)	237

1-79, 2-144, 3-191, 4-204, 5-220, 6-223

M. D. Partridge, J. H. Shackleton and B. M. Brain did not bat.

BOWLING	O	M	R	W
Jarvis	11	2	52	2
Julien	11	0	51	2
Shepherd	11	0	47	1
Woolmer	11	0	42	1
Underwood	11	1	32	0

KENT

R. A. Woolmer	c Shackleton b Graveney	64
G. S. Clinton	b Brain	0
C. J. C. Rowe	c Stovold b Procter	0
*Asif Iqbal	c Sovold b Vernon	5
A. G. E. Ealham	c Stovold b Vernon	11
B. D. Julien	b Graveney	1
J. N. Shepherd	c Procter b Brain	55
†A. P. E. Knott	c Zaheer b Partridge	14
R. W. Hills	c Procter b Shackleton	6
D. L. Underwood	b Brain	8
K. B. S. Jarvis	not out	0
Extras	lb 7, nb 2	9
Total	(47.3 overs)	173

1-4, 2-5, 3-24, 4-64, 5-65, 6-100, 7-122, 8-150, 9-166

BOWLING	O	M	R	W
Procter	7	1	15	1
Brain	7.3	5	9	3
Vernon	11	1	52	2
Shackleton	10	0	40	1
Graveney	9	2	26	2
Partridge	3	0	22	1

Umpires: H. D. Bird and W. L. Budd

It was sad that, after a season of triumph and near-triumph, there should be such a falling off in 1978, when the County finished tenth in the Championship, bottom of the John Player League, were eliminated in the group section of the Benson and Hedges Cup and were beaten in their first Gillette Cup match, again by Lancashire and again at Old Trafford where, after Gloucestershire had rattled up 266 for five, the frailty of their attack was exposed by the Lloyds, David and Clive, who both made unbeaten centuries to set up victory by eight wickets.

The prime weakness again lay in the bowling, where for all the endeavours of Procter and Brain, who had Championship hauls of 69 and 64 wickets respectively, the lack of a penetrative third seamer was critical. Davey had made a fair recovery from his ankle injury but 23 Championship wickets at 32 each in 13 games was not an adequate contribution. Brian Shantry, a left-arm seamer from Bristol, was unsuccessful, as was Shackleton. Graveney fell away badly, his 24 wickets costing over 50 each, but Childs improved, taking 57 wickets at 24 each. The batting was healthier, Procter having one of his best seasons with over 1,600 runs and an average above 50, his three centuries including a spectacular 203 in the match against Essex at Gloucester in which the weakness of the County's attack was exposed as the visitors made 313 for eight in the fourth innings to win the game. Zaheer had a mixed season, hitting six centuries, including 215 against Sussex at Hove but, suffering from a virus infection, he lost form and, finally, fitness and missed the last three matches. Sadiq and Stovold

---

Gloucestershire won by 64 runs. They beat Kent, the holders and six times winners of one-day competitions, with 45 balls to spare in a superb team effort inspired by their splendid captain, Procter. The wicket-keeper batsman, Stovold played a vital part in Gloucestershire taking the Benson and Hedges Cup for the first time. He laid the foundation of their total of 237 for six and held three catches behind the stumps. It was no surprise that Fred Trueman named him Man of the Match.

As soon as Procter won the toss, Gloucestershire assumed command as Stovold and Sadiq helped themselves to 19 runs from the first two overs from Jarvis and Julien. At this stage the Kent bowling was loose and during his brilliant innings of 71 Stovold hit ten 4s. For once Sadiq was overshadowed but his sound defence while he made 24 out of an opening stand of 79 was valuable. Eventually Underwood, bowling in the area of the leg stump with six men on the leg side, slowed down the scoring but Zaheer would not be denied and he hit Shepherd into the Mound Stand for 6.

Kent needed to average just over four runs an over with the bat, not a tall order in this type of cricket, but the opening attack of Procter and Brain wrecked their hopes. Clinton, Rowe and Asif went for 24 and only Woolmer and Shepherd caused Gloucestershire any problems. When 37, Woolmer saw the 50 up in the 35th over, but Ealham fell to a magnificent one-handed diving catch by Stovold and with Julien out to a reckless stroke it was clearly not Kent's day. Shackleton held Woolmer at deep mid-wicket and although Knott hit one spectacular 6, he was caught on the square leg boundary by Zaheer, trying to repeat the stroke. Only four Kent men reached double figures while the Gloucestershire attack under Procter's astute leadership maintained its stranglehold to the end, being supported all through by brilliant fielding.

In the closing stages play was held up several times as fans invaded the pitch in premature excitement. When the presentation took place in front of the pavilion the fans had to be forced back by squads of police. Helmets went flying and a number of fans and police were injured. The M.C.C. secretary, Mr. Jack Bailey, criticised the Gloucestershire supporters. He said: 'I thought the behaviour was disgraceful, but it's a problem endemic to society. How can you control a crowd that size? The only way is with fences and it would be a sad day for cricket if fences ever went up to cage supporters in. The police did well but did not have a chance'.—N.P.

formed a reliable opening pair and Foat and Graveney both batted usefully, but Alan Tait, a left-hand bat from Durham who had joined from Northamptonshire, fared poorly as did Hignell. Andy Brassington, who had established himself as wicket-keeper during the previous season, again maintained a high standard.

The only improvement in the following year was in the Sunday League in which the County improved to joint eighth position. Their Championship position was again tenth and once again no progress was made in either the Gillette Cup or the Benson and Hedges Cup. The batting was very strong, despite the absence of Zaheer and Sadiq during the Prudential World Cup, but once more the bowling was not powerful enough to threaten opponents' composure regularly, despite the fine bowling of Procter. He took 74 Championship wickets (81 in all first-class matches) and had not $10\frac{1}{2}$ of the first 12 days Championship matches been completely washed out by the weather he might well have completed the 'double'. There were signs, though, that Brain's powers were waning, his 42 wickets costing over 28 runs each, and the spin department fell well below expectations, Childs' 46 wickets costing 37 runs each and Graveney's 38 costing 32, an improvement on 1978 but still far too expensive.

The strength of the batting can be illustrated by the fact that 19 centuries were scored in the championship, eight by Sadiq, a tally matched only by Glen Turner of Worcestershire, three each by Zaheer and Procter, two by Alistair Hignell and one each from Chris Broad, in his debut season, Stovold and Foat. Sadiq scored over 1,500 Championship runs, averaging 60, and Zaheer, Procter and Stovold all had good seasons, making around 1,200 runs each, while Hignell was also in fine form later on. David Partridge, from Birdlip, who had appeared occasionally since 1976 without making any impression, advanced markedly, his watchful left-hand batting bringing him over 600 runs at an average of 32. Chris Broad, Bristol born and, like Partridge, left-handed, was tried as an opener in Sadiq's absence but at this time in his career he preferred number four and looked happier when batting there in the last few games.

With due deference again to Sadiq Mohammad, 1979 was Mike Procter's year. Gloucestershire's six wins, five in the Championship, plus the defeat of the Indian touring team at Bristol, all bore the imprint of his enormous talents. When Worcestershire were beaten by 165 runs at Worcester, Procter made 41 and 33 in a comparatively low-scoring match and having taken two for 55 in the first innings, tore the opposition apart in the second with eight for 30. In the innings victory over Hampshire at Bristol he made 29 and took six for 67 and two for 36. Against Hampshire, beaten again by 130 runs at Southampton, he made 33 and 74 and took four for 35 and four for 40.

Against Leicestershire, beaten by eight wickets at Bristol, he did not bowl in the first innings, but then hit a century before lunch on the second day and took seven for 26, including a hat-trick in Leicestershire's second innings. In the defeat of Northamptonshire at Bristol by 135 runs he made 38 and 105, this being the fastest century of the season, made in 56 minutes of which only 16 minutes were needed for the second 50, and took two for 67 and four for 69. In the seven-wicket victory over the Indians at Bristol in July Procter made 17 and 24 not out and, after being wicketless in the Indian first innings, bowled beautifully in their second to return figures of 15.3-8-13-7. Truly, the man was a host in himself, one of the great match-winners in cricket history.

The progress made by younger batsmen during this season meant that there was now no room for David Shepherd, who appeared in only six matches and retired in September. He had been a marvellous servant to his adopted county, for whom he scored 10,672 runs, average 24.47, with 12 centuries. He will be remembered particularly for his courageous batting in the Gillette Cup match against Surrey at Bristol in 1973, without which the County would surely have been beaten, and for a scarcely less important innings of 60 not out which was the decisive factor in the Benson and Hedges semi-final victory over Middlesex in 1977. There was, though, much more to 'Shep' than figures and performances. The Club was never quite the same place without his kindness, his humour and his remarkable evenness of temperament: whether things were going well or badly for him personally, all he ever cared about was his team's success. He, like Barrie Meyer, became an umpire and, again like Meyer, is now a greatly respected arbiter at Test match level.

Jim Foat, after a better season in 1978 and a century against Hampshire at Bristol in June, seemed likely at last to establish himself but his form deteriorated to such an extent that he lost his place in the side and went out of the game altogether at the end of the season.

In 1980, a wet summer again, performances were broadly similar, though the improvement from tenth to seventh in the County Championship really represented something of a triumph, the team being without a Championship victory at the start of the Cheltenham Festival in early August. Again there was an early exit from the Gillette Cup, Surrey winning a tight match at the Oval. Again the County failed to qualify for the knock-out stages of the Benson and Hedges Cup and again there was no impression made in the Sunday League, seven wins earning only tenth place. In the Championship games the batting was generally not so reliable as in recent seasons but the bowling, despite the absence of any spectacular individual totals of wickets, gained 74 bonus points, a total equalled only by Surrey and exceeded only by Middlesex. By contrast only the bottom three clubs, Lancashire, Kent and Hampshire, scored fewer batting bonus points than the County's 39.

Zaheer headed the batting with 1,263 runs, average 39, satisfactory enough but not one of his vintage years. Procter and Sadiq both exceeded 1,000 runs and averaged over 30. Broad confirmed the good impression he had made in 1979, with over 800 Championship runs, including two centuries, and he also scored a century before lunch against Oxford University in The Parks. Stovold, alternating between number four and opener, fell away a little but Hignell, when free from injury, was most effective in his own pugnacious way.

The increased effectiveness of the bowling was partly due to the signing of the former Glamorgan medium-fast left-armer Alan Wilkins. Though he bowled well enough, taking 44 wickets at 27 runs apiece, his greatest effect was to take pressure off Procter and Brain. Procter responded by taking 48 wickets at under 18 each—he was not always fit enough to bowl—while Brain improved on his work of the previous year, his 53 wickets costing below 28. Childs had a better year with 43 wickets at 24 but Graveney's were taken at substantially higher cost.

When Gloucestershire came to Cheltenham they had lost four of their 14 championship games, with nine being drawn and one abandoned. However, they then won all three matches at the Festival and since the final two of these are dominated by match-winning performances from Mike Procter, the last he was to give for the County he had served so faithfully and with such brilliance, it seems appropriate to look at them closely. The first match of the Festival, which brought victory by 147 runs, was dominated by the batting of Chris Broad, who made 116 in the first innings, and Sadiq, with 52 and 90 not out. Wilkins took five for 50 in Hampshire's first innings and Graveney five for 24 in the second, Procter's contribution being limited to a total of three runs and three wickets.

However, in the next match against Worcestershire, he commanded the match. He came in to bat on the first morning with Gloucestershire 27 for three and made a hard-hit 73, helping their total to 178 after they had been put in. Turner and Ormrod put on 72 for Worcestershire's first wicket and things looked a little bleak until, on the second morning, Procter's burst of seven for 9 (he finished with seven for 16 in 15.5 overs) cut them down for 111. The County made 177 at their second attempt, Procter contributing 35. Then, bowling a mixture of seam and off-spin, he took seven for 60 in 27.3 overs to clinch a 96-run victory. In the next match Middlesex, put in, struggled to 220, which looked a formidable total when Vincent Van der Bijl and Wayne Daniel, the best opening attack in the country that season, bowled the county out for 109. Procter, who had taken only two wickets in the first innings, hardly bowled in the second, in which Middlesex made 158 for four between the showers before Mike Brearley's declaration asked Gloucestershire to make 270 in 285 minutes to win. They were 65 for three when Procter came in and looked a beaten side but he proceeded to play one of his greatest innings, making 134 not out and carrying his side to victory with over an hour to spare. He batted for 145 minutes and hit 18 fours and two sixes, all this off an attack spearheaded by Van der Bijl, who took 85 wickets at 14.72 that year, and the formidable West Indies fast bowler Wayne Daniel, and supported by Test bowlers in Fred Titmus and Mike Selvey.

There was no thought, during those six days of triumph, that the days of this great cricketer were numbered. Mike Procter's knee problem, against which he had struggled so valiantly almost throughout his career, finally became too acute for him to continue to play cricket all the year round. He played in only six Championship matches in 1981 and did not appear after the match at Northampton on the first three days of July, the side being captained by senior professional Brian Brain and then by David Graveney, whose tenure was to be confirmed during the close season. To lose their great South African star in mid-season was blow enough to the County's hopes, but this was compounded by Brian Brain's increasingly acute problems with strains and pulls which limited his Championship overs to 188, his wickets to 16 and caused his retirement at the end of the season.

With the attack so crucially weakened, reinforcement was sought in the shape of the fast left-arm Mike Whitney, professional for Northern League side Fleetwood, but after only two Championship appearances he was lost to the County, being needed by the Australian tourists. In these circumstances the drop from seventh to 13th in the Championship was not surprising, nor was 16th position in the Sunday League. Once again no success attended the County's efforts in the Benson and Hedges Cup, while the newly named Natwest 60-over competition (previously the Gillette Cup), though yielding one victory over Ireland in Dublin, brought humiliation in the next round as Essex won by 122 runs at Bristol, bowling Gloucestershire out for 85.

It was not, however, all gloom and doom, for Zaheer had a most wonderful season and younger players in Bainbridge, Broad and Hignell progressed while Graveney, Stovold and Childs also shouldered their increased burdens capably. After rain had caused the abandonment, without a ball being bowled, of all three Championship matches in May, Zaheer, with batting of great brilliance, hit four centuries and scored over 1,000 runs in June, becoming the third

Gloucestershire player, after Grace and Hammond, to record a four-figure total in a calendar month. Against Somerset at Bath in the middle of the month he made 215 not out and 150 not out, the fourth time he had made a double hundred and a hundred in the same match, a record unparalleled in the game's history. In all eight of those innings he was unbeaten, and each first innings double-century was compiled under the 100-overs restriction. Zaheer's total for June was 1,016 runs, average 112.88 and included two more centuries, 101 not out against Hampshire at Southampton and 101 against Warwickshire at Gloucester. Thereafter Zaheer scarcely faltered, scoring six more centuries, including 135 not out and 128 in the match against Northamptonshire. In his 34 Championship innings he scored no fewer than 2,230 runs, averaged 85.76, and comfortably headed the national averages.

In addition to these great feats, Bainbridge's fluent stroke play brought him over 1,000 runs for the first time, at an average above 40. Broad also passed his thousand with an average over 30. Hignell and Andrew Stovold also averaged over 30, though their aggregates both fell just short of four figures. Sadiq had a less prosperous season but against that Graveney improved, hitting a maiden Championship century, 105 not out against Northamptonshire at Bristol. Andy Stovold's younger brother Martin made a good impression with limited opportunities, as did Pinner-born Steve Windaybank but neither was destined to establish himself. Even allowing for the fact that covered wickets now made batting rather easier, Gloucestershire were certainly strong in this department, for despite the considerable interference they experienced through the weather only six sides bettered their tally of 51 batting bonus points.

Not unexpectedly, however, only Worcestershire and Warwickshire gained fewer bonus points for bowling than the County's 55. Childs, though, had his best season, taking 62 Championship wickets and 75 in all. His nine for 56 in Somerset's second innings at Bristol in late August was the best return in the country that year, though Gloucestershire lost the match. Graveney, too, had a satisfactory year and Bainbridge's medium-pace inswing developed but Wilkins, despite taking a career-best eight for 57 against Lancashire at Old Trafford in September, found the going hard and was very expensive. The 26-year-old David Surridge, a Cambridge blue who had played for Hertfordshire and was to have a considerable part to play in the coming seasons, played in five Championship matches and David Lawrence, a 17-year-old Gloucester-born fast bowler, in one. Wicket-keeper Robert 'Jack' Russell made his first-class debut against the Sri Lankan tourists at Bristol, where he gave early notice of his great talent by catching seven batsmen and stumping another.

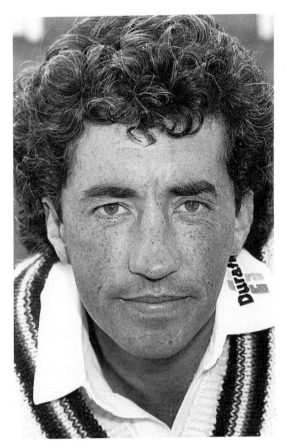

Phil Bainbridge: fluent batsman, useful inswing bowler.
(GCCC)

Here, then, was another watershed. Mike Procter, whose performances over the previous 13 seasons had been so outstanding as to cause
the County to be dubbed 'Proctershire' in certain sections of the
national Press, had finished his English career at the comparatively
early age of 34. Brian Brain, tall, whippy, hostile, who for a couple of
seasons had formed with Procter a feared new-ball combination, had
also come to the end at the age of 41. His control of line, his delivery
from close to the stumps and his high arm had much to do with his
success. He came to Gloucestershire when he was in his 36th year,
virtually in the twilight of his career; to take, as he did, 316 wickets at
below 25 runs each in six seasons, during the last of which injuries
limited his victims to 16, was a fine achievement and an accurate
indication of his high skill.

However, as the poet says, 'the old order changeth, yielding place to new'. The rest of the decade was to see new reputations made, some older ones enhanced and some diminished. There was to be a heart-breaking struggle against odds, followed by a couple of seasons of near-triumph, when the County's reputation stood as high as at any time in its history, and then a few of comparative decline, though fortunately to nothing like the levels of the early 1980s, or of the early and middle 1960s.

GLOUCESTERSHIRE'S DARK HOURS

WHEN DAVID GRAVENEY WAS APPOINTED captain for the last few weeks of 1981, it seemed likely that he would be offered the post full time for the following season. His father, Ken, who had become chairman of the club in succession to Frank Twiselton, pondered the ethics of remaining as chairman if his son was to be captain. After much heart-searching he decided to stand again, but at the spring annual general meeting he found himself deposed in favour of Don Perry, formerly a notable club cricketer from Cheltenham. In view of the storms that were to blow within the next three years, it was perhaps as well that Ken was distanced from the main areas of conflict.

During the close season there had been much recruiting in an attempt to cover the County's areas of weakness. Franklyn Stephenson, the tall Barbadian all-rounder who was later to do such great things for Nottinghamshire, was playing for Rawtenstall in the Lancashire League on Saturdays, but was contracted for mid-week games, of which he played in seven and impressed in taking 25 wickets. However, under the regulations applying, if he played Sadiq could not, and with Zaheer, whose early form had been brilliant, departing to join the Pakistan touring team the batting could ill-afford Sadiq's loss. The former Kent and West Indies all-rounder John Shepherd, released by his county, also joined and was to give yeoman service at the age of 38. Paul Romaines, a right-hand bat from Bishop Auckland who had had an unsuccessful spell with Northamptonshire, also came on to the staff. The former Leicestershire batsman Barry Dudleston, recruited as assistant coach principally to assist with the development of Second XI players, was called on to play late in the season. Also Tony Wright, a Stevenage-born right-hand batsman, who had come to Gloucestershire in 1978 at 16, was given some opportunities, as was Richard Doughty, a Yorkshire-born new-ball bowler and attacking batsman who had played in one match in 1981.

These shifts and stratagems notwithstanding, the achievements of 1982 were modest. Gloucestershire dropped from 13th to 15th in the Championship and were 14th in the Sunday League. They fared a little better, though, in the Benson and Hedges Cup, winning two qualifying matches and losing narrowly in the other two. In the NatWest Trophy, too, they overwhelmed fancied Nottinghamshire at Trent Bridge by nine wickets and, in the quarter-final against Middlesex at Bristol, needed a four off the last ball to win but could manage only a single.

Despite Zaheer's 667 runs in only 11 completed innings and the good batting of Bainbridge, Sadiq and Stovold, the last-named making a career best 212 not out at Northampton, runs were not scored consistently enough. Hignell and Broad both had in-and-out seasons and Romaines, though making a match-saving 186 at Edgbaston, tended to let bowlers dictate to him. John Shepherd and Graveney both played some useful innings but these tended to be repair jobs rather than consolidations of good totals. The bowling, though tidy, was not penetrative enough. Shepherd bowled most overs and took most wickets with 60, but at his age he was not to be expected to combine the roles of strike and stock bowler. Surridge, happily recovered from back trouble, was steady but at his modest pace never did quite enough with the ball to trouble the best players. Graveney was the only bowler apart from Stephenson to take his wickets at below 30 runs apiece but Childs fell away badly, his 33 wickets costing almost 46 apiece. In these circumstances it was not surprising that only two Championship matches were won.

There was some improvement the following season, when 12th place in the Championship was achieved and 14th in the John Player League, while in both the NatWest and the Benson and Hedges competitions the County reached the quarter-finals. With the pitches at Bristol generally very good the batsmen prospered, six of them passing 1,000 runs, not including Zaheer whose 867 Championship runs, average 46, were scored mainly after his return from the World Cup and before his early departure to prepare his side (he was at this time captain of Pakistan) for their tour of India. Stovold, chunky and aggressive, had his best year, with 1,592 Championship runs, including four centuries. Others to pass the 1,000 mark were Paul Romaines, who played valuably whether opening the innings or batting lower down, Alistair Hignell in his final season, John Shepherd and Chris Broad, the last-named averaging over 40 and the other three over 35.

Shepherd, who also took 67 wickets, had an excellent all-round season and was greatly assisted by the steady medium-fast left-arm bowling of Gary Sainsbury, for so long John Lever's understudy at Essex, who took 58 Championship wickets at 32 runs apiece. However, with Stephenson injured and then unable to play after Zaheer's return, the County still lacked a truly penetrative new-ball bowler, Lawrence in his few appearances still lacking control. The spin-bowling, too, was scarcely adequate, Graveney and Childs bowling 1,145 championship overs between them to take 83 wickets at almost 35 runs each. Russell kept wicket brilliantly and was already attracting the attention of those in high places.

Gloucestershire were unfortunate in the NatWest Trophy. They

*John Shepherd, Kent and West Indies all-rounder, later a
valuable player and coach for Gloucestershire. (NCCC)*

comfortably defeated Scotland and then, at Leicester, chasing a
massive 302 for victory, got home with three balls to spare thanks to
Zaheer's brilliant innings of 158. In the quarter-final against
Hampshire at Bristol, Gloucestershire made a useful 252 for eight, but
with John Childs unable to bowl because of a bruised hand Hampshire
made the runs in some comfort. In the Benson and Hedges there was
greater misfortune still. Gloucestershire qualified top of their group
but only four overs were bowled in the quarter-final at Bristol.
Middlesex went through on the toss of a coin, the TCCB being
unsympathetic to the pleas of Graveney and Middlesex skipper Mike
Gatting to have the game decided by some sort of a cricket match at a
later stage in the season.

At the end of the summer Chris Broad's connection with the Club ended. In a newspaper interview he had stated clearly his playing ambitions and, in passing, made slighting reference to some of his senior County colleagues. Since the Club's permission for the interview had not been sought Broad was in clear breach of his contract but the Club quite rightly decided against punitive action, preferring simply to permit a disaffected player to leave. Broad has done well at Trent Bridge on the field but he has not, perhaps, contributed all that much to general harmony off it.

Hopes of further improvements in 1984 were to be swiftly dashed. Despite the arrival of England batsman Bill Athey from strife-torn Yorkshire only one Championship match was won, Gloucestershire finishing bottom of the table. In the NatWest Trophy Staffordshire were beaten at Stone but Lancashire won easily in the next round at Bristol. In the Benson and Hedges Cup the County won only one of their qualifying games, beating Hampshire at Bristol by eight wickets but losing to Essex at Chelmsford, the Combined Universities at Bristol and Surrey at the Oval.

Again, though Zaheer's appearances were limited, the batting was strong, with Athey and Romaines exceeding 1,800 runs in all first-class cricket, Stovold over 1,500, Bainbridge scoring 1,100 and Wright just under 1,000. As John Shepherd made nearly 900 and Jack Russell over 500, runs were rarely in too short supply. Again the problem was the lack of a quality strike bowler. Courtney Walsh, the tall Jamaican, had been signed on the recommendation of Tom Graveney but his success during the winter of 1983–84 in the West Indies' domestic season had earned him a place on their tour party and he was to play in only six matches. David Lawrence had been carefully nursed and was improving, but his 41 wickets at 37 apiece showed how much he still had to learn. John Shepherd and Sainsbury again toiled manfully but each averaged over 30 runs per wicket. Childs' form and confidence so deserted him that he left at the end of the season, to reappear triumphantly for Essex in 1986, having had his action remodelled by Don Wilson and Fred Titmus at Lord's. Once again Graveney took his wickets at below 30, but overall the County didn't possess the capacity to bowl sides out.

There was considerable reaction to the poor results among certain sections of the membership and a petition was got up aimed at rallying members to effect changes in the running of the cricket. At the annual general meeting, held at the Gloucester Leisure Centre on 30 November 1984, R. T. Clark proposed and B. E. Knowles seconded a motion that 'this general meeting has no confidence in the cricket committee'. Clark blamed the cricket committee for inactivity and the captain for lack of imagination. The chairman, Don Perry, blamed the County's poor season on the lack of strike bowlers and rebutted the charge of the cricket committee's slowness by pointing to the signings of Athey and Walsh, plus three more for the 1985 season in Brian Davison, formerly with Leicestershire, the Zimbabwean all-rounder Kevin Curran and Jeremy Lloyds from Somerset. After various other interjections, the proposal was put to the vote and defeated by 224 to 57.

A further motion, 'that this committee has no confidence in David Graveney as captain', was proposed by C. J. Cleverley and seconded by L. B. Hickin. Mr Cleverley maintained that the previous vote laid the blame purely on the captain's shoulders by exonerating the cricket committee, a curious piece of logic. Mr Hickin, too, pressed for an unspecified change in captaincy after which there were numerous expressions of support for Graveney, culminating in Mr Owen's suggestion that 'in the name of decency, the proposers should withdraw the motion'. The motion was, however, put to the vote and defeated by an overwhelming majority.

A BRIGHTER END TO THE
1980s

AFTER SUCH UPHEAVALS, GLOUCESTERSHIRE'S form in 1985 gave great comfort to those who had expressed faith in the existing cricket management and team captaincy. They finished third in the Championship and though, yet again, failing to qualify for the later stages of the Benson and Hedges competition, they reached the quarter-finals of the NatWest, being narrowly defeated in a high-scoring match by Nottinghamshire.

Bowling, and particularly fast bowling, was the key to this rapid change of fortune. The full-time availability of Courtney Walsh coincided happily with the development of David Lawrence into the formidable fast bowler that, bearing in mind his strength and stamina, he had always promised to be. His direct and ferocious assault was a

Left: Courtney Walsh, a relentlessly hostile and inventive quick bowler. (Patrick Eagar). Right: David Lawrence, fast bowler for Gloucestershire and England, pictured here aged 18 in the nets at the County Ground. (GCCC)

perfect foil for the more languid-looking Walsh, who, though capable of bowling a very quick ball, relied less on sheer speed than on subtle changes of pace, ability to move the ball in the air and off the seam, and the disconcerting bounce afforded by his 6 feet $5\frac{1}{2}$ inch (1.97 m) frame and high arm. Between them these two took 161 Championship wickets, 82 to Walsh and 79 to Lawrence. The County had found not one strike bowler but two, or even two and three-quarters, for Curran, medium-fast and making the ball swing and seam, was also a dangerous bowler.

The presence of these three in the side encouraged the County to leave more grass on the Bristol pitches, which could be pretty fiery, particularly in the early stages of a match. For this reason Graveney's spin was sparingly used, though he still took 38 wickets at modest cost. One repercussion of the nature of Bristol's pitches was a gradual decline in run-getting power, which was noticeable during the crucial matches at the end of the season. Exempt from any criticism was Bainbridge, who had his best season, with 1,456 runs for four centuries in the Championship and a batting average not far short of 60. Athey who hit four centuries in the Championship, plus another at Cambridge, played well enough to be called to the Oval as reserve batsman for the sixth Test. He played quite superbly until August, when runs became elusive just as they were most needed. Davison, the Zimbabwean formerly with Leicestershire, played some very important innings and was also a valued adviser to Graveney. His contribution helped to offset the departure of Zaheer, who no longer felt able to play year-round cricket and had announced his retirement during the winter. Brian Davison batted with his customary power and lent Graveney the support of his deep knowledge of the game and his powerful personality. Lloyds, mainly batting at number six or seven, launched some vital rescue acts, and Curran, though wildly impetuous at times, played some valuable innings. Both Stovold and Romaines struggled in the changed conditions, and with Wright also having problems, the County could never be sure of a good start.

The season did not start too promisingly. Walsh missed the first two Championship matches, of which Lancashire won the first while in the second the County beat Worcestershire. Lawrence made an early mark with nine wickets in the Lancashire match and five at Worcester, and then at Hove bowled very fast to take seven for 48 in a match ruined by rain when Gloucestershire were well on top. Two days of the Somerset match at Bristol were lost, but the County then won three of their next four games, winning comprehensively at Derby, Tunbridge Wells and Northampton but having another rain-affected draw with Somerset at Bath. The Derbyshire match illustrated the enormous value of having two quality fast bowlers: 1,070 runs had been scored and only 12 wickets had fallen when Graveney's second declaration asked Derbyshire to make 309 in 125 minutes plus 20 overs. Walsh made the early break, dismissing Maher and Barnett, after which he and Lawrence swept through the opposing batting, taking five wickets apiece and bowling Derbyshire out for 82 in only 34 overs.

This was followed by another rain-affected draw at Bath, after which Kent, bowled out first by Curran and Walsh and then by Walsh and Lawrence, were beaten at Tunbridge Wells, and Northamptonshire were hammered by eight wickets at Northampton. In the latter match Walsh withdrew with a strain and Gary Sainsbury stepped in to take seven for 38 in Northamptonshire's first innings, giving the County a control of the match which they never relaxed. The match at Hove was abandoned without a ball being bowled after which Hampshire had rather the better of a drawn match at Bristol. By now batting problems in the early order were becoming acute. In the earlier match at Bath Gloucestershire were 15 for three in their first innings and 31 for three in their second: in the win at Tunbridge Wells they were 32 for three at one point in each innings, and against Hampshire they were 20 for four in their first innings and 45 for four in the second. There was a limit on how many times the lower order could rescue the side from holes as deep as these, though Lloyds (81 not out) and Lawrence (41) did the trick once more in the next match, at Trent Bridge, after Gloucestershire, facing a Nottinghamshire first innings total of 272, had slumped to 58 for six.

There was more stable batting in the two matches of the Gloucester Week. Yorkshire were beaten by eight wickets, Athey and Bainbridge making centuries and Lawrence bowling at a great pace on a slow surface. He took five wickets in Yorkshire's second innings, in which they were bowled out for 91 in 22.3 overs. Then Worcestershire were beaten by 110 runs, undone by another Athey century and efficient all-round bowling and out-cricket. Thereafter the County's season rather fell away. After the first two games of the Cheltenham Festival had been drawn, rain interfering in each case, Warwickshire were beaten by seven wickets, Gloucestershire having been rescued from 14 for four in their first innings, by Lloyds, Curran and the tail. But successive defeats at the hands of Hampshire at Bournemouth and Essex at Bristol and a draw with Glamorgan at Cardiff (in which the Welshmen took eight points for being the side batting last in a match where scores finished level—this after rain had necessitated the forfeiture of both first innings) reduced their title hopes.

There was still a chance if Northamptonshire could be beaten at Bristol, but again rain intervened. After forfeitures and declarations Northamptonshire chased 245 in 66 overs and faltered to 164 for nine

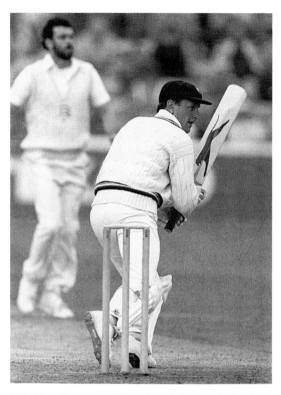

Bill Athey demonstrates his model technique on the bowling of Essex's Don Topley. (Patrick Eagar)

with nine overs remaining, but the County could not part Neil Mallender and Jim Griffiths, the latter one of the poorer batsmen in the side's history. Gloucestershire's prospects of overhauling Middlesex and Hampshire were remote when they started their final match against Surrey at the Oval. They dismissed the home side for 205, mainly through the efforts of Walsh and Curran, and led by 72 in the first innings, despite having been at one time 8 for three, but Monte Lynch's second-innings hundred put them out of the hunt.

This, then was an ultimately disappointing season, though undoubtedly a triumph in view of what had gone before. The County certainly had their chance to secure the Championship, but unstable early batting prevented them from consolidating a number of strong positions and, in all fairness, the weather dealt very harshly with them, for 160 hours, or just over *one third* of their Championship programme, was lost to rain.

If 1986 was also to bring frustration it also confirmed Gloucestershire's position among the leading counties, despite another ineffective one-day season in which they came bottom in the Sunday League, did not progress beyond the zonal stages of the Benson and Hedges and were knocked out in the second round of the NatWest competition. These failures were compensated for by the County's Championship record, which this time brought second place, behind Essex who had ten wins to Gloucestershire's nine. The County lost only three of their Championship matches, and two of these occurred during the final four weeks, when the weather once more played a malign part, forcing Gloucestershire to chase highly improbable targets in matches against Middlesex and Warwickshire involving forfeitures and contrived finishes.

That Gloucestershire did so well in a season in which Curran, having undergone a shoulder operation, bowled only 18 Championship overs, Davison was unable to play owing to registration difficulties caused by the refusal of the Home Office to grant him British citizenship, Athey missed 11 matches through England calls and Lawrence fell away considerably from the high standard he had achieved in 1985, was a tribute to Graveney's leadership and to the excellent spirit of the side generally. Athey batted very consistently when available. Lloyds and Curran both had excellent batting seasons and Stovold recovered much of his former poise. Bainbridge, manfully shouldering the increased burden placed upon him by Curran's inability to bowl through injury, made fewer runs but still batted valuably at times, but Romaines and Wright struggled to impose themselves. Keith Tomlins, recruited from Middlesex, averaged almost 30, but the find of the season was Mark Alleyne, product of the Haringey Cricket School, who scored 116 not out against Sussex in only his eighth first-class innings to become, at just turned 18, the youngest player in the County's history to make a century.

The bowling depended greatly on Courtney Walsh, who responded magnificently, taking 118 Championship wickets at 18.17 each. Bainbridge, with 41 wickets at 26.70, did a fine job, but he did not command the pace or hostility of Curran. Lawrence, perhaps trying to bowl a little too fast, took 20 less wickets than in 1985 and their cost increased from 24 to 36, a reflection of the penalties imposed upon comparatively slight inaccuracies when attacking fields are being consistently set. Lawrence's strength and pace, though, made him a consistently hostile bowler and his figures do not reflect the support he gave Walsh that season. Graveney, though troubled by his back, took useful wickets as did Lloyds with off-spin, and Ian Payne, an all-rounder recruited from Surrey, bowled tidily at medium pace.

In only one of the County's nine Championship wins did Walsh fail to play a major role. In that match, at Leicester, a contrived declaration saw Gloucestershire successfully chase 236 in 46 overs, the major innings coming from Stovold, Athey and Curran. Walsh's impact on the other eight wins was startling. At Bournemouth, where Hampshire lost by 146 runs, he took 11 for 94 in the match; at Gloucester, where Kent lost by four wickets, seven for 107; at Bristol, where Surrey lost by 94 runs, 11 for 113; at Cardiff where Glamorgan were beaten by five wickets, seven for 22; at Bristol, where Sussex were beaten by one wicket, six for 129; again at Bristol, where Somerset lost by an innings and seven runs, ten for 114 (nine for 72 in the first innings, Bainbridge eight for 52 in the second, both career bests); at Worcester, where victory came by 78 runs, six for 97; and at Cheltenham where Hampshire were beaten by 17 runs, 12 for 124. This last match is worth examining in detail.

Gloucestershire had conceded a first-innings lead of 69 as Chris Smith defied Walsh, who took six for 90, by making 72 not out, he and Tim Tremlett adding 112 for Hampshire's ninth wicket. When Malcolm Marshall and Kevan James bowled the County out for 184 at their second attempt, Hampshire's victory target of 116 seemed simple enough, even on a hard, bouncy wicket which had helped the faster bowlers throughout. When Hampshire led off with an opening stand of 39 all seemed lost, but then Walsh bowled Paul Terry and Lawrence had Greenidge caught at slip without addition. Aided by what *Wisden* calls 'close catching of remarkable brilliance' the two fast bowlers swept all before them. Only Robin Smith, apart from the openers, reached double figures, Walsh's final return being 16.5-5-34-6 and Lawrence's 16-2-64-4.

At that point Gloucestershire were 54 points clear at the head of the table but not another match was won. The pitch for the game against Nottinghamshire in the second match of the Festival was just too good to produce a definite result. Then came rain-affected games against Middlesex at Cheltenham and Warwickshire at Nuneaton, both being lost because the opposing captains knew very well that, however steep the target might be, the County would have to chase it, for Essex, apart from a hiccup at Colchester against Northamptonshire, were generally avoiding the worst of the weather and on a winning streak. Gloucestershire were themselves largely outplayed at Colchester, where their former colleague John Childs had 11 for 95 in the match, but rain, for once, was on their side and they hung on for a draw.

At Old Trafford consistent batting enabled Gloucestershire to declare at 354 for eight but with rain washing out the final five sessions there was no chance of exploiting their strong position. The match against Worcestershire at Bristol, again rain-affected, was drawn in the visitors' favour, after which neither Gloucestershire nor Surrey could catch Essex. The match at the Oval, therefore, was for second place, which the County secured with a hard-fought draw.

Gloucestershire could be proud of their challenge in 1986. Their batting had not buckled under pressure, as in the previous year, and they had done well with bowling resources which, despite Walsh's marvellous achievements, had distinct limitations. Russell's brilliance behind the stumps impressed everyone but England's selectors.

Season 1987 was notable for the incidence and variety of injuries suffered by the County's players. Lawrence, who had not been consistently at his best, despite some excellent performances, broke down early in August and missed seven matches. Bainbridge, in good form with bat and ball, missed eight, Graveney missed seven and Curran four. With Athey also missing eight games through England calls, only Stovold and Russell played in all 24 Championship games.

In the circumstances a drop to tenth place in the Championship was predictable, particularly with Walsh looking weary after three years' continuous cricket. The tall Jamaican, who missed three matches when away with the Rest of the World XI, needed careful nursing, his tally of wickets dropping to 59 and his average rising to 24. Vibert Greene, a Barbadian fast-medium bowler signed as cover for him, did useful work with ball and bat, but the bowling, bearing in mind Lawrence's problems and Graveney's, plus the continued inability of Curran to bowl, was simply not strong enough. The batting, though, was attractive and consistent, and only Nottinghamshire and Surrey gained more batting points. Athey finished in a blaze of glory, hitting five centuries—four of them in succession—and a 98 in the last six weeks of the season, having had a very lean start. He, Lloyds and Curran were the leading batsmen, all averaging comfortably above 40 and with Wright and Romaines making their 1,000 runs, Stovold 988 and Jack Russell nearly 800, runs were seldom in short supply.

This made for a much better one-day season. The Sunday League, now sponsored by Refuge Assurance, saw Gloucestershire in third place, the highest in their history. They qualified in a very tough group for the Benson and Hedges quarter-finals only to lose to Kent off the last ball, and reached the NatWest semi-finals, having overcome Lancashire, Sussex and Warwickshire. The win over Lancashire at Old Trafford was particularly sweet for it was the first against these opponents in nine Gillette/NatWest ties. The convincing margin of 41 runs was earned by the fine batting of Wright, Athey and Stovold and by the bowling of Lawrence, Walsh and Graveney. Sadly, the semi-final at Bristol resulted in overwhelming victory for Nottinghamshire, who made 225 and then dismissed Gloucestershire for 82, Andy Pick's five for 22 having been instrumental in reducing them to 33 for six. In mitigation Walsh, Graveney, Bainbridge and Curran were carrying injuries, but it was the batting which, for one of the few times that season, failed utterly.

ROBERT RUSSELL

Robert 'Jack' Russell, born in Stroud on 15 August 1963, has forced himself to the front of English wicket-keepers at a time of fierce competition for the Test spot for which he seemed destined from the moment of his debut as a 17-year-old in 1981. Then, playing for the County against the Sri Lankan tourists at Bristol, he collected eight victims, seven catches and a stumping.

Short, wiry, quick-moving but beautifully balanced, he made a great impression in his first full season in 1983, keeping brilliantly till late August, when weariness induced some uncharacteristic lapses in concentration. Since then his 'off days' have been virtually non-existent. He would from 1985 on have been the choice of most players and umpires for the England place, a virtual unanimity of grass-roots opinion that may have worked against him in the selectors' eyes, for they have an objection to being led by the nose. In any event, unaccountable but persistent doubts over his batting ability delayed his selection for England until 1988. Then, playing against Sri Lanka at the Oval in what was also David Lawrence's Test debut, he went in as night-watchman and made 94, the highest individual score of the match!

Jack Russell demonstrates the elusive secret of the wicket-keeper's art: simultaneous concentration and relaxation. (Patrick Eagar)

In 1989 he held his position throughout the series against Australia. His resolute and well-organised batting did something to salvage his side's dignity and his keeping was of a very high standard. Very safe when standing back he is in a class of his own when standing up, either to medium-pacers or spinners. So complete is his mastery, so simple and economical his movements, that leg-side stumpings of the greatest brilliance are made to look matters of routine.

A similar season-followed in 1988, of modest achievement in the Championship where tenth position was retained, but not without its one-day successes—second position in the Refuge Assurance Sunday League and a quarter-final place in the NatWest. New recruits arrived, most importantly the Australian medium-fast bowler Terry Alderman, signed as replacement for Courtney Walsh who was touring with the West Indies, Ian Butcher from Leicestershire, Kevin Jarvis, the former Kent fast bowler and David Thomas, the fast-medium left-armer from Surrey.

Alderman bowled finely, taking 75 wickets at modest cost, but the averages were headed by Kevin Curran, now fully fit, who took 65 wickets in just over 400 overs of highly penetrative seam bowling. Graveney had 49 Championship wickets, and Lawrence, now bowling very impressively again, 77. Lawrence and Russell both gained England caps against Sri Lanka, Russell having earned selection

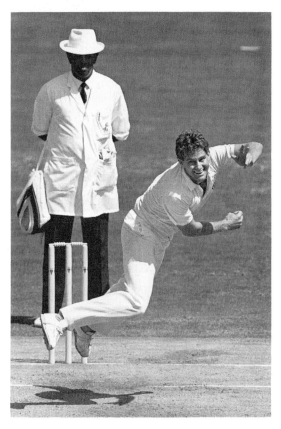

*Terry Alderman, who bowled impressively for
Gloucestershire in 1988. (Patrick Eagar)*

A characteristically violent blow through the off-side from Zimbabwean all-rounder Kevin Curran. (Patrick Eagar)

for the previous winter's ill-fated England tour of Pakistan but not having been selected to play in a Test.

The batting was again very healthy, with Athey in commanding form, averaging 74 in his 12 Championship appearances and Curran, Stovold and Bainbridge all having prosperous seasons. Romaines and Wright both did well enough to offset the loss of form of Jeremy Lloyds, who had batted so valuably in previous seasons. These individual performances looked good enough to have produced more than six Championship wins but after a good run in June, when the County were in third place, a run of 12 successive matches without a win saw them slide slowly down the table, notwithstanding two handsome wins in the last three games.

Three near misses in the past four seasons—third and second in the Championship in 1985 and 1986, second in the Sunday League in 1988, not to mention the NatWest semi-final failure in 1987—prompted an examination by the cricket committee of what had gone wrong. This committee, now chaired by David Allen, voted by four to one for a change of captaincy, the view being that David Graveney had, firstly, been captain for eight seasons and secondly, might not, perhaps, be dynamic enough in pursuit of victory to ensure that trophies were won. However, the manner in which Graveney heard of the intention to replace him was, to say the least, unfortunate. During the penultimate game of the season, against Worcestershire at Bristol, shortly after Graveney left the field with figures of six for 38 in the visitors' second innings—he had taken eight for 127 in their first—Allen informed him of the committee's decision. To the neutral observer there seemed no reason why one of the most respected men in the game should have had the news broken in this way and there was considerable alarm among sections of the membership. Why not wait until the season's end to inform Graveney of his fate? Why not, more importantly, inform so loyal a player of the way in which the cricket committee's thoughts were tending and involve him in the selection of a successor?

In fact, the precipitate action taken by the cricket committee chairman was unconstitutional, for the decision needed to be ratified by the Club's management committee. This was pointed out by Club chairman Don Perry in his attempts to pour oil on troubled waters. Perry apologised to Graveney for the 'distress and embarrassment' caused to himself and his family, but the damage was done and could not be undone. Graveney took some time to consider his future, deciding finally, despite a number of tempting offers from other counties, to continue with Gloucestershire, who would be led in 1989 by Bill Athey.

In the circumstances Athey's was a thankless task. The sort of upheaval that took place during the winter inevitably has an unsettling effect on players and Gloucestershire's were no exception. One of Graveney's unsung skills had been that of getting cricketers who were not temperamentally a particularly harmonious group to forget their personal differences and concentrate on playing cricket. Athey, who had in any event been dealt a poor hand due to the circumstances of Graveney's dismissal and of his own appointment, and having a limited practical experience of leadership, found difficulty in doing this, which was hardly surprising. His own form as a batsman suffered severely because of the problems he encountered, and he resigned the captaincy at the end of the season.

The results achieved during the season mirror the team's lack of cohesion. Six Championship matches were won, a respectable number, and sufficient bonus points were gathered in addition to move up one place in the table, to ninth. However, no fewer than 11 matches were lost of the 21 played—an astonishingly high proportion and among them were several that can only be described as debacles, the worst being against Hampshire at Portsmouth where the County were bowled out for 48 in their second innings on a surface on which their opponents had just declared at 406 for nine. Nor was the one-day cricket much more successful, interest in the NatWest being confined to the first-round tie which Worcestershire won, and 16th being the final position in the Sunday League, in which only three victories were recorded. There was better news in the Benson and Hedges Cup, in which Middlesex, Worcestershire, Surrey and the Combined Universities were defeated in the qualifying matches, only for Nottinghamshire to scrape home by five runs in the quarter-final match at Bristol, thanks mainly to a century by Chris Broad.

Athey's task was not simplified by injuries which kept Graveney out of the side for nine matches, Lawrence for ten and Walsh for four. Russell's absence owing to the Test matches against Australia, in which he enhanced his reputation by keeping wicket beautifully and batting with skill and resolution in testing situations, was also felt, though Geoff Tedstone, the former Warwickshire wicket-keeper, proved a capable deputy. Generally the batting was not reliable, with Athey having a poor time by his own standards, making 900 Championship runs and averaging below 30, and Stovold so completely losing form that he played in only six matches. Curran, though, had a good year, hitting four Championship centuries, making about 1,200 runs and averaging 37. Alleyne, now maturing, was the only other batsman to average over 30. The vice-captain, Tony Wright, started splendidly with two early centuries but rather faded later, but Lloyds recovered some of the confidence he had lost during the previous season.

The bowling, apart from Walsh who took 81 Championship wickets at below 21 runs apiece, was also fairly moderate. Curran, who took 47 wickets, had some good spells and Jarvis, given more opportunity through Lawrence's injury, responded well but generally there was insufficient penetration. Great promise, though, was shown by the young off-spinner Martin Ball, who had played against the Sri Lankans the previous season as an 18-year-old.

Vibert Greene, who had put in some very useful performances when deputising for Walsh, was released at the end of the season having been awarded his county cap, and there was another departure with John Shepherd, who had been coaching the senior players since 1985, with Graham Wiltshire concentrating on the youngsters.

Now wary of the possible dangers of precipitate action, the County took its time over the nomination of a successor to Bill Athey, but finally the cricket committee recommended Tony Wright, who will have as talented a squad of players as any but a couple of the other counties. Courtney Walsh and David Lawrence are a féared pair of opening bowlers, Curran an aggressive and talented all-rounder and though Graveney's problems with recurring back injuries seem likely to cause his retirement sooner rather than later, Martin Ball has much to offer in the spin department. There are fine batsmen, too, in Athey, Bainbridge and Lloyds, while Tony Wright is improving steadily and has it in him to be a really commanding player. Alleyne, still only 21, is as gifted as any young player in the country and needs only a touch more 'run hunger' to move into the top flight. In Jack Russell, almost a veteran in terms of experience but still only 26, Gloucestershire possess probably the best wicket-keeper in the world.

Nonetheless, the Committee has recognised that Wright, who has only just established himself as a senior player, faces a formidable task in restoring the side's unity of purpose. Accordingly they have engaged the tough former South African Test all-rounder Eddie Barlow as Chief Coach on a three-year contract. Barlow's brief is initially concerned primarily with first XI cricket, though he will in due course examine thoroughly the structure of cricket within club and county and where necessary recommend modifications to ensure that the best is made of available talent.

Apart from the basically healthy playing side, the County is in an era of greater financial stability than at any time in its long history. Profits have been returned in every year but one of the last nine, and have averaged in excess of £20,000 per annum. Strict financial management, together with a marked increase in revenue from sponsorship and advertising have been the major factors in the attainment of this happy position, which is in great contrast to the days just prior to the First World War, when Gloucestershire almost ceased

W.G.'s memorial plaque on the main gate at the County Ground. (GCCC)

to exist, and to the period before the involvement with Phoenix Assurance.

Gloucestershire, then, seem poised for a future to match and, perhaps, excel their glamorous if, at times, maddeningly erratic past. Great cricketers and great deeds adorn its history, but some of the achievements of the side during the 1970s and 1980s have been fit to compare with those of the Graces, Gilbert Jessop, Charlie Parker, Walter Hammond and the rest. The winning of the County Championship remains an elusive goal, but Gloucestershire are not alone in never having taken the title in modern times. Ambition burns brightly within the County and in its players who will surely leave their mark on the proud pages of its story.

STATISTICAL SECTION

BIOGRAPHICAL DETAILS
OF GLOUCESTERSHIRE PLAYERS

NAME AND EXTENT OF CAREER	BIRTHPLACE	DATE OF BIRTH	DATE OF DEATH
Dennis George A'Court 1960–1963	Tredegar	27. 7.1937	
Terence Michael Alderman 1988–	Subiaco, W. Australia	12. 6.1956	
Ernest Ewart Gladstone Alderwick	Bristol	14. 4.1886	26. 8.1917
Basil Oliver Allen 1932–1951	Bristol	13.10.1911	1. 5.1981
Charles Allen 1909		1878	22. 5.1958
David Arthur Allen 1953–1972	Bristol	29.10.1935	
Mark Wayne Alleyne 1986–	Tottenham	23. 5.1968	
Herbert John Hampden Alpass 1926–1928	Thornbury	7. 8.1906	
Frederick James Andrew 1959–1963	Bristol	29. 5.1937	
Martin J. Ashenden 1962–1965	Bexhill	4. 8.1937	
Alfred John Atfield 1893	Ightham, Kent	3. 3.1868	1. 1.1949
Charles William Jeffery Athey 1984–	Middlesborough	27. 9.1957	
Sir Derrick Thomas Louis Bailey 1949–1952	London	15. 8.1918	
William Hunter Baillie 1870	Cheltenham	1838	17. 3.1895
Philip Bainbridge 1977–	Staffordshire	16. 4.1958	
Francis Baker 1875	Cirencester	5.12.1847	15. 4.1901
Edward William Ball 1880–1881	Bristol	10. 2.1859	31. 7.1917
Martyn Charles John Ball 1988–	Bristol	26. 4.1970	
Charles John Barnett 1927–1948	Cheltenham	3. 7.1910	
Charles Sherborne Barnett 1904–1926	Cheltenham	24. 2.1884	20.11.1962
Edgar Playle Barnett 1903–1921	Cheltenham	22. 3.1885	1. 1.1922
Percival Playle Barnett 1908–1909	Cheltenham	1889	1966
Arthur William Barrow 1919	Cheltenham	1897	19. 7.1943
Adrian William Bay Becher 1925–1929	Stow-on-the-Wold	12. 5.1897	29. 3.1957
Charles Belcher 1890–1892	Thornbury	1872	1. 4.1938
Percy Harrison Bell 1911–1912	Headington, Oxon	1892	4. 2.1956
Gerald Harry Beloe 1898–1899	Bristol	21.11.1877	1.10.1944
Frederick George Bendall 1887	Cheltenham	18.12.1865	27. 4.1941
Clement Stuart Bengough 1880	Bristol	14. 1.1861	19.11.1934
Edward Turk Benson 1929–1931	Cardiff	20.11.1907	11. 9.1967
John Richard Bernard 1956–1961	Bristol	9.12.1938	
John Bessant 1921–1928	New Forest, Hants	11.11.1895	18. 1.1982
David George Bevan 1964–1970	Gloucester	11. 6.1943	
Alfred William George Bewick 1903	Gloucester	25. 1.1876	15.10.1949
Frederick Nash Bird 1899–1900	Framlingham, Suffolk	13.12.1875	3. 3.1965
Michael Bissex 1961–1972	Bath	25. 9.1944	
Ernest George Blackmore 1925	Bristol	21. 5.1895	10.1955
Herbert Henry Gratwicke Blagrave 1922	Cheltenham	3. 3.1899	4. 7.1981
Bernard Sydney Bloodworth 1919–1932	Cheltenham	12.1893	19. 2.1967
James Henry Bloor 1887	Bristol	1857	9. 3.1935
John Henry Board 1891–1914	Bristol	23. 2.1867	16. 4.1924
Allan Robert Border 1977	Australia	27. 7.1955	

NAME AND EXTENT OF CAREER	BIRTHPLACE	DATE OF BIRTH	DATE OF DEATH
William Frederick Borroughs *1899–1901*	Cheltenham, Glos	1865	16. 1.1943
Hubert James Boughton *1884–1888*	Westbury-on-Severn	11.10.1858	26. 3.1902
William Albert Boughton *1979–1883*	Westbury-on-Severn	23.12.1854	26.11.1936
John Jesse Bowles *1911–1920*	Lower Slaughter	3. 4.1890	27.11.1971
Frederick Charles Bracher *1895–1897*	Bristol	25.10.1868	23.12.1947
Brian Maurice Brain *1976–1981*	Worcester	13. 9.1940	
Joseph Hugh Brain *1883–1889*	Bristol	11. 9.1863	26. 6.1914
William Henry Brain *1893*	Bristol	21. 7.1870	20.11.1934
Andrew James Brassington *1974–1988*	Bagnall, Staffs	9. 8.1954	
Edward Archibald Brice *1872–1873*	Secunderabad, India	1. 9.1848	14.11.1918
Brian Christopher Broad *1979–1983*	Bristol	29. 9.1957	
Arthur Hugh Brodhurst *1939–1946*	Buenos Aires	21. 7.1916	
Richard Hubert John Brooke *1931*	Eton	6. 6.1909	3. 5.1973
J. Brooks *1892*			
Rowland Brotherhood *1875*	Brinkworth, Wilts	18.11.1841	4. 3.1883
Anthony Stephen Brown *1953–1976*	Bristol	24. 6.1936	
David Wyndham James Brown *1964–1967*	Cheltenham	26. 2.1942	
H. W. Brown *1890–1894*			
Walter Medlicott Rodney Brown	Benares, India	31. 7.1868	13. 8.1954
William Stanley Alston Brown *1896–1919*	Bristol	23. 5.1877	12. 9.1952
Elliott Kenworthy Browne *1872*	Goldington, Beds	10.10.1847	10. 3.1915
Gerald Elliott Kenworthy Browne *1874*	Goldington, Beds	14. 5.1850	6. 7.1910
Leigh Dunlop Brownlee *1901–1909*	Bristol	17.12.1882	12. 9.1955
Wilfred Methven Brownlee *1909–1914*	Bristol	18. 4.1890	12.10.1914
Charles Lamb Bruton *1922*	Gloucester	6. 4.1890	26. 3.1969
John Bryan *1873*	Lower Slaughter	17.10.1841	24. 6.1909
John Wilson Burrough *1924–1937*	Headington, Oxon	17. 6.1904	11. 9.1969
Dean Andrew Burrows *1984–1987*	Peterlee	20. 6.1966	
James Arthur Bush *1870–1890*	Cawnpore, India	28. 7.1850	21. 9.1924
Robert Edwin Bush *1874–1877*	Bristol	11.10.1855	29.12.1939
Ian Paul Butcher *1988–*	Farnborough, Kent	1. 7.1962	
David Carpenter *1954–1963*	Stroud	12. 9.1935	
Frederic Asgill Carter *1871–1873*	Newnham	13. 6.1853	1. 8.1924
Walter Frederick Cave *1883*	Bristol	17. 9.1863	7. 1.1939
Claude Edward Bateman Champain *1898–1907*	Richmond, Surrey	30. 3.1875	13.10.1956
Francis Henry Bateman Champain *1895–1914*	Richmond, Surrey	17. 6.1877	29.12.1942
Hugh Frederick Bateman Champain *1888–1902*	Ashford, Middlesex	6. 4.1869	7.10.1933
John Norman Bateman Champain *1899*	Richmond, Surrey	14. 3.1880	22.10.1950
Herbert William Chard *1889*	Bristol	1869	9. 1.1932
Hon. Hugo Francis Charteris *1910*	Wilbury, Wilts	28.12.1884	23. 4.1916
Algernon William Chester-Master *1870*	Almondsbury	27.10.1851	1. 9.1897
Edgar Chester-Master *1911*	London	6. 5.1888	17. 9.1979
John Henry Childs *1975–1984*	Plymouth	15. 8.1951	
Basil Frederick Clarke *1914–1920*	Madras	26. 9.1885	4. 5.1940
Howard Cleaton *1971*	Merthyr Tydfil	15.11.1949	
Henry Clowes *1884*	Cheadle, Cheshire	1. 7.1863	6. 4.1899

NAME AND EXTENT OF CAREER	BIRTHPLACE	DATE OF BIRTH	DATE OF DEATH
Arthur Edward Coates *1873*	Wigan	2. 8.1848	19. 8.1898
Halsted Sayer Cobden *1872*	London	20.11.1845	5. 1.1909
Frederick Livesey Cole *1879–1890*	Patricroft, Lancs	4.10.1852	1. 7.1941
Gilbert Farraday Collett *1900–1914*	Gloucester	18. 7.1879	26. 2.1945
Algernon William Collings *1874*	Guernsey	4. 9.1853	14. 5.1945
Cecil Cook *1946–1964*	Tetbury	8. 8.1921	
Nicholas Henry Charles Cooper *1975–1978*	Bristol	14.10.1953	
Leonard James Corbett *1920–1925*	Bristol	12. 5.1897	26. .1983
Norman Stanley Cornelius *1910–1911*	Lancashire	5. 6.1887	21.10.1963
Alan Edward Cripps Cornwall *1920*	Monmouth	12. 8.1898	
Wilfred Hartland Craddy *1928*	Bristol	1. 9.1905	1.1979
Lionel Lord Cranfield *1903–1922*	Brixton	11.10.1883	17. 5.1968
Lionel Montague Cranfield *1934–1951*	Bristol	29. 8.1909	
Sir Eric Norman Spencer Crankshaw *1909*	Macclesfield	1. 7.1885	24. 6.1966
James Cranston *1876–1899*	Birmingham	9. 1.1859	10.12.1904
John Frederick Crapp *1936–1956*	St Columb, Cornwall	14.10.1912	15. 2.1981
Ian Cunningham Crawford *1975–1978*	Bristol	13. 9.1954	
Frederick James Crooke *1874–1875*	Liverpool	21. 4.1844	6. 8.1923
Arthur Capel Molyneux Croome *1885–1892*	Stroud	21. 2.1866	11. 9.1930
Joseph John Cross *1870*	Chard, Som	2.1949	2.11.1918
George Lytton Crossman *1896*	Bristol	18. 2.1877	17. 1.1947
Martin Henry Cullimore *1929*	Stroud	4.12.1908	
Edward James Cunningham *1982–1985*	Oxford	16. 5.1962	
Kevin Malcolm Curran *1985–*	Rusapa, Rhodesia	7. 9.1959	
Francis Algernon Curteis *1884*	Bideford	26. 6.1856	1. 5.1928
Charles Christian Ralph Dacre *1928–1936*	Devenport, N.Z.	15. 5.1899	2.11.1975
Christopher Stephen Dale *1984*	Canterbury, Kent	15.12.1961	
John Giles Upton Daniels *1964*	Birmingham	25. 1.1942	
Jack Davey *1966–1978*	Tavistock	4. 9.1944	
Brian Fettes Davison *1985*	Bulawayo, Rhodesia	21.12.1946	
Leonard Morrison Day *1880–1882*	York	24.12.1859	25. 4.1943
T. Dean *1908*			
Alfred John Dearlove *1895–1900*	Bristol	1869	17. 3.1955
Edward George Dennett *1903–1926*	Upway, Dorset	27. 4.1879	15. 9.1937
Ernest George Dewfall *1938*	Bristol	12. 8.1911	
George Seton de Winton *1890–1901*	Bristol	5. 9.1869	28. 6.1930
Robert Anthony Diment *1952*	Falfield	9. 2.1927	
Andrew Dindar *1962–1963*	Johannesburg S.A.	26. 6.1942	
Alfred Ernest Dipper *1908–1932*	Deerhurst	9.11.1885	9.11.1945
Charles Ronald Disney *1923*	Stourbridge, Worcs	21.11.1894	11. 4.1963
John Henry Dixon *1973–1981*	Bournemouth	3. 4.1954	
Richard James Doughty *1981–1984*	Bridlington, Yorks	17.11.1960	
Arthur Houssemayne Du Boulay *1908*	Chatham, Kent	18. 6.1880	25.10.1918
Barry Dudleston *1981–1983*	Stockport, Cheshire	16. 7.1945	
Malcolm Stephen Thomas Dunstan *1971–1974*	Redruth, Cornwall	14.10.1950	

NAME AND EXTENT OF CAREER	BIRTHPLACE	DATE OF BIRTH	DATE OF DEATH
Edward Desmond Russell Eagar *1935–1939*	Cheltenham	8.12.1917	13. 9.1977
Michael Anthony Eagar *1957–1961*	Kensington	20. 3.1934	
E. Eden *1921*	Worcestershire		
Charles William Edwards *1911–1912*	Burton on Trent	18.10.1884	22. 5.1938
Frank Edgar Ellis *1914–1921*	Bristol	1893	29. 4.1961
Richard Gary Peter Ellis *1985–1986*	Paddington	20. 2.1960	
George Malcolm Emmett *1936–1959*	Agra, India	2.12.1912	18.12.1976
Ernest Robert Maling English *1909*	Cheltenham	2.12.1874	18. 8.1941
Robert James Etheridge *1955–1966*	Gloucester	25. 3.1934	4. 4.1988
David Linzee Evans *1889–1891*	West Down	13. 4.1869	12.11.1907
Walter Fairbanks *1877–1884*	Chatham, Kent	13. 4.1852	25. 8.1924
Archibald Hugh Conway Fargus *1900–1901*	Bristol	15.12.1878	1963
John James Ferris *1892–1895*	Sydney N.S.W.	21. 5.1867	17.11.1900
James Fewings *1872*	Bristol	1849	20. 8.1920
Charles Roden Filgate *1870–1877*	Ireland	16.10.1849	1. 9.1930
Nicholas Henry Finan *1975–1979*	Bristol	3. 7.1954	
James Clive Foat *1972–1979*	Warwickshire	21.11.1952	
Ernest Claudius Bramhall Ford *1874–1875*	Cheltenham	23. 7.1855	19. 6.1900
John Kenneth Ford *1951*	Bristol	5. 3.1934	
Percy Hadley Ford *1906–1908*	Wheatenhurst	5. 7.1877	2.12.1920
Reggie Gilbert Ford *1929–1936*	Bristol	3. 3.1907	Oct 1981
Theodore Humphrey Fowler *1901–1914*	Cirencester	25. 9.1879	17. 8.1915
John Charles Ker Fox *1872*	Ireland	10. 3.1851	10. 8.1929
Conway James Francis *1895*	Bristol	1870	15. 4.1924
Guy Francis *1884–1888*	Maugersbury	16. 8.1860	18. 5.1948
Howard Henry Francis *1890–1894*	Bristol	26. 5.1868	7. 1.1936
Sidney Thomas Freeman *1920–1921*	Gloucester	21. 8.1888	6. 6.1971
Henry George Gallop *1877–1883*	Bristol	21. 8.1857	21. 8.1940
Thomas Henry Gange *1913–1920*	Pietermaritzburg	15. 4.1891	11. 7.1947
Henry William Garne *1884*	Islington	9. 5.1860	25. 5.1895
Michael Anthony Garnham *1979*	Johannesburgh	20. 8.1960	
Walter Raleigh Gilbert *1876–1886*	London	16. 9.1853	26. 7.1924
Godwin Merryweather Giles *1903*	Mere, Wilts	1876	1955
Thomas William John Goddard *1922–1952*	Gloucester	1.10.1900	22. 5.1966
Richard Thomas Godsell *1903–1910*	Stroud	9. 1.1880	11. 4.1954
Harry Smyth Goodwin *1896–1907*	Merthyr Tydfil	30. 9.1870	13.11.1955
Frederick Wyldman Goodwyn *1871–1873*	Calicut, India	20. 1.1850	23. 4.1931
Charles Steward Gordon *1870–1875*	Oakleaze, Glos	8. 9.1849	24. 3.1930
William Robert Gouldsworthy *1921–1929*	Bristol	20. 5.1892	4. 2.1969
Alfred Henry Grace *1886–1891*	Chipping Sodbury	10. 3.1866	16. 6.1929
Edward Mills Grace *1870–1896*	Bristol	28.11.1841	20. 5.1911
George Frederick Grace *1870–1880*	Bristol	13.12.1850	22. 9.1880
Henry Grace *1871*	Bristol	31. 1.1833	13.11.1895
William Gilbert Grace *1870–1899*	Bristol	18. 7.1848	23.10.1915
William Gilbert Grace (Jnr) *1893–1898*	London	6. 7.1874	2. 3.1905
William St Clair Grant *1914*	Bhagalpur, India	8. 9.1894	26. 9.1918
David Anthony Graveney *1972–*	Bristol	2. 1.1953	
John Kenneth Richard Graveney *1947–1964*	Hexham	16.12.1924	

NAME AND EXTENT OF CAREER	BIRTHPLACE	DATE OF BIRTH	DATE OF DEATH
Thomas William Graveney *1948–1960*	Riding Mill, Northumberland	16. 6.1927	
David Michael Green *1968–1971*	Llanengan, Carms	10.11.1939	
Michael Arthur Green *1912–1928*	Bristol	3.10.1891	28.12.1971
Robert Lawrence Herbert Green *1924*	Chippenham, Wilts	11.12.1895	13. 9.1969
Alan Douglas Greene *1876–1886*	Brandeston, Suffolk	15. 4.1856	18. 6.1928
Robin Morton Greene *1951*	Durban	1.11.1930	
Victor Sylvester Greene *1987–1989*	Barbados	24. 9.1960	
Charles H. Greenway *1890–1891*		1862	1949
Thomas Gregg *1884–1889*	Wilford, Notts	18.11.1859	25. 3.1939
Herbert Willis Reginald Gribble *1878–1882*	Bristol	23.12.1860	12. 6.1943
Edward Llewellyn Griffiths *1885–1889*	Winchcombe	17. 3.1892	20. 4.1893
John Vesey Claude Griffiths *1952–1957*	Blackheath, Kent	19. 1.1931	1981
Edward Richmond Gurney *1911*	Kidderminster, Worcs	16. 4.1868	17. 6.1938
William Stamford Hacker *1899–1901*	Chipping Sodbury	8.12.1879	8.12.1925
Alfred Hubert Haines *1901–1910*	Long Sutton, Lincs	27. 8.1877	30. 5.1935
Harold Hale *1886–1889*	Perth, Australia	27. 3.1867	2. 8.1947
Ivor Edward Hale *1947–1948*	Worcester	6.10.1922	
Walter Henry Hale *1895–1909*	West Bromwich	6. 3.1870	12. 8.1956
John Halford *1870–1874*	Newent	1846	1901
Walter Reginald Hammond *1920–1951*	Dover, Kent	19. 6.1903	2. 7.1965
Leonard Harbin *1949–1951*	Trinidad	30. 4.1915	
Frank Albert Harris *1929–1931*	Bristol	19. 3.1907	21. 2.1936
Stanley Shute Harris *1902*	Bristol	19. 7.1881	4. 5.1926
Rev Percy Hattersley-Smith *1878–1879*	Cambridge	19. 5.1847	1. 1.1918
John Hatton *1884*	Monmouth	1858	1915
Derek Graham Hawkins *1952–1962*	Alveston	18. 5.1935	
Edward Brownlow Haygarth *1883*	Cirencester	26. 4.1854	14. 4.1915
Carleton Haynes *1878–1879*	Barbados	7. 2.1858	20.11.1945
Richard William Haynes *1930–1939*	Shipston on Stour	27. 8.1913	16.10.1976
John Alfred Healing *1899–1906*	Tewkesbury	14. 6.1873	4. 7.1933
Percival Healing *1911*	Tewkesbury	16. 7.1878	1. 2.1915
Arthur Howard Heath *1875*	Newcastle Under Lyme, Staffs	29. 5.1856	21. 4.1930
Walter Heath *1886*	Tewkesbury	1860	7. 3.1937
Lionel Paget Hedges *1926–1929*	London	13. 7.1900	12. 1.1933
George Edmund Hemingway *1898*	Sutton, Cheshire	1.1872	11. 3.1907
William McGregor Hemingway *1893–1900*	Sutton, Cheshire	12.11.1873	11. 2.1967
Reginald James Hewlett *1909–1922*	Bristol	12. 8.1885	7. 5.1950
Antony Francis Hignall *1947*	Kroonstad, O.F.S.	6. 7.1928	
Alastair James Hignell *1974–1983*	Cambridge	4. 9.1955	
Alfred William Hill *1904–1905*	Little Rissington	1866	27. 5.1936
Frank Langford Hinde *1895*	Dublin	1869	22. 8.1931
Ernest Stanley Hoare *1929*	Andover, Hants	21. 6.1903	
Norman Frederick Charles Hobbs *1924*	Cheltenham	1900	6. 4.1966

206

NAME AND EXTENT OF CAREER	BIRTHPLACE	DATE OF BIRTH	DATE OF DEATH
Henry Joseph Jordan Hodgkins *1900–1901*	Cheltenham	11.11.1868	24. 6.1952
Geoffrey Dean Hodgson *1989–*	Carlisle	22.10.1966	
Cyril Hollinshead *1946*	Timberland, Lincs	26. 5.1902	
George James Warner Sinclair Holloway *1908–1911*	Stroud	26. 4.1884	22. 9.1966
Reginald Frank Price Holloway *1923–1926*	Dursley	31.10.1904	12. 2.1979
Victor Hopkins *1934–1948*	Dumbleton	21. 1.1911	6. 8.1984
Reginald Arthur Hopwood *1924*	London	1903	3. 6.1969
Sir James Nockells Horlick *1907–1910*	Brooklyn, N.Y.	22. 3.1886	31.12.1972
R. Horton *1925*			
Worthington Wynn Hoskins *1912*	South Africa	8. 5.1885	4. 3.1956
John Howman *1922–1923*	Stow-on-the-Wold	26. 4.1895	4. 4.1958
Henry James Huggins *1901–1921*	Headington, Oxon	15. 3.1877	19.11.1942
Kenneth Hunt *1926*	Bristol	4.12.1902	16. 3.1971
James Hubert Hussey-Hunt *1880*	Castle Cary, Som	20. 4.1853	13. 5.1924
Kassem Ben Khalid Ibadulla *1987–1989*	Birmingham	13.10.1964	
John Henry Iles *1890–1891*	Bristol	17. 9.1871	29. 5.1951
Alan Durant Imlay *1905–1911*	Bristol	14. 2.1885	3. 7.1959
Ratan Chand Jaidka *1927*	Malaya	1904	
Burnet George James *1914*	Bristol	26.10.1886	26. 9.1915
Harold James Jarman *1961–1971*	Bristol	4. 5.1939	
Kevin Bertram Sidney Jarvis *1988–*	Dartford, Kent	23. 4.1953	
W. Jeffries *1919*			
Herbert Jenner-Fust *1875*	Beckenham, Kent	14. 8.1841	11.11.1940
Gilbert Laird Jessop *1894–1914*	Cheltenham	19. 5.1874	11. 5.1955
Hylton Jessop *1896*	Cheltenham	1868	19. 7.1924
Osman Walter Temple Jessop *1901–1911*	Cheltenham	3. 1.1878	25. 5.1941
Walter Hylton Jessop *1920–1921*	Cheltenham	22. 3.1899	25.12.1960
Hugh Jones	Lydney	1889	10.11.1918
Richard Prescott Keigwin *1921–1923*	Colchester, Essex	8. 4.1883	26.11.1972
Cuthbert Reeves Kempe *1877*	Bristol	1856	18. 4.1953
Edmund Poole King *1927*	Bristol	21. 1.1907	
James Morris Roy King *1966*	Bristol	15. 9.1942	
Charles John King-Turner *1922*	Cirencester	13.12.1904	4. 4.1972
Henry Bloonfield Kingscote *1877*	Kingscote	28. 2.1843	1. 8.1915
William Miles Nairn Kington *1875–1876*	Bristol	24. 9.1838	21. 4.1898
Sidney Austyn Paul Kitcat *1892–1904*	Tetbury	20. 7.1868	17. 6.1942
Edward Michael Knapp *1871–1880*	Bath, Som	28. 4.1848	24.11.1903
Roger David Verdun Knight *1971–1975*	Surrey	6. 9.1946	
William Knightley-Smith *1955–1957*	West Smithfield	1. 8.1932	31. 7.1962
Graham J. Lake *1956–1958*	Croydon	15. 5.1935	
Arthur Lamb *1895–1896*	Cheltenham	1869	26. 7.1908
George E. E. Lambert *1938–1957*	London	5. 5.1919	
Robert John Lanchbury *1971*	Evesham, Worcs	11. 2.1950	
Sivell Lane *1901*	Ledbury, Hrfds	21. 8.1881	10. 2.1961
Thomas William Lang *1871–1874*	Selkirk	22. 6.1854	30. 5.1902

NAME AND EXTENT OF CAREER	BIRTHPLACE	DATE OF BIRTH	DATE OF DEATH
Thomas Langdon *1900–1914*	Brighton	8. 1.1879	30.11.1944
David Valentine Lawrence *1981*	Gloucester	28. 1.1964	
Joseph Frank Lawson *1914*	Stroud	13.11.1893	1970
Albert Edward Leatham *1883–1884*	Wakefield, Yorks	9. 8.1859	13. 7.1948
Solomon Levy *1910–1911*	Stroud	18. 5.1886	
Jeremy William Lloyds *1985–*	Penang, Malaya	17.11.1954	
Arthur John Hamilton Luard *1892–1907*	Watlair, India	3. 9.1861	22. 5.1944
Frank Mowbray Luce *1901–1911*	Gloucester	26. 4.1878	9. 9.1962
Beverley Hamilton Lyon *1921–1947*	Surrey	19. 1.1902	22. 6.1970
James Edward McDonnell *1881*	Ireland	23. 4.1841	26.11.1891
Claude Lysaght MacKay *1914*	Satara, India	29.10.1894	7. 6.1915
Robert Theodore Hope MacKenzie *1907*	Poona, India	8.10.1886	20. 3.1934
John Francis MacLean *1930–1932*	Northumberland	1. 3.1901	
William Douglas Lawson MacPherson *1870–1871*	Cheltenham	1841	24. 4.1920
Maurice Alfred McCanlis *1929*	Quetta, India	17. 6.1906	
William Kerr McClintock *1920–1921*	Newcastle on Tyne	7. 3.1896	30. 3.1946
Francis P. McHugh *1952–1956*	Leeds, Yorks	15.11.1925	
Humphrey Mainprice *1905*	Cheshire	27.11.1882	24.11.1958
Geoffrey Mains *1951–1954*	Bristol	24. 1.1934	
Herbert Cecil Manners *1902–1911*	Hampshire	16. 4.1877	30.12.1955
Charles Henry Margretts *1886*	Cheltenham	1862	22.11.1941
Edmund Marsden *1909*	Madras, India	18. 4.1881	26. 5.1915
Alan Ivor Matthews *1933–1938*	Keynsham, Som	3. 5.1913	
John Leonard Matthews *1872*	Bristol	1847	25. 9.1912
Thomas Gadd Matthews *1870–1878*	Bristol	9.12.1845	6. 1.1932
Bernard Meakin *1906*	Stone, Staffs	5. 3.1885	17. 2.1964
Robert George William Melsome *1925–1934*	Christchurch, Hants	16. 1.1906	
Michael David Mence *1966–1967*	Newbury, Berks	13. 4.1944	
Horace Merrick *1909–1911*	Bristol	21.12.1887	16. 8.1961
Samuel Paul Meston *1906*	Loughton, Essex	19.11.1882	9. 1.1960
Barrie John Meyer *1957–1971*	Bournemouth	21. 8.1932	
William Eustace Meyer *1909–1910*	Bristol	12. 1.1883	1.10.1953
William Midwinter *1877–1882*	St Briavels	19. 6.1851	3.12.1890
Robert Fenton Miles *1870–1879*	Bingham, Notts	24. 1.1846	26. 2.1930
Thomas Miller *1902–1914*	St Vincente, Cape Verde Islands	8. 3.1883	20.10.1962
Anthony O. H. Mills *1939–1948*	Sherston, Wilts	1920	
David Cecil Mills *1958*	Camborne, Cornwall	23. 4.1937	
John Mills *1870*		1848	14. 4.1935
Percy Thomas Mills *1902–1929*	Cheltenham	7. 5.1882	8.12.1950
Clement Arthur Milton *1948–1974*	Bristol	10. 3.1928	
William Edward Mirehouse *1872*	Bristol	29.10.1844	16. 6.1925
Ian Norman Mitchell *1950–1952*	Bristol	17. 4.1925	
William Octavius Moberly *1876–1887*	Shoreham, Sussex	14.11.1850	2. 2.1914
Edgar Robert Moline *1878*	Austria	2. 1.1855	16.12.1943
Francis George Monkland *1874–1879*	Trichinopoly, India	8.10.1854	15. 1.1915

NAME AND EXTENT OF CAREER	BIRTHPLACE	DATE OF BIRTH	DATE OF DEATH
Clifford Ivon Monks *1935–1952*	Bristol	4. 3.1912	23. 1.1974
Dennis Neville Moore *1930–1936*	Tewkesbury	26. 9.1910	
Donald Lindsay Morgan *1907*	Tientsin, China	5.11.1888	22. 1.1969
Edward Silvester Morris *1870*	Bristol	1849	1928
Ewart Gladstone Morrison *1926–1933*	Ceylon	7.10.1899	
John Brian Mortimore *1950–1975*	Bristol	14. 5.1933	
William Murch *1889–1903*	Bristol	18.11.1867	1. 5.1928
Ernest George Murdock *1889*	Keynsham, Som	14.11.1864	18. 5.1926
William Wallace Hayward Nash *1905–1906*	Gloucester	22. 9.1884	24. 7.1971
John William Washington Nason *1913–1914*	Corse Green	4. 8.1889	26.12.1916
Reginald George Neal *1922*	Bristol	1901	2.10.1964
William Legge Neale *1923–1948*	Berkeley	3. 3.1904	26.10.1955
Arthur Tristram Herbert Newnham *1887–1894*	Dharwar, India	17. 1.1861	29.12.1941
Ronald Bernard Nicholls *1951–1975*	Sharpness	4.12.1933	
George Benjamin Nichols *1883–1885*	Bristol	14. 6.1862	19. 2.1911
James Norley *1877*	Canterbury, Kent	5. 1.1847	24.10.1900
Albert Edward Charles North *1912*	Bristol	1878	4. 6.1933
Arthur Samuel Nott *1903–1912*	Bristol	1881	1959
Dallas Alexander Chencellor Page *1933–1936*	Cheltenham	11. 4.1911	2. 9.1936
Herbert Vivian Page *1883–1895*	Lancaster	30.10.1862	1. 8.1927
John Richard Painter *1881–1897*	Bourton on the Water, Glos	11.11.1856	16. 9.1900
Arthur James Paish *1898–1903*	Gloucester	5. 4.1874	16. 8.1948
Charles Warrington Lennard Parker *1903–1935*	Prestbury	14.10.1882	11. 7.1959
Grahame Wilshaw Parker *1932–1951*	Gloucester	11. 2.1912	
Martin David Partridge *1976–1980*	Birdlip	25.10.1954	
Ian Roger Payne *1985–1986*	Kennington	9. 5.1958	
Edward Peake *1881–1889*	Tidenham	29. 3.1860	3. 1.1945
Guy Richard Pedder *1925*	London	7. 7.1892	6. 4.1964
Arthur E. Penduck *1908–1909*		1885	1924
George Pepall *1896–1904*	Stow-on-the-Wold	29. 2.1986	8. 1.1953
John Douglas Percival *1923*	London	5. 8.1902	
Roy Wycliffe Phillips *1968–1970*	Barbados	8. 4.1941	
Arthur Pickering *1908*	Bristol	1878	15.12.1939
Alfred Pontifex *1871*	London	17. 3.1842	25. 8.1930
Malcolm William Pooley *1988*	Truro, Cornwall	27. 7.1969	
Andrew Noble Pope *1911*	Bristol	14.11.1881	18. 4.1942
Dudley Fairbridge Pope *1925–1927*	Barnes	28.10.1908	8. 9.1934
Charles John Price *1919*	Newent	1890	
Frederic Richard Price *1872*	Llewes Hall, Denbigh	2. 2.1840	1895
Hubert Cecil Prichard *1896*	Bristol	6. 2.1865	12.11.1942
Donald Lacey Priestley *1909–1910*	Tewkesbury	28. 7.1887	30.10.1917
Michael John Procter *1965–1981*	Durban, S.A.	15. 9.1946	
Charles Thomas Michael Pugh *1959–1962*	London	13. 3.1937	
Geoffrey Pullar *1969–1970*	Swinton, Lancs	1. 8.1935	
William Wade Fitzherbert Pullen *1882–1892*	Itchington	24. 6.1866	9. 8.1937

NAME AND EXTENT OF CAREER	BIRTHPLACE	DATE OF BIRTH	DATE OF DEATH
George Augustus Frederick Quentin *1874*	Kirkee, India	3.11.1848	6. 5.1928
Octavius Goldney Radcliffe *1886–1893*	North Newnton, Wilts	20.10.1859	13. 4.1940
Douglas Charles Gordon Raikes *1932*	Bristol	26. 1.1910	
Gilbert Leach Rattenbury *1902–1909*	Cardiff	28. 2.1878	14. 8.1958
Henry Albert Reed *1921–1923*	Bristol	1892	3. 5.1963
Reginald William Rice *1890–1903*	Tewkesbury	14.11.1868	11. 2.1938
Barry Anderson Richards *1965*	Durban S.A.	21. 7.1945	
Alfred Graham Richardson *1897–1901*	Sandy, Beds	24. 7.1875	17.12.1934
Terence Michael Noel Riley *1964*	Birmingham	25.12.1939	
George Lionel Robathan *1922*	Brighton, Sussex	1878	3. 8.1951
Arthur Wilson Roberts *1908–1913*	Bombay, India	23. 9.1874	27. 6.1961
Francis Bernard Roberts *1906–1914*	Nasik, India	20. 5.1882	8. 2.1916
Frederick George Roberts *1887–1905*	Mickleton	1. 4.1862	7. 4.1936
Lambert Lloyd Roberts *1900*	Brentford, Middlesex	1878	26. 6.1919
Arthur Robinson *1878*		1855	24. 2.1913
Douglas Charles Robinson *1905–1926*	Bristol	20. 4.1884	30. 7.1963
Sir Foster Gotch Robinson *1903–1923*	Bristol	19. 9.1880	31.10.1967
John Foster Robinson *1929*	Bristol	2. 2.1909	
Percy Gotch Robinson *1904–1921*	Bristol	2.11.1881	30. 1.1951
Vivian John Robinson *1923*	Bristol	16. 5.1897	28. 2.1979
Peter Rochford *1952–1957*	Halifax, Yorks	27. 8.1928	
Paul Gerrard Peter Roebuck *1984*	Bath, Som	13.10.1963	
Francis Galpin Rogers *1924–1931*	Bristol	7. 4.1897	28. 7.1967
Joseph Alfred Rogers *1929–1933*	Oxford	1. 2.1908	25. 3.1965
Lawson Macgregor Rolls *1984*	Bristol	8. 3.1965	
Paul William Romaines *1982–*	Bishop Auckland, Co. Durham	25.12.1955	
George Romans *1899–1903*	Gloucester	30.11.1876	2. 1.1946
Arthur William Frederick Roper *1920–1921*	Bristol	1890	21. 6.1956
Frank Rowlands *1920–1922*	Bristol	26. 7.1889	6. 9.1975
William Henry Rowlands *1901–1928*	Bristol	30. 7.1883	29. 6.1948
Robert Charles Russell *1981–*	Stroud	15. 8.1963	
Sydney Edward James Russell *1965–1968*	Feltham, Middlesex	4.10.1937	
Thomas Henry Rust *1914*	Gloucester	3. 3.1881	9. 8.1962
Sadiq Mohammad *1972–1982*	Junagadh, India	3. 5.1945	
Edward Sainsbury *1891–1892*	Bath, Som	5. 7.1851	28.10.1930
Gary Edward Sainsbury *1983–1987*	Wanstead, Surrey	17. 1.1958	
Malcolm Gurney Salter *1907–1925*	Cheltenham	10. 5.1887	15. 6.1973
Henry Jarvis Savory *1937*	Chipping Sodbury	4. 3.1914	
Colin J. Scott *1938–1954*	Bristol	1. 5.1919	
Edward Keith Scott *1937*	Truro, Cornwall	14. 6.1918	
Osmond Scott *1905*	Wareham, Dorset	24. 3.1876	9. 9.1948
Frederick James Seabrook *1919–1935*	Gloucester	9. 1.1899	7. 8.1979
Walter George Seabrook *1928*	Gloucester	12. 2.1904	
Arthur Samuel Sellick *1903–1904*	Gloucester	6.1878	1958

NAME AND EXTENT OF CAREER	BIRTHPLACE	DATE OF BIRTH	DATE OF DEATH
Arthur Thomas Serjeant *1883*	Clifton	1856	1916
Cyril Otto Hudson Sewell *1895–1919*	Pietermaritzburg S.A.	19.12.1874	19. 8.1951
Frederic John Sewell *1937*	Stow-on-the-Wold	29. 9.1913	
Julian Howard Shackleton *1971–1978*	Todmorden, Yorks	29. 1.1952	
Brian Keith Shantry *1978–1979*	Bristol	26. 5.1955	
David Robert Shepherd *1965–1979*	Bideford, Devon	27.12.1940	
John Neil Shepherd *1982–1987*	Barbados	9.11.1943	
Edward Cecil J. Sheppard *1921–1922*	Bristol	1891	23.12.1962
Herbert John Donald Shrimpton *1923*	Worcester	12. 4.1903	12. 3.1979
William Henry Simmonds *1924–1925*	Bristol	1892	11. 3.1957
David Paul Simpkins *1982–1983*	Chippenham, Wilts	28. 3.1962	
Reginald Albert Sinfield *1924–1939*	Stevenage, Herts	24.12.1900	
David Robert Smith *1956–1970*	Bristol	5.10.1934	
Edwin George Smith *1875–1876*	Cheltenham	29. 8.1850	5. 4.1880
Harry Smith *1912–1935*	Bristol	21. 5.1891	12.11.1937
Oliver Charles Kennedy Smith *1987–*	Meriden, Warwicks	29.10.1967	
Kenneth Hannam Soutar *1908*	Gloucester	11.10.1888	2. 9.1914
Edward James Spry *1899–1921*	Bristol	31. 7.1881	19.11.1958
Ernest Henry Staddon *1912*	Bristol	1883	23. 7.1965
John Latham Stanton *1921–1922*	Bristol	8. 3.1901	27. 6.1973
Eric James Stephens *1927–1937*	Gloucester	23. 3.1909	
Franklyn Dacosta Stephenson *1982–1983*	Barbados	8. 4.1959	
James Parker Stephenson-Jellie *1896–1908*		1875	1960
Richard William Stewart *1966*	Portland, Jamaica	28. 2.1945	
Andrew Willis Stovold *1973–*	Bristol	19. 3.1953	
Martin Willis Stovold *1979–1982*	Bristol	28.12.1955	
George Strachan *1870–1882*	Prestbury	21.11.1850	29.12.1901
Edward Basil Turnour Studd *1919*	India	20.10.1878	2. 3.1951
John Patrick Sullivan *1968–1977*	Bristol	11. 3.1948	
Geoffrey Pearce Surman *1936–1937*	Uckington	18. 7.1914	
David Surridge *1980–1982*	Bishops Stortford	6. 1.1956	
Roy Swetman *1972–1974*	Croydon, Surrey	25.10.1933	
Noel Ongley Tagart *1900–1901*	London	24.12.1878	8.10.1913
Alan Tait *1978*	Washington, Co Durham	27.12.1953	
Frederick Ernest Tayler *1911*	Aston-Blank	18. 7.1889	30. 4.1954
Herbert William Tayler *1914*	Aldsworth	6.12.1887	
Edmund Junkin Taylor *1876–1886*	Bristol	30.12.1854	25.12.1936
Frank Taylor *1873*	Rochdale, Lancs	4. 5.1855	16. 8.1936
John Clifford Taylor *1899–1900*	Bristol	1. 8.1875	10.11.1952
Philip H. Taylor *1938*	Bristol	18. 9.1917	
Geoffrey Alan Tedstone *1961–*	Southport, Lancs	19. 1.1929	
David James Thomas *1988*	Solihull, B'ham	30. 6.1959	
Edgar Lang Thomas *1895–1907*	Bristol	2.11.1875	1936
Frank Edgecumbe Thomas *1901–1906*	Bristol	5. 4.1877	20. 5.1924
Philip Leslie Thorn *1974*	Bristol	17.11.1951	

NAME AND EXTENT OF CAREER	BIRTHPLACE	DATE OF BIRTH	DATE OF DEATH
Herbert Henry Timms *1911–1912*	Moreton-in-Marsh	6. 7.1890	1. 3.1973
Keith Patrick Tomlins *1986–1987*	Kingston upon Thames	23.10.1957	
William Corrie Tonge *1880*	Edenbridge, Kent	14. 4.1862	2. 5.1943
Thomas Hector Toogood *1900–1914*	Bristol	1873	9.1953
Wilson Gardner Tovey *1901*	Cirencester	1874	4. 3.1950
Arthur Fenton Miles Townsend *1903–1906*	Bristol	1. 8.1885	1948
Charles Lucas Townsend *1893–1922*	Bristol	7.11.1876	17.10.1958
Frank Townsend *1870–1891*	Bristol	17.10.1847	25.10.1920
Frank Norton Townsend *1896–1900*	Bristol	16. 9.1875	25. 5.1901
Sean Robert Tracy *1983*	Auckland N.Z.	7. 6.1963	
Christopher Richard Trembath *1982–1984*	London	27. 9.1961	
James Henry Apperley Tremenheere *1872*	Poona, India	30.10.1853	28.10.1912
Frank Colin Troup *1914–1921*	India	27. 9.1896	19. 1.1924
Walter Troup *1887–1911*	Meerut, India	16.10.1869	12.1940
Thomas Archibald Truman *1910–1913*	Newton Abbot, Devon	1881	14. 9.1918
Bertrand Turnbull *1911*	Cardiff	1887	17.1.1943
Charles Lane Turnbull *1873*	Gloucester	1851	24. 3.1920
Charles Turner *1886–1889*		1861	20. 5.1926
Ronald Turner *1906*	Medway, Kent	1885	15. 8.1915
Peter Henry Twizell *1985–1986*	Northumberland	18. 6.1959	
Cyril Tyler *1936–1938*	Ossett, Yorks	26. 1.1911	
Paul Ian Van der Gucht *1932–1933*	Sparken, Worksop	2.11.1911	
Martin Jeffrey Vernon *1977*	Marylebone, London	9. 7.1951	
Walter Oswald Vizard *1882–1890*	Bellary, India	16.11.1861	10. 1.1929
Nesbit Willoughby Wallace *1871*	Halifax, Nova Scotia	20. 4.1839	31. 7.1931
Courtney Andrew Walsh *1984–*	Kingston, Jamaica	30.10.1962	
Albert Edward Waters *1923–1925*	Bristol	8. 5.1902	
Bert Thomas Lewis Watkins *1932–1938*	Gloucester	25. 6.1902	22.12.1982
Frederick Arthur Watts *1905*	Westbury on Severn	1884	20. 2.1968
Lawrence Dursley Watts *1958*	Bristol	2. 5.1935	
Frederick Charles Weaver *1897–1909*	Gloucester	10. 3.1878	29.12.1949
George Wedel *1925–1929*	Leigh, Lancs	18. 5.1900	
Frederick James Weeks *1925–1928*	Bristol	7. 1.1903	
Brian Douglas Wells *1951–1959*	Gloucester	27. 7.1930	
Stuart Alkar Westley *1969–1971*	Preston, Lancs	21. 3.1947	
Richard Kingscote Whiley *1954*	Gloucester	10.10.1935	
Alison Kingsley Gordon White *1912–1919*		2. 1.1881	20. 3.1962
Raymond Christopher White *1962–1964*	Johannesburg, S.A.	29. 1.1941	
Michael Roy Whitney *1981*	Sydney, Australia	24. 2.1959	
Frank Cowlin Wicks *1912*	Bristol	ˈ1891	26. 4.1965
Eric W. E. Wignall *1952–1953*	Edgware, Middlesex	25.12.1932	

NAME AND EXTENT OF CAREER	BIRTHPLACE	DATE OF BIRTH	DATE OF DEATH
Alfred George Sidney Wilcox *1939–1949*	Cheltenham	10. 7.1920	
Alan Haydn Wilkins *1980–1982*	Cardiff	22. 8.1953	
John Wilkinson *1899–1920*		16. 7.1876	15. 5.1948
John Nathaniel Williams *1908*	St Austell, Cornwall	24. 1.1878	25. 4.1915
Leoline Williams *1922*	Dursley	15. 5.1900	
Philip Francis Cunningham Williams *1919–1925*	Kensington, London	6. 7.1884	6. 5.1958
Stephen Williams *1978*	Swindon, Wilts	11. 3.1954	
Arthur Edward Wilson *1936–1955*	Paddington, London	18. 5.1910	
Graham George Morley Wiltshire *1953–1960*	Chipping Sodbury	16. 4.1931	
Stephen James Windaybank *1979–1982*	Pinner, Middlesex	20.10.1956	
Anthony Robin Windows *1960–1968*	Bristol	25. 9.1942	
Alex Ethelbert Winstone *1906–1909*	Keynsham, Som	1879	29. 3.1963
James Percival Winterbotham *1902*	Cheltenham	21. 6.1883	2.12.1925
Arthur Strachan Winterbottom *1885*	Dursley	28. 6.1864	15. 6.1936
Henry Gough Witchell *1923*	Dursley	8. 4.1906	24. 8.1965
Russell Brown Wood *1950–1951*	Bristol	15.12.1929	
Reginald George Woodman *1925*	Bristol	11. 8.1905	
William Alfred Woof *1878–1902*	Gloucester	9. 7.1858	4. 4.1937
Gilbert George Wooley *1920*		1896	8. 2.1953
Claud Neville Woolley *1909*	Tunbridge Wells	5. 5.1886	3.11.1962
Simon Howard Wootton *1984*	Perivale, Middlesex	24. 2.1959	
Harry Wrathall *1894–1907*	Cheltenham	1. 2.1869	1. 6.1944
Charles Wreford-Brown *1886–1898*	Bristol	9.10.1866	26.11.1951
Oswald Eric Wreford-Brown *1900*	Bristol	21. 7.1877	7. 7.1916
Anthony John Wright *1982–*	Stevenage, Herts	27. 6.1962	
Edward Campbell Wright *1894–1898*	South Shields	23. 4.1874	28. 7.1949
Edward Fortescue Wright *1878*	Chudleigh, Devon	23.11.1904	
George Nevil Wyatt *1871–1876*	Champaran, India	25. 8.1850	16. 2.1926
William Stanley Yalland *1910*	Bristol	27. 6.1889	23.10.1914
Gerald Joseph Yorke *1925*	Tewkesbury	10.12.1901	
Vincent Wodehouse Yorke *1898*	London	21. 5.1869	27.11.1957
Douglas Martin Young *1949–1964*	Coalville, Leics	15. 4.1924	
Syed Zaheer Abbas *1972–1985*	Sialkot, Pakistan	24. 7.1947	

CAREER AVERAGES IN ALL
FIRST-CLASS MATCHES 1870–1989

Name	M	Inns	NO	Runs	HS	Avge	100s	Runs	Wkts	Avge	Best	5wI
A'Court, D. G.	49	68	31	420	47★	1.35	—	3890	145	26.82	6/25	5
Alderman, T. M.	20	22	11	135	43★	12.27	—	1711	75	22.81	8/59	3
Alderwick, E. E. G.	2	3	—	7	5	2.33	—					
Allen, B. O.	285	471	20	13265	220	29.41	14	429	3	143.00	2/80	—
Allen, C.	2	3	—	51	35	17.00	—					
Allen, D. A.	349	514	110	7510	121★	18.58	1	19515	882	22.12	8/34	42
Alleyne, M. W.	64	97	17	2042	116★	25.52	2	1138	21	54.19	4/48	—
Alpass, H. J. H.	7	9	2	36	18★	5.14	—	114	4	28.50	2/42	—
Andrew, F. J.	21	26	7	54	7	2.84	—	1366	57	23.96	5/8	2
Ashenden, M. J.	15	14	3	21	7★	1.90	—	889	26	34.19	3/32	—
Atfield, A. J.	3	6	—	74	45	12.33	—					
Athey, C. W. J.	115	196	24	7365	171★	42.81	18	634	15	42.26	3/3	—
Bailey, Sir D. T. L.	60	95	12	2029	111	24.44	2	388	12	32.33	2/19	—
Baillie, W. H.	1	1	—	7	7	7.00	—					
Bainbridge, P.	235	392	57	11174	169	33.35	20	9439	262		8/53	7
Baker, F.	1	2	—	31	27	15.50	—					
Ball, E. W.	3	3	—	0		—	—					
Ball, M. C. J.	10	9	3	33	17★	5.50	—	594	20	29.70	4/53	—
Barnett, C. J.	424	700	38	21222	232	32.05	38	11265	371	30.36	6/17	11
Barnett, C. S.	108	191	18	3690	157	21.32	2	66	—	—	—	—
Barnett, E. P.	63	119	8	1925	95	17.34	—					
Barnett, P. P.	4	7	—	36	16	5.14	—					
Barrow, A. W.	6	11	1	162	37	16.20	—	196	3	65.33	2/51	—
Becher, A. W. B.	9	15	—	238	64	15.86	—	112	—	—	—	—
Belcher, C.	7	12	2	157	60★	15.70	—	55	1	55.00	1/13	—
Bell, P. H.	8	14	1	244	64	18.76	—					
Beloe, G. H.	6	11	2	153	52★	17.00	—					
Bendall, F. G.	1	2	—	3	3	1.50	—	42	1	42.00	1/42	—
Bengough, C. S.	2	3	—	8	8	2.66	—					
Benson, E. T.	5	8	1	71	42	10.14	—					
Bernard, J. R.	11	20	3	225	65	13.23	—	271	8	33.87	3/20	—
Bessant, J.	113	170	53	1200	50	10.25	—	4615	130	35.50	5/29	5
Bevan, D. G.	33	52	3	605	63	12.34	—					
Bewick, A. W. G.	1	2	—	5	5	2.50	—	51	1	51.00	1/31	—
Bird, F. N.	6	11	2	135	40	15.00	—					
Bissex, M.	203	343	34	6360	104★	20.57	2	6491	231	28.09	7/50	11
Blackmore, E. G.	3	5	—	11	5	2.20	—	140	2	70.00	1/38	—
Blagrave, H. H. G.	1	2	—	12	12	6.00	—					
Bloodworth, B. S.	142	237	9	3714	115	16.28	1	47	—	—	—	—
Bloor, J. H.	3	5	—	44	22	8.80	—	14	—	—	—	—
Board, J. H.	430	755	74	13092	214	19.22	8	32	—	—	—	—
Border, A. R.	1	1	1	15	15★	—	—					
Borroughs, W. F.	5	7	3	45	25	11.25	—					
Boughton, H. J.	7	12	2	114	41	11.40	—					
Boughton, W. A.	3	3	—	3	3	1.00	—					
Bowles, J. J.	18	34	1	237	25	7.18	—	458	11	41.63	3/47	—

Name	M	Inns	NO	Runs	HS	Avge	100s	Runs	Wkts	Avge	Best	5wI
Bracher, F. C.	13	23	I	163	21	7.40	—					
Brain, B. M.	110	114	27	897	57	10.31	—	7896	316	24.98	7/51	13
Brain, J. H.	68	119	6	2323	143	20.55	2	239	7	34.14	4/54	—
Brain, W. H.	7	13	5	95	36	11.87	—					
Brassington, A. J.	128	156	46	882	35	8.01	—	10	0	—	—	—
Brice, E. A.	4	5	—	15	13	3.00	—	102	13	7.84	6/34	2
Broad, B. C.	89	159	9	4804	145	32.02	8	656	11	59.63	2/14	—
Brodhurst, A. H.	6	10	I	72	54	8.00	—					
Brooke, R. H. J.	I	I	—	37	37	37.00	—					
Brooks, J.	I	2	—	0	—	—	—	31	I	31.00	1/31	—
Brotherhood, R.	3	6	2	3	2	0.75	—	67	2	33.50	2/49	—
Brown, A. S.	489	797	98	12684	116	18.14	3	31159	1223	25.47	8/80	54
Brown, D. W. J.	88	152	11	2862	142	20.29	I					
Brown, H. W.	16	31	5	210	41	8.07	—	522	13	40.15	3/3	—
Brown, W. M. R.	I	2	—	19	11	9.50	—					
Brown, W. S. A.	161	272	23	4787	155	19.22	2	6401	192	33.33	6/56	3
Browne, E. K.	4	6	I	136	52	27.20	—	19	I	19.00	1/7	—
Browne, G. E. K.	2	3	—	20	12	6.66						
Brownlee, L. D.	65	109	3	1572	103	14.83	I	362	14	25.85	3/40	—
Brownlee, W. M.	32	51	4	764	68	16.25	—	1172	40	29.30	6/84	2
Bruton, C. L.	3	6	I	60	24	12.00	—					
Bryan, J.	2	3	I	34	24	17.00	—					
Burrough, J. W.	7	12	3	136	46	15.11	—	250	5	50.00	2/26	—
Burrows, D. A.	2	I	—	0	—	—	—	93	—	—	—	—
Bush, J. A.	136	207	61	1186	57	8.12	—	65	—	—	—	—
Bush, R. E.	16	22	I	217	42	10.33	—					
Butcher, I. P.	18	29	3	535	105★	20.51	I	15	—	—	—	—
Carpenter, D.	117	210	6	3741	95	18.33	—	36	—	—	—	—
Carter, F. A.	10	13	3	75	13★	7.50	—	88	2	44.00	1/15	—
Cave, W. F.	3	6	—	65	42	10.83	—					
Champain, C. E. B.	16	25	4	212	29	10.09	—	14	—	—	—	—
Champain, F. H. B.	83	144	8	3307	149	24.31	4	324	15	21.60	6/62	I
Champain, H. F. B.	11	16	I	134	35	8.93	—					
Champain, J. N. B.	2	3	—	2	2	0.66	—					
Chard H. W.	2	4	—	35	32	8.75	—	136	3	45.33	2/27	—
Charteris, Hon. H. F.	I	I	—	I	I	1.00	—					
Chester-Master, A. W.	2	2	I	5	5	5.00	—					
Chester-Master, E.	I	2	I	4	4	4.00	—	25	I	25.00	1/9	—
Childs, J. H.	165	151	72	535	34★	6.77	—	13468	421	31.99	9/56	21
Clarke, B. F.	12	19	I	249	108★	13.83	· I					
Cleaton, H.	I	I	—	I	I	1.00	—	23				
Clowes, H.	4	8	—	82	22	10.25	—					
Coates, A. E.	I	I	—	2	2	2.00	—					
Cobden, H. S.	4	4	I	11	5★	3.66	—	22	I	22.00	1/22	—
Cole, F. L.	15	25	2	188	36	8.17	—	41	—	—	—	—
Collett, G. F.	9	16	—	155	41	9.68	—	144	4	36.00	2/37	—
Collings, A. W.	I	I	—	I	I	1.00	—					
Cook, C.	498	601	244	1936	35★	5.42	—	35929	1768	20.32	9/42	98
Cooper, N. H. C.	17	31	I	561	106	18.70	I	61	I	61.00	1/4	—
Corbett, L. J.	9	18	—	373	55	20.72	—	19	—	—	—	—
Cornelius, N. S.	6	9	I	99	40	12.37	—					

Name	M	Inns	NO	Runs	HS	Avge	100s	Runs	Wkts	Avge	Best	5wI
Cornwall, A. E. C.	1	2	—	5	3	2.50	—					
Craddy, W. H.	3	5	—	47	29	9.40	—					
Cranfield, L. L.	25	44	5	547	51★	14.02	—	1645	57	28.85	6/67	2
Cranfield, L. M.	162	228	55	2466	90	14.25	—	7671	233	32.92	8/45	8
Crankshaw, Sir E. N. S.	1	2	—	2	1	1.00	—					
Cranston, J.	103	168	17	3102	152	20.54	5	19	—	—	—	—
Crapp, J. F.	422	708	73	22195	175	34.95	36	306	6	51.00	3/24	—
Crawford, I. C.	5	7	—	104	73	14.85	—	174	3	58.00	1/18	—
Crooke, F. J.	8	11	—	165	36	15.00	—	12	—	—	—	—
Croome, A. C. M.	30	49	8	499	71	12.17	—	372	7	53.14	2/25	—
Cross, J. J.	2	2	—	5	5	2.50	—					
Crossman, G. L.	2	4	—	11	5	2.75	—					
Cullimore, M. H.	3	3	—	19	15	6.33	—					
Cunningham, E. J.	14	23	6	271	61★	15.94	—	264	4	66.00	2/55	—
Curran, K. M.	116	179	28	5498	142	36.41	13	4348	175	24.85	7/54	8
Curteis, F. A.	6	10	1	72	27★	8.00	—	127	—	—	—	—
Dacre, C. C. R.	191	309	17	8271	223	28.32	16	240	7	34.28	2/8	—
Dale, C. S.	8	8	2	100	49	16.66	—	467	7	66.71	3/10	—
Daniels, J. G. U.	1	2	—	19	15	9.50	—					
Davey, J.	175	209	91	918	53★	7.77	—	11720	411	28.51	6/95	9
Davison, B. F.	24	35	7	984	111	35.14	1					
Day, L. M.	15	21	8	159	34★	12.23	—					
Dean, T.	1	2	—	15	11	7.50	—					
Dearlove, A. J.	6	10	1	129	34★	14.33	—	141	5	28.20	3/56	—
Dennett, E. G.	388	628	244	3966	71	10.32	—	41408	2082	19.88	10/40	206
Dewfall, E. G.	2	2	—	0	—	—	—	148	4	37.00	3/82	—
de Winton, G. S.	28	51	9	669	80	15.92	—	3	—	—	—	—
Diment, R. A.	1	2	—	3	3	1.50	—					
Dindar, A.	7	10	2	100	55	12.50	—	70	3	23.33	3/32	—
Dipper, A. E.	478	860	68	27948	252★	35.28	53	4903	161	30.45	7/46	5
Disney, C. R.	1	2	—	2	2	1.00	—					
Dixon, J. H.	16	20	7	79	13★	6.07	—	1136	21	54.09	5/44	2
Doughty, R. J.	14	19	7	214	32★	17.83	—	939	23	40.82	6/43	1
Du Boulay, A. H.	3	5	1	35	21	8.75	—	40	1	40.00	1/4	—
Dudleston, B.	9	16	2	530	111	37.85	1	302	7	43.14	3/36	—
Dunstan, M. S. T.	12	20	3	283	52	16.64	—					
Eagar, E. D. R.	21	30	2	465	82	16.60	—					
Eagar, M. A.	6	10	—	159	35	15.90	—					
Eden, E.	1	2	—	3	3	1.50	—					
Edwards, C. W.	7	14	—	184	42	13.14	—	28	—	—	—	—
Ellis, F. E.	26	44	19	241	24★	9.64	—	2185	70	31.21	6/90	4
Ellis, R. G. P.	1	2	—	23	20	11.50	—	7	1	7.00	1/7	—
Emmett, G. M.	454	770	44	22806	188	31.41	34	2455	57	43.07	6/137	2
English, E. R. M.	1	2	—	2	2	1.00	—					
Etheridge, R. J.	39	64	14	796	48	15.92	—					
Evans, D. L.	7	13	1	91	50★	7.58	—	13	1	13.00	1/7	—
Fairbanks, W.	24	35	7	280	46	10.00	—					
Fargus, A. H. C.	15	27	4	210	42	9.13	—	876	33	26.54	7/55	2
Ferris, J. J.	63	114	8	1845	106	17.40	1	3448	130	26.52	6/37	8
Fewings, J.	2	4	1	4	3★	1.33	—					
Filgate, C. R.	15	24	4	405	93	20.25	—					

Name	M	Inns	NO	Runs	HS	Avge	100s	Runs	Wkts	Avge	Best	5wI
Finan, N. H.	8	4	2	26	18	13.00	—	313	4	78.25	2/57	—
Foat, J. C.	91	150	15	2512	126	18.60	5	40	—	—	—	—
Ford, E. C. B.	6	9	2	75	32★	10.71	—					
Ford, J. K.	1	1	—	0	—	—	—	44	1	44.00	1/44	—
Ford, P. H.	29	51	9	419	36	9.97	—	2148	87	24.68	6/24	7
Ford, R. G.	51	70	23	496	37★	10.55	—	493	10	49.30	2/11	—
Fowler, T. H.	46	78	4	1057	114	14.28	1	36	—	—	—	—
Fox, J. C. K.	2	3	1	13	11★	6.50	—					
Francis, C. J.	1	1	—	8	8	8.00	—	11	—	—	—	—
Francis, G.	31	55	6	642	89	13.10	—	16	1	16.00	1/16	—
Francis, H. H.	18	31	3	344	55	12.28	—					
Freeman, S. T.	3	4	1	55	45	18.33	—					
Gallop, H. G.	6	10	2	43	16	5.37	—	104	5	20.80	3/47	—
Gange, T. H.	37	64	7	571	39	10.01	—	3265	103	31.69	7/91	6
Garne, H. W.	1	2	—	2	2	1.00	—					
Garnham, M. A.	3	4	2	50	21	25.00	—					
Gilbert, W. R.	108	180	15	3141	102	19.03	1	3272	175	18.69	6/30	7
Giles, G. M.	1	2	—	8	8	4.00	—	31	—	—	—	—
Goddard, T. W. J.	558	743	207	5026	71	9.37	—	56062	2862	19.58	10/113	246
Godsell, R. T.	51	96	4	1132	98★	12.30	—	8	—	—	—	—
Goodwin, H. S.	31	50	6	546	46	12.40						
Goodwyn, F. W.	3	3	—	69	38	23.00	—					
Gordon, C. S.	13	19	—	361	96	19.00	—	162	5	32.40	3/67	—
Gouldsworthy, W. R.	26	44	10	277	65★	8.14	—	1729	62	27.88	6/47	4
Grace, A. H.	2	3	—	5	4	1.66	—	42	1	42.00	1/42	—
Grace, E. M.	253	445	11	7859	122	18.10	3	4023	171	23.52	7/46	4
Grace, G. F.	85	129	13	3279	180★	28.26	4	3204	165	19.41	8/43	9
Grace, H.	2	2	—	—	—	—	—					
Grace, W. G.	360	612	49	22808	318★	40.51	50	24774	1340	18.48	9/55	115
Grace, W. G. jr.	29	46	2	526	62	11.95	—	565	15	37.66	4/59	—
Grant, W. St C.	4	7	—	55	16	7.85	—	22	—	—	—	—
Graveney, D. A.	366	473	137	6000	119	17.85	2	22499	784	28.69	8/85	5
Graveney, J. K. R.	110	165	26	1991	62	14.32	—	4706	171	27.52	10/66	7
Graveney, T. W.	296	506	48	19705	222	43.02	50	2001	57	35.11	5/28	1
Green, D. M.	81	146	1	4703	233	32.43	7	475	9	52.77	4/61	—
Green, M. A.	91	155	17	1969	64★	14.26	—	65	—	—	—	—
Green, R. L. H.	1	2	—	5	3	2.50	—					
Greene, A. D.	21	33	4	239	32	8.24	—					
Greene, R. M.	1	2	2	49	26★	—	—	59	1	59.00	1/56	—
Greene, V. S.	16	21	4	218	62★	12.82	—	1484	54	27.48	7/96	3
Greenway, C. H.	3	6	—	8	6	1.33	—	196	4	38.25	2/40	—
Gregg, T.	32	54	4	490	62	9.80	—	1370	41	33.41	4/19	—
Gribble, H. W. R.	29	40	7	342	37	10.36	—	—	—	—	—	—
Griffiths, E. L.	30	52	9	499	40★	11.60	—	11	—	—	—	—
Griffiths, J. V. C.	34	53	10	396	32	9.20	—	1167	48	24.31	4/74	—
Gurney, E. R.	1	2	—	10	8	5.00	—					
Hacker, W. S.	3	4	1	7	6	2.33	—	287	4	71.75	2/29	—
Haines, A. H.	7	13	2	117	23	10.63	—					
Hale, H.	19	34	6	331	44★	11.82	—	851	30	28.36	7/90	1
Hale, I. E.	13	23	3	287	61	14.35	—	18	1	18.00	1/18	—
Hale, W. H.	60	103	7	1975	135	20.57	2	356	6	59.33	2/16	—

Name	M	Inns	NO	Runs	HS	Avge	100s	Runs	Wkts	Avge	Best	5wI
Halford, J.	10	15	2	150	42	11.53	—	12	—	—	—	—
Hammond, W. R.	405	664	74	33664	317	57.05	113	14801	504	29.36	9/23	15
Harbin, L.	4	5	—	34	13	6.80	—	168	10	16.80	5/80	1
Harris, F. A.	10	13	1	68	33	5.66	—	33	—	—	—	—
Harris, S. S.	1			did not bat				did not bowl				
Hattersley-Smith, Rev P.	11	15	2	198	56	15.23						
Hatton, J.	3	6	1	28	11*	6.60	—					
Hawkins, D. G.	134	220	14	3755	106	18.22	3	1153	38	30.34	6/81	1
Haygarth, E. B.	2	3	—	8	7	2.66	—					
Haynes, C.	5	10	2	76	21	9.50	—	—	—			
Haynes, R. W.	74	121	6	1673	89	14.54	—	815	15	54.33	4/76	—
Healing, J. A.	10	16	—	174	37	10.87	—					
Healing, P.	1	2	—	38	30	19.00	—					
Heath, A. H.	6	10	—	52	25	5.20	—					
Heath, W.	1	1	—	0	—	—	—					
Hedges, L. P.	30	46	—	816	85	17.73	—	36	1	36.00	1/23	—
Hemingway, G. E.	1	2	—	0	—	—	—					
Hemingway, W. McG.	48	83	1	1186	78	14.46	—					
Hewlett, R. J.	5	10	—	80	24	8.00	—					
Hignell, A. F.	1	1	—	7	7	7.00	—	48	—	—	—	—
Hignell, A. J.	137	231	35	5678	149*	28.96	7	98	3	32.66	2/13	—
Hill, A. W.	2	2	1	30	29*	30.00	—	54	1	54.00	1/47	—
Hinde, F. L.	1	2	—	5	3	2.50	—					
Hoare, E. S.	3	4	—	16	10	4.00	—					
Hobbs, N. F. C.	6	10	1	53	28	5.88	—					
Hodgkins, H. J. J.	10	17	1	209	44	13.06	—	183	5	36.60	3/68	—
Hodgson, G. D.	3	4	—	60	25	15.00	—					
Hollinshead, C.	1			did not bat			—	7	—	—	—	—
Holloway, G. J. W. S.	10	20	1	187	34*	9.84	—					
Holloway, R. F. P.	7	12	3	108	28*	12.00	—	19	—	—	—	—
Hopkins, V.	139	210	34	2608	83*	14.81	—					
Hopwood, R. A.	1	2	—	2	2	1.00	—	8	—	—	—	—
Horlick, Sir J. N.	2	3	—	17	9	5.66	—					
Horton, R.	3	5	2	13	7	4.33	—	149	1	149.00	1/97	—
Hoskins, W. W.	5	9	—	62	25	6.88	—	67	—	—	—	—
Howman, J.	13	21	1	128	23	6.40	—					
Huggins, H. J.	200	347	44	4375	92	14.43	—	16952	584	29.02	9/34	24
Hunt, K.	1	2	—	7	7	3.50	—					
Hussey-Hunt, J. H.	2	3	—	13	6	4.33	—					
Ibadulla, K. B.	9	15	4	269	77	24.45	—	299	7	42.71	3/37	—
Iles, J. H.	3	6	1	13	7	2.60	—	152	3	50.66	3/79	—
Imlay, A. D.	7	12	—	88	17	7.33	—					
Jaidka, R. C.	2	1	—	5	5	5.00	—	160	2	80.00	1/57	—
James, B. G.	3	6	1	27	10	5.40	—					
Jarman, H. J.	45	74	18	1041	67*	18.58	—	131	—	—	—	—
Jarvis, K. B. S.	16	15	4	66	32	6.00	—	1074	37	29.02	5/15	1
Jeffries, W.	2	4	1	0	—	—	—	93	5	18.60	3/38	—
Jenner-Fust, H.	1	2	1	1	1	1.00	—					
Jessop, G. L.	345	605	23	18936	286	32.53	36	13867	620	22.36	8/29	30

Name	M	Inns	NO	Runs	HS	Avge	100s	Runs	Wkts	Avge	Best	5wI
Jessop, H.	3	6	—	75	41	12.50	—	29	1	29.00	1/12	—
Jessop, O. W. T.	2	4	1	61	29	20.33	—					
Jessop, W. H.	5	10	1	118	25	13.11	—					
Jones, H.	1	2	—	11	11	5.50	—					
Keigwin, R. P.	9	17	1	270	65	16.87	—	189	5	37.80	4/40	—
Kempe, C. R.	2	3	—	28	15	9.33	—					
King, E. P.	3	4	—	14	6	3.50	—					
King, J. M. R.	3	5	—	47	28	9.40	—					
King-Turner, C. J.	6	9	—	29	10	3.22	—					
Kingscote, H. B.	3	3	1	4	4	2.00	—					
Kington, W. M. N.	2	4	—	27	17	6.75	—					
Kitcat, S. A. P.	50	90	8	1805	95*	22.01	—	481	14	34.35	2/0	—
Knapp, E. M.	12	17	3	215	90*	15.35	—	48	2	24.00	2/27	—
Knight, R. D. V.	105	186	13	5610	144	32.42	11	3561	100	35.61	6/44	1
Knightley-Smith, W.	29	54	1	791	64	14.92	—					
Lake, G. J.	13	18	4	106	18	7.57	—	464	17	27.29	4/39	—
Lamb, A.	2	4	—	24	10	6.00	—	32	—	—	—	—
Lambert, G. E. E.	334	480	61	6288	100*	15.00	1	25831	908	28.44	8/35	37
Lanchbury, R. J.	5	9	—	112	38	12.44	—					
Lane, S.	3	5	1	16	8	4.00	—	296	7	42.28	5/139	1
Lang, T. W.	8	10	1	126	44	14.00	—	427	21	20.33	4/49	—
Langdon, T.	279	513	14	10621	156	21.28	6	835	19	43.94	2/8	—
Lawrence, D. V.	129	147	30	1146	65*	9.79	—	11390	353	32.36	7/47	14
Lawson, J. F.	1	2	—	4	3	2.00	—					
Leatham, A. E.	7	13	2	63	23	5.72	—	131	1	131.00	1/25	—
Levy, S.	4	8	2	43	22	7.16	—	147	4	41.66	2/41	—
Lloyds, J. W.	114	169	25	4797	130	33.31	5	4771	129	36.98	7/134	6
Luard, A. J. H.	45	81	2	1140	75*	14.43	—					
Luce, F. M.	25	46	5	754	57	18.39	—	20	—	—	—	—
Lyon, B. H.	238	395	20	9550	189	25.46	15	2218	50	44.36	5/72	1
MacDonnell, J. E.	1	1	—	0	—	—	—					
MacKay, C. L.	1	2	—	28	15	14.00	—	24	—	—	—	—
MacKenzie, R. T. H.	2	4	—	29	21	7.25	—	4	—	—	—	—
MacLean, J. F.	6	7	2	124	46	24.80	—					
MacPherson, W. D. L.	3	4	1	7	5	2.33	—					
McCanlis, M. A.	1			did not bat				32	—	—	—	—
McClintock, W. K.	8	13		98	24	7.53	—					
McHugh, F. P.	92	110	43	179	18	2.67	—	6710	272	24.66	7/32	15
Mainprice, H.	1q	2	—	108	60	54.00	—	77	4	19.25	4/77	—
Mains, G.	6	10	1	19	8	2.11	—	305	6	50.83	2/42	—
Manners, H. C.	5	8	—	60	32	7.50	—					
Margretts, C. H.	1	2	—	14	14	7.00	—					
Marsden, E.	2	4	—	79	38	19.75	—					
Matthews, A. I.	16	25	6	185	51	9.73	—	980	14	70.00	4/81	—
Matthews, J. L.	1			did not bat				did not bowl				
Matthews, T. G.	29	47	—	769	201	16.36	1					
Meakin, B.	1	2	1	4	4*	4.00	—					
Melsome, R. G. W.	16	26	3	351	47	15.26	—	366	10	36.60	2/34	—
Mence, M. D.	22	35	7	482	78	17.21	—	1067	25	42.68	4/27	—
Merrick, H.	12	23	5	257	58	14.27	—					
Meston, S. P.	3	6	—	40	22	6.66	—	17	—	—	—	—

Name	M	Inns	NO	Runs	HS	Avge	100s	Runs	Wkts	Avge	Best	5wI
Meyer, B. J.	405	569	191	5368	63	14.20	—	28	—	—	—	—
Meyer, W. E.	9	16	—	136	43	8.50	—					
Midwinter, W. E.	58	88	8	1605	107*	20.06	2	3673	231	15.90	7/27	17
Miles, R. F.	59	79	17	508	79	8.19	—	2630	168	15.65	7/38	12
Miller, T.	18	32	1	406	35	13.09	—	253	4	63.25	2/5	—
Mills, A. O. H.	4	5	—	81	39	16.20	—	62	3	20.66	2/28	—
Mills, D. C.	1	1	—	17	17	17.00	—					
Mills, J.	1	2	—	17	15	8.50	—					
Mills, P. T.	346	546	116	5052	95	11.74	—	20736	824	25.16	7/30	39
Milton, C. A.	584	1017	119	30218	170	33.65	52	3567	79	45.15	5/64	1
Mirehouse, W. E.	1			did not bat				did not bowl				
Mitchell, I. N.	9	15	1	97	24	6.92	—					
Moberly, W. O.	64	101	7	2072	121	22.04	3					
Moline, E. R.	2	3	—	31	28	10.33	—					
Monkland, F. G.	26	37	6	458	59	14.77	—					
Monks, C. I.	65	101	17	1589	120	18.91	1	1629	36	45.25	4/70	—
Moore, D. N.	31	46	2	1187	206	26.97	1	19	—	—	—	—
Morgan, D. L.	2	4	—	3	2	0.75	—					
Morris, E. S.	2	2	—	30	17	15.00	—					
Morrison, E. G.	20	34	1	340	59	10.30	—	209	3	69.66	1/30	—
Mortimore, J. B.	594	928	114	14918	149	18.32	4	38496	1696	22.69	8/59	72
Murch, W.	77	129	12	1060	49	9.05	—	5052	204	24.76	8/68	11
Murdock, E. G.	3	6	—	15	8	2.50	—	11	1	11.00	1/11	—
Nash, W. W. H.	3	6	1	81	34	16.20	—					
Nason, J. W. W.	19	37	1	623	139	17.30	1	204	4	51.00	2/52	—
Neal, R. G.	1	1	1	2	2*	—	—					
Neale, W. L.	452	700	79	14751	145*	23.75	14	3970	100	39.70	6/9	1
Newnham, A. T. H.	16	28	5	242	56	10.52	—	892	42	21.23	6/64	3
Nicholls, G.B.	5	10	1	54	36	6.00	—	187	3	62.33	1/22	—
Nicholls, R. B.	534	954	52	23612	217	26.17	18	719	11	65.36	2/19	—
Norley, J.	1	1	—	0	—	—	—					
North, A. E. C.	2	4	1	49	27	16.33	—	27	1	27.00	1/18	—
Nott, A. S.	15	25	3	182	44*	8.27	—	77	—	—	—	—
Page, D. A. C.	106	167	7	2993	116	18.70	1	45	—	—	—	—
Page, H. V.	102	165	16	2538	116	17.03	1	2701	112	24.11	6/34	3
Painter, J. R.	192	341	15	5839	150	17.91	5	1209	46	26.28	8/67	2
Paish, A. J.	79	123	38	967	66	11.37	—	8610	354	24.32	8/68	27
Parker, C. W. L.	602	916	185	7616	82	10.41	—	61614	3170	19.43	10/79	273
Parker, G. W.	70	112	9	1954	210	18.97	4	1366	32	42.68	5/57	1
Partridge, M. D.	46	66	21	1202	90	26.71	—	2076	41	50.63	5/29	1
Payne, I. R.	18	18	5	212	37	16.30	—	790	19	41.57	3/48	—
Peake, E.	26	43	7	392	33	10.88	—	1166	53	22.20	6/47	2
Pedder, G. R.	1	1	—	9	9	9.00	—					
Penduck, A. E.	5	8		18	8	3.00	—	294	6	49.00	3/98	—
Pepall, G.	14	24	7	99	45	5.82	—	725	20	36.25	5/63	1
Percival, J. D.	1	2	—	10	10	5.00	—					
Phillips, R. W.	16	25	—	431	82	17.24	—	6	—	—	—	—
Pickering, A.	1	2	—	5	4	2.50	—	20	—	—	—	—
Pontifex, A.	1	2	1	12	6*	12.00	—					
Pooley, M. W.	11	15	6	155	38	15.50	—	497	13	39.23	4/80	—
Pope, A. N.	2	4	—	46	29	11.50	—					

Name	M	Inns	NO	Runs	HS	Avge	100s	Runs	Wkts	Avge	Best	5wI
Pope, D. F.	11	20	5	114	46★	7.60	—					
Price, C. J.	1	2	—	19	13	9.50	—					
Price, F. R.	2	2	1	10	10★	10.00	—					
Prichard, H. C.	2	4	—	46	23	11.50	—					
Priestley, D. L.	7	13	1	154	51	12.83	—					
Procter, M. J.	259	437	38	14441	203	36.19	32	16299	833	19.56	8/30	42
Pugh, C. T. M.	76	134	8	2324	137	18.44	1	30	1	30.00	1/12	—
Pullar, G.	25	41	8	1038	109	31.45	1	—	—	—	—	—
Pullen, W. W. F.	91	162	8	2655	161	17.24	1	93	3	31.00	1/11	—
Quentin, G. A. F.	1	1	—	22	22	22.00	—					
Radcliffe, O. G.	119	219	7	4408	117	20.79	4	2677	95	28.17	5/43	2
Raikes, D. C. G.	5	7	1	32	23	5.33	—					
Rattenbury, G. L.	2	4	—	7	7	1.75	—	129	1	129.00	1/54	—
Reed, H. A.	6	12	—	1100	45	9.16	—					
Rice, R. W.	123	215	18	4157	111	21.10	2	4	—			—
Richards, B. A.	1	1	—	59	59	59.00	—	—	—	—	—	—
Richardson, A. G.	20	32	1	500	89	16.12	—	18	—			—
Riley, T. M. N.	11	20	—	238	51	11.90	—					
Robathan, G. L.	3	6	—	118	42	19.66	—					
Roberts, A. W.	28	44	3	727	90	17.73	—	396	11	36.00	2/20	—
Roberts, F. B.	67	115	7	2280	157	21.11	5	1868	50	37.36	5/69	1
Roberts, F. G.	260	410	151	1922	38	7.42	—	21154	963	21.96	8/40	62
Roberts, L. L.	2	3	—	4	4	1.33	—					
Robinson, A.	3	4	3	38	34★	38.00	—					
Robinson, D. C.	124	216	12	3584	150★	17.56	1					
Robinson, Sir F. G.	68	116	2	2075	144	18.20	2					
Robinson, J. F.	1	did not bat						50	—	—	—	—
Robinson, P. G.	26	46	1	790	66	17.55	—	585	11	53.18	5/60	1
Robinson, V. J.	1	2	—	2	2	1.00	—					
Rochford, P.	80	113	22	479	31★	5.26	—					
Roebuck, P. G. P.	1	2	—	25	20	12.50	—					
Rogers, F. G.	26	43	3	798	79	19.95	—					
Rogers, J. A.	45	57	2	461	59	8.38	—	1644	45	36.53	4/50	—
Rolls, L. M.	1	—	—	—	—	—	—	49	—	—	—	—
Romaines, P. W.	151	272	19	7272	186	28.74	12	217	3	72.3	3/42	—
Romans, G.	11	19	3	218	62	13.62	—					
Roper, A. W. F.	13	21	2	226	55	11.89	—	7	—			—
Rowlands, F.	11	21	—	308	50	14.66	—					
Rowlands, W. H.	138	207	14	3248	113	16.82	2	281	10	28.10	1/0	—
Russell, R. C.	160	211	51	3818	72	23.86	—	19	—			
Russell, S. E. J.	80	141	11	2743	107	21.10	2	3	—			
Rust, T. H.	1	2	—	2	2	1.00	—					
Sadiq Mohammad	193	346	19	12012	203	36.73	25	4666	138	33.81	5/37	1
Sainsbury, E.	18	32	3	359	36	12.37	—					
Sainsbury, G. E.	71	68	36	177	14★	5.53	—	5449	164	33.22	7/38	7
Salter, M. G.	34	65	3	1168	135	18.83	1					
Savory, H. J.	1	1	—	16	16	16.00	—					
Scott, C. J.	235	326	43	3376	90	11.92	—	16775	531	31.59	8/90	22
Scott, E. K.	2	2	—	0	—	—	—	101	1	101.00	1/42	—
Scott, O.	2	4	1	29	23★	9.66	—	11	—	—	—	—
Seabrook, F. J.	104	160	100	3371	136	22.47	5	168	5	33.60	4/77	—

Name	M	Inns	NO	Runs	HS	Avge	100s	Runs	Wkts	Avge	Best	5wI
Seabrook, W. G.	1	2	—	0	—	—	—	10	—	—	—	—
Sellick, A. S.	11	20	6	258	49	18.42	—	37	—	—	—	—
Serjeant, A. T.	3	6	—	41	25	6.83	—					
Sewell, C. O. H.	158	278	12	6850	165	25.75	8	304	5	60.80	2/35	—
Sewell, F. J.	4	7	—	113	56	16.14	—					
Shackleton, J. H.	48	64	20	596	41★	13.54	—	2242	49	45.75	4/38	—
Shantry, B. K.	3			did not bat				167	3	55.66	2/63	—
Shepherd, D. R.	282	476	40	10672	153	24.47	12	106	2	53.00	1/1	—
Shepherd, J. N.	71	109	22	2506	168	28.80	2	6431	204	31.52	7/50	7
Sheppard, E. C. J.	5	9	—	117	29	13.00	—					
Shrimpton, H. J. D.	3	6	1	26	14	5.20	—					
Simmonds, W. H.	2	3	—	57	44	19.00	—					
Simpkins, D. P.	1	2	1	1	1★	1.00	—	15	—	—	—	—
Sinfield, R. A.	423	684	83	15561	209★	25.89	16	28394	1165	24.37	9/111	66
Smith, D. R.	357	488	110	4640	74	12.27	—	27449	1159	23.68	7/20	48
Smith, E. G.	2	3	—	26	14	8.66	—					
Smith, H.	393	645	55	13330	149	22.59	10	7	—	—	—	—
Smith, O. C. K.	1	2	—	15	14	7.50	—					
Soutar, K. H.	3	5	—	59	16	11.80	—	—	—	—	—	—
Spry, E. J.	89	154	24	1447	76	11.13	—	4307	149	28.90	8/52	13
Staddon, E. H.	1	2	—	16	12	8.00	—					
Stanton, J. L.	4	7	—	80	47	11.42	—					
Stephens, E. J.	216	313	54	4593	92	17.73	—	1171	29	40.37	6/59	1
Stephenson, F. D.	9	10	1	63	21	7.00	—	682	36	18.94	5/56	2
Stephenson-Jellie, J. P.	6	10	—	88	27	8.80	—					
Stewart, R. W.	1	1	—	9	9	9.00	—	53	4	13.25	3/27	—
Stovold, A. W.	344	613	35	17356	212★	30.02	20	218	4	54.50	1/0	—
Stovold, M. W.	25	37	6	518	75★	16.70	—	19	—	—	—	—
Strachan, G.	13	18	3	248	50	16.53	—	381	25	15.24	5/46	1
Studd, E. B. T.	2	4	—	56	25	14.00	—					
Sullivan, J. P.	23	40	1	480	53	12.30	—	50	2	25.00	2/50	—
Surman, G. P.	2	4	3	11	5★	11.00	—	99	2	49.50	2/60	—
Surridge, D.	25	20	10	63	12	6.30	—	2016	60	33.60	5/78	1
Swetman, R.	45	62	15	529	37	11.25	—	36	—	—	—	—
Tagart, N. O.	6	9	—	93	28	10.33	—					
Tait, A.	11	19	1	348	53	19.33	—	—	—	—	—	—
Tayler, F. E.	4	8	—	53	21	6.62	—	7	—	—	—	—
Tayler, H. W.	2	4	1	84	43★	28.00	—					
Taylor, E. J.	24	35	3	319	33	9.96	—					
Taylor, F.	3	4	—	41	36	10.25	—					
Taylor, J. C.	4	5	—	72	25	14.40	—	44	2	22.00	2/33	—
Taylor, P. H.	1	2	—	14	12	7.00	—					
Tedstone, G. A.	12	17	2	206	50	13.75	—					
Thomas, D. J.	3	4	1	77	57★	25.66	—	174	7	24.85	2/39	—
Thomas, E. L.	27	45	—	571	109	12.68	1					
Thomas, F. E.	51	87	3	1874	138	22.30	3	330	10	33.00	3/22	—
Thorn, P. L.	4	6	2	45	25	11.25	—	227	4	56.75	2/53	—
Timms, H. H.	3	6	—	33	12	5.50	—					
Tomlins, K. P.	24	40	6	997	100	29.32	1	34	—	—	—	—
Tonge, W. C.	2	2	—	8	5	4.00	—					
Toogood, T. H.	8	11	3	30	12	3.75	—	488	16	30.50	6/115	1

Name	M	Inns	NO	Runs	HS	Avge	100s	Runs	Wkts	Avge	Best	5wI
Tovey, W. G.	1	2	—	8	8	4.00	—	42	2	21.00	2/42	—
Townsend, A. F. M.	9	14	—	200	28	14.28	—	171	3	57.00	1/23	—
Townsend, C. L.	161	275	19	7754	224★	30.28	19	14307	655	21.84	9/48	64
Townsend, F.	169	271	20	4826	136	19.22	2	2276	91	25.01	6/31	2
Townsend, F. N.	11	18	4	208	56	14.85	—					
Tracy, S. R.	1	1	—	0	—	—	—	55	2	27.50	2/55	—
Trembath, C. R.	4	4	3	33	17★	33.000	—	444	11	40.36	5/91	1
Tremenheere, J. H. A.	1	1	—	7	7	7.00	—					
Troup, F. C.	3	5	—	7		2.00	—					
Troup, W.	80	135	13	3252	180	26.65	7	4	—	—	—	—
Truman, T. A.	4	8	2	39	12★	6.50	—	11	1	11.00	1/10	—
Turnbull, B.	1	2	1	35	28★	35.00	—					
Turnbull, C. L.	1	1	—	0	—	—	—					
Turner, C.	3	5	—	33	17	6.60	—	119	3	39.66	1/16	—
Turner, R.	3	6	—	30	19	5.00	—					
Twizell, P. H.	2	1	—	0	—	—	—	136	2	68.00	2/65	—
Tyler, C.	16	22	4	113	22	6.27	—	1122	33	34.00	5/116	1
Van der Gucht, P. I.	33	50	9	701	81	17.09	—	5	—	—	—	—
Vernon, M. J.	5	6	—	13	4	2.16	—	217	3	72.33	1/21	—
Vizard, W. O.	18	32	2	256	49★	8.53	—					
Wallace, N. W.	2	3	1	1	1	0.50	—	6	—	—	—	—
Walsh, C. A.	85	98	19	1032	52	13.066	—	7581	361	21.00	9/72	24
Waters, A. E.	16	24	3	270	42	12.85	—	377	5	75.40	2/13	—
Watkins, B. T. L.	30	44	9	211	25	6.02						
Watts, F. A.	1	2	—	0	—	—	—	125	3	41.66	3/125	—
Watts, L. D.	1	2	—	46	46	23.00	—					
Weaver, F. C.	5	10	3	31	18★	4.42	—	177	8	22.12	5/63	1
Wedel, G.	45	71	10	545	53	8.93	—	1629	51	31.94	4/4	—
Weeks, F. J.	7	12	1	122	35★	11.09	—	22	—	—	—	—
Wells, B. D.	141	191	35	1041	42★	6.67	—	11524	544	21.18	8/31	29
Westley, S. A.	10	17	9	138	35★	17.25	—					
Whiley, R. K.	1	2	2	11	7★	—						
White, A. K. G.	11	20	1	376	54	19.78	—					
White, R. C.	40	75	1	1443	102★	19.50	1	4	1	4.00	1/4	—
Whitney, M. R.	3	2	—	0	—	—	—	399	13	30.69	4/86	—
Wicks, F. C.	1	2	—	2	2	1.00	—					
Wignall, E. W. E.	3	4	1	24	14	8.00	—	63	2	31.50	2/50	—
Wilcox, A. G. S.	39	58	5	835	73	15.75	—					
Wilkins, A. H.	40	47	6	379	44	9.24	—	3137	104	30.16	8/57	3
Wilkinson, J.	10	16	7	64	17★	7.11	—	587	17	34.52	4/39	—
Williams, J. N.	3	5	—	31	16	6.20	—					
Williams, L.	11	18	2	194	57★	12.12	—					
Williams, P. F. C.	112	198	10	3081	87	16.38	—	173	2	86.50	1/0	—
Williams, S.	1	1	—	0	—	—	—					
Wilson, A. E.	318	486	73	10534	188	25.50	7	1	—	—	—	—
Wiltshire, G. G. M.	19	30	4	218	39	8.38	—	835	25	33.40	7/52	1
Windaybank, S. J.	15	19	4	385	53	25.66	—					
Windows, A. R.	98	158	27	1953	74	14.90	—	4948	184	26.89	8/78	6
Winstone, A. E.	44	80	3	975	58	12.66	—	130	4	32.50	1/12	—
Winterbotham, J. P.	1	2	—	2	2	1.00	—	77	1	77.00	1/44	—
Winterbottom, A. S.	3	5	1	53	35	13.25	—	28	—	—	—	—

Name	M	Inns	NO	Runs	HS	Avge	100s	Runs	Wkts	Avge	Best	5wI
Witchell, H. G.	1	1	—	4	4	4.00	—					
Wood, R. B.	8	12	3	110	48	12.22	—					
Woodman, R. G.	2	3	—	4	4	1.33	—					
Woof, W. A.	140	224	53	1105	35	6.46	—	11838	644	18.38	8/70	57
Wooley, G. G.	1	2	—	0	—	—	—					
Woolley, C. N.	1	1	—	22	22	22.00	—	45	—	—	—	—
Wootton, S. H.	4	8	1	194	97	27.71	—	—	—	—	—	—
Wrathall, H.	263	465	18	10289	176	23.01	8	1288	27	47.70	4/37	—
Wreford-Brown, C.	4	6	1	45	21*	9.00	—	82	2	41.00	2/26	—
Wreford-Brown, O. E.		1	1	—	5	5	5.00	—				
Wright, A. J.	138	240	14	6058	161	26.80	7	29	1	29.00	1/16	—
Wright, E. C.	7	12	5	95	30*	13.57	—	266	9	29.55	4/32	—
Wright, E. F.	4	8	—	81	32	10.12	—	38	1	38.00	1/26	—
Wyatt, G. N.	10	17	1	194	37	12.12	—	4	1	4.00	1/4	—
Yalland, W. S.	1	1	—	1	1	1.00	—					
Yorke, G. J.	1	2	—	6	6	3.00	—					
Yorke, V. W.	1	1	—	10	10	10.00	—					
Young, D. M.	435	777	35	23400	198	31.53	40	130	3	43.33	2/35	—
Zaheer Abbas	206	360	37	16083	230*	49.79	49	332	6	55.38	3/32	—

RESULTS OF ALL INTER-COUNTY FIRST-CLASS MATCHES 1870–1989

	DY	EX	GM	HA	KT	LA	LE	MX	NR	NT	SM	SY	SX	WA	WO	YO
1870												WW				
1871										DL		WW				
1872										DD		LW	DW			W–
1873												WD	WD			WW
1874												LW	WD			WW
1875										LD		LW	LW			LW
1876										WW		WD	WD			WD
1877										WW		WW	WW			DW
1878						DW				DW		LD	WW			LD
1879						LD		DD		DL		WD				LD
1880						DW		DW		DD		LW				DW
1881						LD		WD		DL		WW				WD
1882						LL		LL		LD	W–	DW				LW
1883						LW		LD		LD	WW	LL				DL
1884						DW		LD		LL		LD	LL			LL
1885						LL		WW		LL	WW	WW	LL			LD
1886	W–					DW		LL		DD		LL	LW			DL
1887				DD	LL			DL		LL		LL	LW			DL
1888			WW	DL				WL		LW		LD	DW			LD
1889			DL	LW				LD		LL		LD	DW			WL
1890				LD	DD			LW		WW		LL	LW			LW
1891				DD	LL			LD		WD	LL	LL	WL			LL
1892				WL	LD			LD		LD	LD	LL	LD			DD
1893				WD	LL			WL		LL	LL	LW	LD			LL
1894				LL	LL			LD		WL	LL	LL	WL	DD		LL
1895				WD	LD			WD		WW	WL	LD	LW	LW		LW
1896				WL	LL			LW		LW	LW	LD	DW	DL		LL
1897				WW	LL			DD		WW	WD	WL	DD	LD		LW
1898		WW		DW	DL			WD		DD	WW	LW	DD	WW		DL
1899		WW		WD	LL			LL		DD	DL	DL	WD	DW		LL
1900		LW		DW	DW			WL		LD	WW	LW	DD	DW	LW	LL
1901	DD	DD		LD	LD			DL		DD	LL	LD	WL	WW	DL	LL
1902				LL	LD			DL		DL	WW	DD	WD	DL	LD	LL
1903				DW	DD			LL		DL	LL	LW	DD	LD	WL	LL
1904				LD	LL			DW		LW	WL	DL	DW		WD	DD
1905				LL	LW			WW		WD	LW	DW	LW	WL		LL
1906		LW		LL	LL			WW		DL	DL	LL	WL		WD	DW
1907		LW	WW	WW				LL	DW	LL	DL	LW	WL		LL	LL
1908		LW	LW	LL				LL	WD	LW	DW	DW	DD	WW	LL	LL
1909		DD	DD	LL				LL	WL	LL	LL	DL	LD	DL	LD	
1910			LL	LL	DL			LL	DW	DL	WD	WL		LL	WW	
1911			LD	LL	LD			LL	LW	LL	WW	LD		WL	WL	
1912			WD	LD						AW	LD	LA	LL	LD	WD	LL
1913			LL	WL	DL				WL	WL	DW	LL	DL	LW	LW	LW
1914			DL	LL	LL				LL	DL	LW	LL	LD	L–	LD	LL
1919		DD	DL		LL	LW					LD		WW	DW	DD	LL
1920		WD	LW	LL	DL	WW					WW		LL	WL	LW	LD

	DY	*EX*	*GM*	*HA*	*KT*	*LA*	*LE*	*MX*	*NR*	*NT*	*SM*	*SY*	*SX*	*WA*	*WO*	*YO*
1921	WW	WL	WW	LL	LL	LL	WW				WW		LL	WW	LW	LL
1922	LW	LW	DW	LL	LL	LL	LL	LL			WD	LL	WW	LW	DW	LL
1923	WW	DL	WL	DD	LL	LD	WW	LL			LL	DL	LL	LL	WW	LL
1924	DW	WW	DW	DD	LD	LD	LW	LW			DD	DL	LW		WW	LD
1925	WW	LW	WW	LD	LL	LD	LL	DD		LL	WD	LL	WL		WW	LL
1926	DL	LD	LW	LL	LL	DL	DW	LL	WL	DL	WL	LL	LD		WD	DL
1927	DD	DD	DD	DW	WA	DL	LD	LD	WW	LD	DD	DD	DL		WW	LL
1928	DD	WD	DW	WD	LL	LD	DL	WD	DD	DL	WD	DW	WL		WW	
1929		WD	WW	WW	LD	WD	LW	WW	WW	LL	WD	DD	LL	DW	WW	
1930	DW	DW	WW	LW	WD	LD	DW	WW			WW	DW	WL	DW	WD	LD
1931	WW		DD	LW		LW	DW	DW	DD	WD	DD	WD	DD	DW	LW	WL
1932		WL	LD	DD	LW	WD		LW	DW	DL	DD	LD	LL	AL	WL	LL
1933	LW	LL	WD	DW	WL	DD	WW	LL		DD	LW	LW	LL	WL	DW	LL
1934	DD	WD	DD	DD	LW	LL	LW	WD		LW	LW	LW	LW	LL	WD	WW
1935	WL	LL	WW	LL	LL	LL	DW	DL		DD	WL	DD	LL	DD	WL	LL
1936	LL	DW	WW	DD	LD	WD	WD	DL		LW	DD	LW	WW	WD	LD	DD
1937	LW	WW	DW	WW	WL	LW	DW	WL		DW	WW	DW	LD	LL	LW	LL
1938	WD	LL	DW	LW	WL	DW	LW	LL		NA	LD	DL	LL	DL	WW	DL
1939	DL	WW	DL	WW	WL	LD		WW		WA	DW	WL	WD	WL	WL	WW
1946	W–	WD	WL	WW	W–	L–	WW	LW	W–	WD	DD	W–	DD	D–	LL	DL
1947	W–	WW	DW	WD	W–	L–	WW	LL	W–	WD	WW	W–	DL	D–	WW	WW
1948	LL	L–	D–	LL	DW	DD	W–	D–	DL	W–	WD	LD	WW	DW	DW	W–
1949	WW	W–	D–	DD	WW	WW	W–	L–	LD	D–	LD	WL	DW	LL	DD	L–
1950	WD	W–	LD	LW	DD	LD	D–	D–	DD	D–	DD	LL	WW	DD	WD	DL
1951	WD	W–	DD	DD	DL	DD	D–	L–	DL	D–	WW	DL	LD	LL	LW	LD
1952	L–	LD	WW	WL	D–	D–	DW	LL	D–	DL	DD	LL	DW	WD	DW	LL
1953	D–	WL	DD	DD	W–	L–	WL	WW	W–	DL	WW	DW	DL	DL	DD	DL
1954	WL	W–	LD	LD	DD	DA	A–	L–	LL	W–	WD	LL	DD	LD	DW	LL
1955	DL	L–	DW	DL	LD	LW	L–	W–	WW	W–	DD	LL	LW	WL	WL	LL
1956	D–	LW	WW	DD	W–	L–	WW	DL	D–	WD	WW	WD	WL	LW	LW	LW
1957	L–	LL	WW	WL	L–	D–	WD	LD	L–	WL	DW	LW	LDD	LL	LD	DW
1958	DW	W–	LL	LD	DD	LW	W–	D–	DL	D–	DD	LD	LD	DD	LL	WD
1959	WW	T–	LL	LW	WW	DL	W–	W–	WW	D–	WW	LL	DL	LL	LL	DW
1960	W–	W–	WD	LW	DL	DL	DW	WD	DL	D–	WL	D–	DD	WD	LW	LD
1961	D–	W–	WW	LL	WL	LL	DW	LL	WW	W–	LL	D–	WD	WL	DD	WL
1962	L–	L–	LW	DW	DW	DW	DW	WL	DD	W–	L	WW	LL	WL	LL	
1963	W–	DL	WL	LD	W–	W–	WW	DL	D–	WW	LW	DD	DL	DL	DD	DD
1964	D–	LD	LD	LD	D–	D–	LW	DL	L–	LL	LW	LL	DW	DL	LL	DL
1965	WL	D–	LD	DW	LL	WW	W–	L–	DD	D–	DW	DL	DW	DD	DL	LD
1966	WW	D–	WD	LL	LW	DL	D–	L–	WL	L–	LD	LD	DL	DW	DL	LD
1967	W–	WL	DD	LD	D–	D–	LL	AW	L–	DD	DD	DL	LD	DL	DL	LL
1968	L–	DD	DD	LD	D–	L–	LL	DD	D–	DL	LD	DD	WD	WA	DL	DD
1969	W–	W–	LL	DW	D–	D–	W–	L–	W–	D–	DW	DL	WL	DD	WW	LW
1970	L–	D–	LL	LD	L–	D–	D–	L–	D–	L–	WL	DD	WD	DD	DD	WD
1971	DW	D–	DA	DD	W–	L–	D–	DL	DD	WW	DD	L–	D–	W–	WD	W–
1972	W–	W–	DD	DW	W–	D–	L–	L–	W–	L–	DD	D–	W–	D–	DW	L–
1973	W–	D–	–	DW	DL	D–	D–	A–	D–	D–	D–	LW	W–	L–	W–	D–
1974	D–	D–	WA	LD	L–	D–	L–	D–	L–	D–	WW	W–	L–	L–	LL	L–
1975	D–	L–	LD	LL	D–	L–	D–	W–	D–	L–	LD	W–	W–	W–	LL	L–
1976	L–	W–	DW	WW	W–	D–	L–	L–	L–	L–	WW	D–	D–	W–	AW	D–
1977	W–	W–	LW	WL	L–	D–	W–	D–	AL	D–	DL	D–	WW	D–	WW	A–

226

	DY	EX	GM	HA	KT	LA	LE	MX	NR	NT	SM	SY	SX	WA	WO	YO
1978	W–	L–	DW	WD	W–	L–	L–	L–	AD	D–	LD	W–	DL	D–	DD	L–
1979	D–	L–	DD	WW	L–	D–	W–	D–	DW	L–	AD	L–	AD	D–	WD	D–
1980	A–	D–	LL	DW	W–	D–	D–	W–	LL	D–	DD	D–	LD	D–	DW	D–
1981	L–	A–	AD	DW	D–	D–	D–	D–	DD	L–	DL	W–	AD	D–	DW	W–
1982	D–	D–	DL	WL	D–	D–	L–	D–	LD	L–	DD	L–	LL	D–	LD	W–
1983	DD	L–	WW	LD	D–	L–	D–	L–	L–	D–	DD	DL	A–	DL	DL	WD
1984	D–	L–	DD	DD	DW	DD	DL	DL	D–	L–	LL	D–	L–	L–	DL	L–
1985	W–	DL	DD	DL	W–	L–	D–	D–	WD	DD	DD	D–	DA	W–	WW	W–
1986	DD	D–	DW	WW	W–	D–	W–	L–	D–	D–	LW	WD	W–	DL	WD	DD
1987	T–	L–	WW	DL	DD	DL	LL	DW	D–	D–	LD	W–	D–	W–	DL	L–
1988	W–	W–	WA	DW	D–	D–	L–	L–	LL	W–	LW	L–	DD	D–	DL	D–
1989	D–	L–	DW	LD	W–	W–	W–	L–	LL	L–	WW	L–	DL	L–	LL	D–

RESULTS OF ALL SUNDAY LEAGUE MATCHES 1969–1989

	DY	EX	GM	HA	KT	LA	LE	MX	NR	NT	SM	SY	SX	WA	WO	YO	P	W	L	T	NR
1969	L	L	W	L	W	L	W	L	L	L	W	W	W	L	W	W	16	8	8	–	–
1970	L	L	W	W	L	L	A	W	W	L	W	W	W	A	L	W	16	7	7	–	2
1971	W	L	W	W	L	L	L	L	W	A	L	L	L	W	L	A	16	5	9	–	2
1972	L	W	L	T	L	L	L	L	T	W	L	L	W	A	L	L	16	3	10	2	1
1973	L	W	L	A	L	L	L	W	L	W	W	A	W	W	A	W	16	7	6	–	3
1974	W	W	W	L	A	L	L	L	L	W	L	A	L	L	A	A	16	4	8	–	4
1975	W	L	L	L	L	W	L	L	L	W	L	W	L	W	L	L	16	5	11	–	–
1976	L	W	L	W	L	L	L	L	W	L	L	L	W	L	L	L	16	4	12	–	–
1977	L	A	L	W	W	L	L	A	W	W	L	W	W	A	A	A	16	6	5	–	5
1978	L	L	L	L	L	L	L	L	L	A	L	W	W	W	L	A	16	3	11	–	2
1979	W	L	W	L	L	W	A	L	A	L	L	W	W	L	W	W	16	7	7	–	2
1980	L	W	W	W	L	L	L	W	L	W	L	W	A	L	W	L	16	7	8	–	1
1981	L	A	L	L	W	A	A	W	W	L	L	L	L	L	L	A	16	3	9	–	4
1982	A	W	A	W	L	L	L	L	L	L	W	L	L	W	W	L	16	5	9	–	2
1983	L	L	W	W	L	L	A	W	L	A	L	A	L	W	A	L	16	4	8	–	4
1984	W	L	L	L	W	L	W	L	W	A	W	A	L	L	L	L	16	5	9	–	2
1985	L	L	W	L	L	W	L	L	W	W	L	W	L	W	W	W	16	8	8	–	–
1986	L	L	L	A	L	W	L	A	L	L	W	L	L	L	L	W	16	3	11	–	2
1987	L	W	W	T	W	L	L	W	A	W	L	W	W	W	A	W	16	9	4	1	2
1988	W	W	W	W	W	L	W	L	L	W	W	L	W	A	AA	W	16	10	4	–	2
1989	L	L	W	W	L	L	W	L	L	L	L	L	L	L	L	L	16	3	13	–	–

RESULTS OF GILLETTE CUP/NATWEST TROPHY MATCHES 1963–1989

1963 *1st Round*: lost to Middlesex
1964 *1st Round*: lost to Surrey
1965 *1st Round*: lost to Northamptonshire
1966 *2nd Round*: beat Berkshire; *3rd Round*: lost to Warwickshire
1967 *2nd Round*: lost to Lancashire
1968 *2nd Round*: beat Kent; *3rd Round*: beat Nottinghamshire; *S/Final*: lost to Sussex
1969 *2nd Round*: lost to Sussex
1970 *1st Round*: lost to Lancashire
1971 *2nd Round*: beat Sussex; *3rd Round*: beat Surrey; *S/Final*: lost to Lancashire
1972 *2nd Round*: lost to Kent
1973 *1st Round*: beat Glamorgan; *2nd Round*: beat Surrey; *3rd Round*: beat Essex; *S/Final*: beat Worcestershire; *Final*: beat Sussex
1974 *1st Round*: lost to Lancashire
1975 *2nd Round*: beat Oxfordshire; *3rd Round*: beat Leicestershire; *S/Final*: lost to Lancashire
1976 *1st Round*: beat Worcestershire; *2nd Round*: beat Yorkshire; *3rd Round*: beat Worcestershire; *2nd Round*: beat Yorkshire; *3rd Round*: lost to Lancashire
1977 *2nd Round*: lost to Northamptonshire
1978 *2nd Round*: lost to Lancashire
1979 *1st Round*: lost to Hampshire
1980 *2nd Round*: lost to Surrey
1981 *1st Round*: beat Ireland; *2nd Round*: lost to Essex
1982 *2nd Round*: beat Nottinghamshire; *3rd Round*: lost to Middlesex
1983 *1st Round*: beat Scotland; *2nd Round*: beat Leicestershire; *3rd Round*: lost to Hampshire
1984 *1st Round*: beat Staffordshire; *2nd Round*: lost to Lancashire
1985 *1st Round*: beat Bedfordshire; *2nd Round*: beat Northamptonshire; *3rd Round*: lost to Nottinghamshire
1986 *1st Round*: beat Berkshire; *2nd Round*: lost to Leicestershire
1987 *1st Round*: beat Lancashire; *2nd Round*: beat Sussex; *3rd Round*: beat Warwickshire; *S/Final*: lost to Nottinghamshire
1988 *1st Round*: beat Ireland; *2nd Round*: beat Leicestershire; *3rd Round*: lost to Worcestershire
1989 *1st Round*: beat Oxfordshire; *2nd Round*: lost to Lancashire

RESULTS IN
BENSON AND HEDGES
CUP 1972–1989

1972 Beat Glamorgan
      Lost to Hampshire
      Beat Minor Counties (South)
      Beat Somerset
      Beat Middlesex
      S/F: Lost to Yorkshire
1973 Beat Somerset
      Lost to Glamorgan
      Beat Minor Counties (South)
      Lost to Hampshire
1974 Lost to Hampshire
      Lost to Somerset
      Beat Glamorgan
      Beat Minor Counties (South)
1975 Lost to Hampshire
      Lost to Somerset
      Lost to Glamorgan
      Beat Surrey
1976 Beat Minor Counties (West)
      Lost to Somerset
      Lost to Worcestershire
      Beat Leicestershire
1977 Beat Somerset
      Beat Lancashire
      Beat Leicestershire
      Beat Hampshire
      Q/Final: Beat Middlesex
      S/Final: Beat Hampshire
      Final: Beat Kent
1978 Beat Minor Counties (West)
      Lost to Derbyshire
      Lost to Lancashire
      Lost to Warwickshire
1979 Beat Minor Counties (South)
      Lost to Worcestershire
      Lost to Somerset
      Lost to Glamorgan
1980 Lost to Glamorgan
      Lost to Sussex
      Beat Essex
      Lost to Minor Counties
1981 Lost to Leicestershire
      Drew with Northamptonshire (abandoned no start)
      Beat Worcestershire
      Lost to Nottinghamshire

1982 Beat Glamorgan
      Beat Combined Universities
      Lost to Middlesex
      Lost to Somerset
1983 Beat Scotland
      Beat Worcestershire
      Beat Northamptonshire
      Drew with Leicestershire (match abandoned)
      Q/Final: Lost to Middlesex (toss of coin)
1984 Lost to Essex
      Beat Hampshire
      Lost to Combined Universities
      Lost to Surrey
1985 Beat Nottinghamshire
      Lost to Northamptonshire
      Beat Scotland
      Lost to Derbyshire
1986 Beat Somerset
      Lost to Essex
      Lost to Sussex
      Beat Glamorgan
1987 Beat Nottinghamshire
      Beat Leicestershire
      Lost to Northamptonshire
      Beat Derbyshire
      Lost to Kent
1988 Beat Combined Universities
      Beat Hampshire
      Beat Somerset
      Lost to Glamorgan
1989 Beat Middlesex
      Beat Worcestershire
      Beat Surrey
      Beat Combined Universities
      Lost to Nottinghamshire

GROUNDS USED BY GLOUCESTERSHIRE 1870–1989

BRISTOL *(Durdham Down)*

Only first-class match was against Surrey on 2, 3 and 4 June 1870. The ground was in a large public open space. The square was used by Clifton CC until 1929, and for other cricket until the 1960s; a football pitch is now on the site.

BRISTOL *(Clifton College)*

First first-class match was against Nottinghamshire on 3, 4 and 5 August 1871, and the last against All India on 6, 8 and 9 August 1932. Present College Ground.

BRISTOL *(Ashley Down)*

First first-class matches against Lancashire on 1 and 2 July 1889. The ground laid out to W. G. Grace's specification, was purchased by 'Fry's' in 1916 to get the Cricket Club out of debt, and became known as 'Fry's Ground'.
The County Cricket Club re-purchased the ground in 1932, the money being raised by forming a Company, Gloucestershire County Cricket Club Ltd.
The Phoenix Assurance Company purchased the ground in 1976, and it is now run by a Joint Amenity Company.
Current Ground and County Headquarters.

BRISTOL *(Greenbank)*

First first-class match was against Sussex on 13 and 15 May 1922, and the last against Derbyshire on 28, 30 and 31 July 1928. The ground was owned by H. J. Packer (Chocolate Manufacturers), and known as 'Packer's Ground'. Later became an education committee playing field.

CHELTENHAM *(College Ground)*

First first-class match was against Surrey on 18 and 19 July 1872. Present college ground, still used by the County.

CHELTENHAM *(East Gloucestershire Ground)*

First first-class match was against Nottinghamshire on 14, 15 and 16 June 1888, and the last against Philadelphians on 15 and 16 June 1903. These were the only first-class matches played on the ground. The ground was not used for cricket after 1923, but is still the East Gloucestershire Club, and used for hockey, squash and tennis. It was known as 'Charlton Park'.

CHELTENHAM *(Victoria Ground)*

First first-class match was against Glamorgan on 27, 28 and 29 June 1923. The County did not play on this ground after 1937. Gloucestershire CCC returned on 10, 11 and 12 May 1986, when the Indians were the visitors. Present ground used by Cheltenham Cricket Club.

CIRENCESTER

Only first-class match was against Surrey on 28, 29 and 30 August 1879. Present ground used by Cirencester Cricket Club.

STATISTICAL SECTION

GLOUCESTER *(Spa Ground)*

First first-class match was against Yorkshire on 12, 13 and 14 July 1883, and the last against Leicestershire on 30, 31 May and 1 June 1923. Present ground used by Gloucester City Cricket Club.

GLOUCESTER *(Wagon Works)*

First first-class match was against Lancashire on 2, 3 and 4 June 1923. The present ground has changed hands, and is now owned by the Council. It is still used by Gloucestershire CCC.

LYDNEY

First first-class match was against Surrey on 24, 26 and 27 August 1963, and the last against Sussex on 28 and 30 June 1969. Present ground used by Lydney CC.

MORETON-IN-MARSH

First first-class match was against Yorkshire on 8, 9 and 10 May 1884, and the last against Worcestershire on 22 and 23 June 1914. Present ground used by Moreton-in-March CC and by the County for one Sunday game per season.

STROUD *(Erinoid)*

First first-class match was against Nottinghamshire on 9, 11 and 12 June 1956, and the last against Glamorgan on 29, 30 and 31 May 1963. The ground was lost due to industrial expansion.

SWINDON *(County Ground)*

First used by Gloucestershire against Sussex on 3 May 1970 for a JPL match. Resumed playing here in 1985 for one Sunday match per season. Present ground used by Swindon CC and Wiltshire CCC.

TEWKESBURY *(The Swilgate)*

Used by the County for two Sunday matches, against Yorkshire on 3 September 1972, and against Lancashire on 9 September 1973. Present ground used by Tewkesbury CC.

INDIVIDUAL BATTING RECORDS

(1) DOUBLE CENTURIES IN FIRST-CLASS MATCHES

Score	Batsman	Opponents	Venue	Year
318*	W. G. Grace	Yorkshire	Cheltenham	1876
317	W. R. Hammond	Nottinghamshire	Gloucester	1936
302	W. R. Hammond	Glamorgan	Bristol	1934
302	W. R. Hammond	Glamorgan	Newport	1939
301	W. G. Grace	Sussex	Bristol	1896
290	W. R. Hammond	Kent	Tunbridge Wells	1934
288	W. G. Grace	Somerset	Bristol	1895
286	G. L. Jessop	Sussex	Brighton	1903
271	W. R. Hammond	Lancashire	Bristol	1938
265*	W. R. Hammond	Worcestershire	Dudley	1934
264	W. R. Hammond	Lancashire	Liverpool	1932
264	W. R. Hammond	West Indians	Bristol	1933
257	W. G. Grace	Kent	Gravesend	1895
252	W. R. Hammond	Leicestershire	Leicester	1935
252	A. E. Dipper	Glamorgan	Cheltenham (Vict)	1923
250*	W. R. Hammond	Lancashire	Old Trafford	1925
247	A. E. Dipper	Oxford University	Bristol	1924
244	W. R. Hammond	Essex	Chelmsford	1928
243*	W. G. Grace	Sussex	Hove	1896
240	G. L. Jessop	Sussex	Bristol	1907
239	W. R. Hammond	Glamorgan	Gloucester	1933
238*	W. R. Hammond	Warwickshire	Edgbaston	1929
237	W. R. Hammond	Derbyshire	Bristol	1938
234	G. L. Jessop	Somerset	Bristol	1905
233	D. M. Green	Sussex	Hove	1968
232	C. J. Barnett	Lancashire	Gloucester	1937
231	W. R. Hammond	Derbyshire	Cheltenham	1933
230*	Zaheer Abbas	Kent	Canterbury	1976
228	C. J. Barnett	Leicestershire	Gloucester	1947
224	C. L. Townsend	Essex	Clifton College	1899
223	C. C. R. Dacre	Worcestershire	Worcester	1930
222	T. W. Graveney	Derbyshire	Chesterfield	1954
221*	W. G. Grace	Middlesex	Clifton College	1885
220	B. O. Allen	Hampshire	Bournemouth	1947
218*	W. R. Hammond	Glamorgan	Bristol	1928
217	W. R. Hammond	Nottinghamshire	Bristol	1934
217	W. R. Hammond	Leicestershire	Gloucester	1933
217	R. B. Nicholls	Oxford University	Oxford	1962
216*	Zaheer Abbas	Surrey	The Oval	1976
215	W. G. Grace	Sussex	Hove	1888
215*	Zaheer Abbas	Somerset	Bath	1981
214	W. R. Hammond	Somerset	Bristol	1946
214	C. L. Townsend	Worcestershire	Cheltenham	1906
214	J. H. Board	Somerset	Bristol	1900
213	Zaheer Abbas	Sussex	Hove	1978
212	A. E. Dipper	Worcestershire	Bristol	1927

Score	Batsman	Opponents	Venue	Year
212*	A. W. Stovold	Northamptonshire	Northampton	1982
211*	W. R. Hammond	Oxford University	Oxford	1930
211*	W. R. Hammond	Nottinghamshire	Bristol	1946
211	T. W. Graveney	Kent	Gillingham	1953
210	G. W. Parker	Kent	Dover	1937
209	R. A. Sinfield	Glamorgan	Cardiff	1935
207	W. R. Hammond	Essex	Westcliff	1939
206	W. R. Hammond	Leicestershire	Leicester	1933
206	G. L. Jessop	Nottinghamshire	Bristol	1904
206	D. N. Moore	Oxford University	Oxford	1930
205*	W. R. Hammond	Surrey	The Oval	1928
205*	Zaheer Abbas	Sussex	Cheltenham	1977
204*	C. J. Barnett	Leicestershire	Leicester	1936
203	M. J. Procter	Essex	Gloucester	1978
203	Sadiq Mohammed	Sri Lankans	Bristol	1981
201	T. G. Matthews	Surrey	Clifton	1871
201	T. W. Graveney	Sussex	Worthing	1950
201	T. W. Graveney	Oxford University	The Parks	1951
200	T. W. Graveney	Glamorgan	Newport	1956

(2) CENTURIES IN LIMITED-OVERS MATCHES

(a) Sunday League (John Player/Refuge Assurance)

Score	Batsman	Opponents	Venue	Year
131	Sadiq Mohammad	Somerset	Bristol (Imp Grd)	1975
129*	Zaheer Abbas	Middlesex	Lord's	1981
127*	D. M. Green	Hampshire	Bristol	1970
121*	C. W. J. Athey	Northamptonshire	Moreton-in-Marsh	1985
116*	R. W. Phillips	Lancashire	Old Trafford	1970
114*	Zaheer Abbas	Hampshire	Bristol	1976
115*	C. W. J. Athey	Surrey	The Oval	1985
112*	Zaheer Abbas	Worcestershire	Bristol	1980
109*	M. J. Procter	Warwickshire	Cheltenham	1972
108	R. C. Russell	Worcestershire	Hereford	1986
106*	Zaheer Abbas	Middlesex	Lord's	1983
106*	P. Bainbridge	Somerset	Bristol	1986
105	P. W. Romaines	Northamptonshire	Northampton	1985
104*	Zaheer Abbas	Yorkshire	Hull	1980
103	Zaheer Abbas	Glamorgan	Swansea	1980
103	B. F. Davison	Yorkshire	Gloucester	1985
102	Zaheer Abbas	Northamptonshire	Bristol	1984
100	D. R. Shepherd	Glamorgan	Cardiff	1978

(b) Benson and Hedges Cup

Score	Batsman	Opponents	Venue	Year
154*	M. J. Procter	Somerset	Taunton	1972
128	Sadiq Mohammad	Minor Counties (S)	Bristol	1974
125	P. W. Romaines	Nottinghamshire	Bristol	1985
123	A. W. Stovold	Combined Univ	Oxford	1982
122	Sadiq Mohammad	Somerset	Bristol	1973

Score	Batsman	Opponents	Venue	Year
115	M. J. Procter	Lancashire	Liverpool	1978
108	Sadiq Mohammad	Glamorgan	Swansea	1972
104	A. W. Stovold	Leicestershire	Leicester	1977
101*	A. W. Stovold	Nottinghamshire	Bristol	1987

(c) NatWest Trophy/Gillette Cup

Score	Batsman	Opponents	Venue	Year
158	Zaheer Abbas	Leicestershire	Leicester	1983
131*	Zaheer Abbas	Leicestershire	Leicester	1975
128	Zaheer Abbas	Worcestershire	Bristol	1976
127	R. B. Nicholls	Berkshire	Reading	1966
122	Sadiq Mohammad	Lancashire	Old Trafford	1975
111	Sadiq Mohammad	Leicestershire	Leicester	1975
111	Zaheer Abbas	Yorkshire	Headingley	1976
107	M. J. Procter	Sussex	Hove	1971
104*	A. W. Stovold	Ireland	Bristol	1988
101	M. J. Procter	Worcestershire	Worcester	1973

(3) CARRYING BAT THROUGH A COMPLETED FIRST-CLASS INNINGS

The following opening batsmen have batted throughout a completed innings in which all ten of their partners have been dismissed:

Batsman	Score	Total	Opponents	Venue	Year
W. G. Grace	318*	528	Yorkshire	Cheltenham	1876
W. R. Gilbert	40*	110	Lancashire	Clifton	1885
W. G. Grace	221*	348	Middlesex	Clifton	1885
E. L. Griffiths	24*	123	Nottinghamshire	Trent Bridge	1885
O. G. Radcliffe	104*	207	Middlesex	Lord's	1886
W. G. Grace	113*	186	Nottinghamshire	Clifton	1887
W. G. Grace	37*	87	Lancashire	Bristol	1889
W. G. Grace	127*	282	Middlesex	Cheltenham	1889
O. G. Radcliffe	101*	214	Kent	Canterbury	1889
W. G. Grace	109*	231	Kent	Maidstone	1890
W. G. Grace	61*	105	Surrey	The Oval	1893
J. J. Ferris	34*	77	Sussex	Bristol	1894
W. G. Grace	102*	238	Lancashire	Bristol	1896
W. G. Grace	243*	463	Sussex	Hove	1896
C. L. Townsend	36*	117	Surrey	Clifton	1897
C. O. H. Sewell	88*	127	Yorkshire	Bramall Lane	1898
S. A. P. Kitcat	18*	70	Yorkshire	Hull	1901
R. W. Rice	38*	101	Yorkshire	Cheltenham	1900
R. W. Rice	58*	147	Essex	Clifton	1901
W. Troup	127*	388	Worcestershire	Bristol	1902
E. P. Barnett	52*	141	Yorkshire	Bradford	1905
R. T. Godsell	98*	269	Nottinghamshire	Bristol	1905
T. Langdon	78*	151	South Africans	Bristol	1907
C. S. Barnett	62*	235	Worcestershire	Cheltenham	1913
A. E. Dipper	168*	343	Somerset	Taunton	1914

Batsman	Score	Total	Opponents	Venue	Year
A. E. Dipper	37*	104	Lancashire	Old Trafford	1919
A. E. Dipper	99*	185	Worcestershire	Cheltenham	1919
A. E. Dipper	120*	175	Warwickshire	Edgbaston	1920
A. E. Dipper	37*	138	Kent	Cheltenham	1922
A. E. Dipper	22*	72	Leicestershire	Ashby de la Zouch	1922
A. E. Dipper	87*	192	Warwickshire	Bristol	1923
A. E. Dipper	126*	211	West Indians	Bristol	1923
A. E. Dipper	85*	210	Northamptonshire	Northampton	1926
A. E. Dipper	66*	119	Kent	Bristol	1929
A. E. Dipper	64*	192	Glamorgan	Swansea	1930
R. A. Sinfield	39*	104	Sussex	Cheltenham	1931
R. A. Sinfield	161*	374	Oxford University	The Parks	1931
R. A. Sinfield	100*	290	Sussex	Bristol	1935
R. A. Sinfield	38*	106	Derbyshire	Buxton	1937
R. A. Sinfield	69*	165	Worcestershire	Bristol	1939
C. J. Barnett	228*	363	Leicestershire	Gloucester	1947
G. M. Emmett	104*	156	Oxford University	The Parks	1948
C. A. Milton	51*	117	Lancashire	Bristol	1955
C. A. Milton	28*	69	Middlesex	Gloucester	1956
C. A. Milton	138*	253	Leicestershire	Bristol	1966
R. B. Nicholls	26*	87	Hampshire	Bristol	1966
A. W. Stovold	59*	161	Yorkshire	Scarborough	1978

(4) CENTURY IN EACH INNINGS OF A FIRST-CLASS MATCH

Batsman	Scores	Opponents	Venue	Year
W. G. Grace	101 and 103	Kent	Clifton	1887
W. G. Grace	148 and 153	Yorkshire	Clifton	1888
G. L. Jessop	101 and 109	Yorkshire	Bradford	1900
G. L. Jessop	143 and 133*	Somerset	Bath	1908
G. L. Jessop	161 and 129	Hampshire	Bristol	1909
G. L. Jessop	153 and 123*	Hampshire	Southampton	1911
H. Smith	120 and 102*	Hampshire	Southampton	1919
A. E Dipper	117 and 103	Sussex	Horsham	1922
W. R. Hammond	108 and 128	Surrey	The Oval	1927
W. R. Hammond	139 and 143	Surrey	Cheltenham	1928
B. H. Lyon	115 and 101*	Essex	Bristol	1930
C. C. R. Dacre	119 and 125*	Worcestershire	Worcester	1933
W. R. Hammond	122 and 111*	Worcestershire	Worcester	1933
W. R. Hammond	110 and 123	Derbyshire	Burton-on-Trent	1938
G. M. Emmett	115 and 103*	Leicestershire	Leicester	1947
G. M. Emmett	110 and 102*	Somerset	Bristol	1951
T. W. Graveney	103 and 105*	Northamptonshire	Bristol	1951
D. M. Young	121 and 117*	Northamptonshire	Kettering	1955
T. W. Graveney	106 and 101*	Warwickshire	Edgbaston	1957
C. A. Milton	150 and 100*	Sussex	Eastbourne	1961
C. A. Milton	110* and 102*	Kent	Bristol	1962
Sadiq Mohammad	163* and 150	Derbyshire	Bristol	1976
Zaheer Abbas	216* and 156*	Surrey	The Oval	1976

Batsman	Scores	Opponents	Venue	Year
Zaheer Abbas	230* and 104*	Kent	Canterbury	1976
Zaheer Abbas	205* and 108*	Sussex	Cheltenham	1977
Sadiq Mohammad	171 and 103	Glamorgan	Bristol	1979
Zaheer Abbas	215* and 150*	Somerset	Bath	1981
Zaheer Abbas	135* and 128	Northamptonshire	Northampton	1981
Zaheer Abbas	162* and 107	Lancashire	Gloucester	1982
C. W. J. Athey	115 and 114*	Warwickshire	Edgbaston	1987

(5) CENTURY ON FIRST-CLASS DEBUT FOR GLOUCESTERSHIRE

Batsman	Score	Opponents	Venue	Year
D. R. Shepherd	108	Oxford University	The Parks	1965
D. N. Moore	206	Oxford University	The Parks	1930

(6) 2,000 FIRST-CLASS RUNS IN A SEASON FOR GLOUCESTERSHIRE

Batsman	Runs	Average	Year
W. R. Hammond	2,860	69.75	1933
W. R. Hammond	2,637	71.27	1927
W. R. Hammond	2,583	78.27	1928
W. R. Hammond	2,571	65.92	1937
Zaheer Abbas	2,554	75.11	1976
A. E. Dipper	2,365	55.00	1928
Zaheer Abbas	2,306	88.69	1981
C. J. Barnett	2,282	45.64	1934
W. R. Hammond	2,269	84.03	1938
A. E. Dipper	2,246	49.91	1927
A. E. Dipper	2,218	47.19	1929
W. R. Hammond	2,176	68.00	1939
C. J. Barnett	2,161	41.55	1933
W. R. Hammond	2,141	57.86	1932
T. W. Graveney	2,139	53.47	1951
D. M. Green	2,137	40.32	1968
W. R. Hammond	2,101	48.64	1935
D. M. Young	2,090	42.65	1959
C. A. Milton	2,089	46.42	1967
W. R. Hammond	2,081	122.41	1934
A. E. Dipper	2,072	37.00	1926
R. B. Nicholls	2,059	36.76	1962
A. E. Dipper	2,048	40.15	1923
D. M. Young	2,035	33.91	1955
C. J. Barnett	2,024	44.97	1937
J. F. Crapp	2,014	45.77	1949
G. M. Emmett	2,005	40.91	1949

INDIVIDUAL BOWLING RECORDS

(1) HAT-TRICKS IN FIRST-CLASS MATCHES

Bowler	Opponents	Venue	Year
C. L. Townsend	Somerset	Cheltenham	1893
H. J. Huggins	Nottinghamshire	Trent Bridge	1907
E. G. Dennett	Northamptonshire	Gloucester	1907
E. G. Dennett	Surrey	Bristol	1913
C. W. L. Parker	Yorkshire	Bristol	1922
T. W. J. Goddard	Sussex	Eastbourne	1922
C. W. L. Parker	Middlesex (1st inns)	Bristol	1924
C. W. L. Parker	Middlesex (2nd inns)	Bristol	1924
C. W. L. Parker	Surrey	The Oval	1924
C. W. L. Parker	Yorkshire	Hull	1926
C. W. L. Parker	Essex	Chelmsford	1930
T. W. J. Goddard	Glamorgan	Swansea	1930
T. W. J. Goddard	Glamorgan	Swansea	1947
T. W. J. Goddard	Somerset	Bristol	1947
G. G. M. Wiltshire	Yorkshire	Headingley	1958
D. G. A'Court	Derbyshire	Gloucester	1961
A. S. Brown	Glamorgan	Swansea	1973
M. J. Procter	Essex	Westcliff	1972
J. Davey	Oxford University	The Parks	1976
M. J. Procter	Essex	Southend on Sea	1977
M. J. Procter	Leicestershire	Bristol	1979
M. J. Procter	Yorkshire	Cheltenham	1979
D. A. Graveney	Leicestershire	Leicester	1983

(2) NINE OR MORE WICKETS IN AN INNINGS FOR GLOUCESTERSHIRE

Bowler	Analysis	Opponents	Venue	Year
E. G. Dennett	10-40	Essex	Bristol	1906
J. K. R. Graveney	10-66	Derbyshire	Chesterfield	1949
C. W. L. Parker	10-79	Somerset	Bristol	1921
T. W. J. Goddard	10-113	Worcestershire	Cheltenham	1937
T. W. J. Goddard	9-21	Cambridge University	Cheltenham	1929
W. R. Hammond	9-23	Worcestershire	Cheltenham	1928
H. J. Huggins	9-34	Sussex	Bristol	1934
C. W. L. Parker	9-35	Leicestershire	Cheltenham	1920
C. W. L. Parker	9-36	Yorkshire	Bristol	1922
T. W. J. Goddard	9-37	Leicestershire	Bristol	1934
T. W. J. Goddard	9-38	Kent	Bristol	1939
T. W. J. Goddard	9-41	Nottinghamshire	Bristol	1947
C. Cook	9-42	Yorkshire	Bristol	1947
C. W. L. Parker	9-44	Essex	Gloucester	1925
C. W. L. Parker	9-44	Warwickshire	Cheltenham	1930

Bowler	Analysis	Opponents	Venue	Year
T. W. J. Goddard	9-44	Somerset	Bristol	1939
C. W. L. Parker	9-46	Northamptonshire	Northampton	1927
C. L. Townsend	9-48	Middlesex	Lord's	1898
W. G. Grace	9-55	Nottinghamshire	Cheltenham	1877
J. H. Childs	9-56	Somerset	Bristol	1981
T. W. J. Goddard	9-61	Derbyshire	Bristol	1949
E. G. Dennett	9-63	Surrey	Bristol	1913
C. A. Walsh	9-72	Somerset	Bristol	1986
T. W. J. Goddard	9-82	Surrey	Cheltenham	1946
C. W. L. Parker	9-87	Derbyshire	Gloucester	1922
C. W. L. Parker	9-103	Somerset	Bristol	1927
R. A. Sinfield	9-111	Middlesex	Lord's	1936
C. W. L. Parker	9-118	Surrey	Gloucester	1925
C. L. Townsend	9-128	Warwickshire	Cheltenham	1898

(3) 15 WICKETS IN A MATCH FOR GLOUCESTERSHIRE

Bowler	Analysis	Opponents	Venue	Year
C. W. L. Parker	17-56	Essex	Gloucester	1925
W. G. Grace	17-89	Nottinghamshire	Cheltenham	1877
T. W. J. Goddard	17-106	Kent	Bristol	1939
T. W. J. Goddard	16-99	Worcestershire	Bristol	1939
E. G. Dennett	16-146	Hampshire	Bristol	1912
T. W. J. Goddard	16-181	Worcestershire	Cheltenham	1937
C. W. L. Parker	16-109	Middlesex	Cheltenham	1930
C. L. Townsend	16-122	Nottinghamshire	Trent Bridge	1895
C. W. L. Parker	16-154	Somerset	Bristol	1927
E. G. Dennett	15-21	Northamptonshire	Gloucester	1907
W. G. Grace	15-79	Yorkshire	Bramall Lane	1872
T. W. J. Goddard	15-81	Nottinghamshire	Bristol	1947
E. G. Dennett	15-88	Essex	Bristol	1906
C. W. L. Parker	15-91	Surrey	Cheltenham	1930
E. G. Dennett	15-96	Middlesex	Bristol	1904
E. G. Dennett	15-97	Northamptonshire	Northampton	1907
T. W. J. Goddard	15-107	Derbyshire	Bristol	1949
C. W. L. Parker	15-109	Derbyshire	Derby	1924
C. W. L. Parker	15-113	Nottinghamshire	Bristol	1931
W. G. Grace	15-116	Surrey	Cirencester	1879
W. R. Hammond	15-128	Worcestershire	Cheltenham	1928
C. L. Townsend	15-134	Middlesex	Lord's	1898
T. W. J. Goddard	15-134	Leicestershire	Gloucester	1947
E. G. Dennett	15-140	Worcestershire	Cheltenham	1906
C. L. Townsend	15-141	Essex	Clifton	1898
T. W. J. Goddard	15-156	Middlesex	Cheltenham	1947
C. W. L. Parker	15-173	Northamptonshire	Gloucester	1927
C. L. Townsend	15-184	Yorkshire	Cheltenham	1895
E. G. Dennett	15-195	Surrey	Bristol	1913
C. L. Townsend	15-205	Warwickshire	Cheltenham	1898

(4) SIX WICKETS IN LIMITED-OVERS MATCHES

(a) Sunday League (John Player/Refuge Assurance)

Bowler	Analysis	Opponents	Venue	Year
J. N. Shepherd	6-52	Kent	Bristol	1983

(b) Benson and Hedges Cup

Bowler	Analysis	Opponents	Venue	Year
M. J. Procter	6-13	Hampshire	Bristol	1977

(c) NatWest Trophy/Gillette Cup

Nil

(5) 125 WICKETS IN A SEASON FOR GLOUCESTERSHIRE

Bowler	Wickets	Average	Year
T. W. J. Goddard	222	16.80	1937
T. W. J. Goddard	222	16.37	1947
C. W. L. Parker	219	14.26	1931
C. W. L. Parker	206	14.75	1925
C. W. L. Parker	200	17.97	1926
T. W. J. Goddard	200	20.36	1935
T. W. J. Goddard	196	14.58	1939
C. W. L. Parker	195	13.17	1922
C. W. L. Parker	193	13.68	1924
C. W. L. Parker	191	19.58	1927
E. G. Dennett	188	15.84	1907
T. W. J. Goddard	183	17.41	1933
T. W. J. Goddard	176	16.68	1946
T. W. J. Goddard	175	14.98	1929
C. W. L. Parker	172	11.94	1930
C. W. L. Parker	170	18.66	1923
T. W. J. Goddard	170	19.16	1932
C. W. L. Parker	162	17.51	1921
C. W. L. Parker	162	22.23	1928
E. G. Dennett	160	17.97	1906
T. W. J. Goddard	160	19.18	1949
R. A. Sinfield	158	19.50	1936
T. W. J. Goddard	153	20.30	1936
E. G. Dennett	153	20.51	1913
E. G. Dennett	149	20.46	1908
C. Cook	149	14.16	1956
E. G. Dennett	148	19.18	1909
E. G. Dennett	144	21.26	1905
T. W. J. Goddard	141	19.31	1930
C. Cook	139	20.17	1950
C. W. L. Parker	138	17.41	1929
C. Cook	138	19.94	1947
A. J. Paish	137	18.54	1899
E. G. Dennett	137	15.54	1912
T. W. J. Goddard	137	19.99	1950

240

Bowler	Wickets	Average	Year
D. R. Smith	136	20.90	1960
C. W. L. Parker	134	20.94	1932
T. W. J. Goddard	132	18.55	1931
C. Cook	131	18.00	1946
C. L. Townsend	130	19.96	1898
E. G. Dennett	129	20.00	1904
R. A. Sinfield	129	22.92	1937
R. A. Sinfield	129	24.23	1938
T. W. J. Goddard	126	24.05	1934
C. W. L. Parker	125	15.79	1920
T. W. J. Goddard	125	21.49	1948

The following have taken 100 wickets since the reduction of first-class county matches in 1969:

Bowler	Wickets	Average	Year
C. A. Walsh	118	18.17	1986
M. J. Procter	109	18.04	1977
M. J. Procter	108	15.02	1969

RECORD WICKET PARTNERSHIPS

(1) IN FIRST-CLASS MATCHES

First Wicket (Qualification 250)

395	D. M. Young *and* R. B. Nicholls *v* Oxford University *at* The Parks	1962
315	D. M. Green *and* C. A. Milton *v* Sussex *at* Hove	1968
277	T. H. Fowler *and* H. Wrathall *v* London Co. *at* Crystal Palace	1903
261	Sadiq Mohammad *and* A. W. Stovold *v* Hampshire *at* Southampton	1979
250	R. A. Sinfield *and* C. J. Barnett *v* Glamorgan *at* Cardiff	1935

Second Wicket (Qualification 250)

256	C. T. M. Pugh *and* T. W. Graveney *v* Derbyshire *at* Chesterfield	1960
251	C. J. Barnett *and* W. R. Hammond *v* Sussex *at* Cheltenham	1934

Third Wicket (Qualification 250)

336	W. R. Hammond *and* B. H. Lyon *v* Leicestershire *at* Leicester	1933
330	A. E. Dipper *and* W. R. Hammond *v* Lancashire *at* Old Trafford	1925
318	T. W. Graveney *and* J. F. Crapp *v* Kent *at* Gillingham	1953
305	C. W. J. Athey *and* P. Bainbridge *v* Derbyshire *at* Derby	1985
273	W. R. Hammond *and* B. O. Allen *v* Leicestershire *at* Leicester	1935
269	B. O. Allen *and* W. R. Hammond *v* Worcestershire *at* Cheltenham	1937
259	C. L. Townsend *and* W. Toup *v* Essex *at* Clifton	1899
255★	W. G. Grace *and* E. M. Knapp *v* Surrey *at* Clifton	1873
254	Zaheer Abbas *and* A. J. Hignell *v* Somerset *at* Taunton	1980

Fourth Wicket (Qualification 250)

321	W. R. Hammond *and* W. L. Neale *v* Leicestershire *at* Gloucester	1937

Fifth Wicket (Qualification 225)

261	W. G. Grace *and* W. O. Moberley *v* Yorkshire *at* Cheltenham	1876
245	J. F. Crapp *and* A. E. Wilson *v* Worcestershire *at* Dudley	1953
242	W. R. Hammond *and* B. O. Allen *v* Somerset *at* Bristol	1946
228	B. C. Broad *and* A. J. Hignell *v* Northamptonshire *at* Bristol	1979

Sixth Wicket (Qualification 225)

320	J. H. Board *and* G. L. Jessop *v* Sussex *at* Hove	1903
285	W. R. Hammond *and* B. H. Lyon *v* Surrey *at* The Oval	1928
268	J. N. Shepherd *and* D. A. Graveney *v* Warwickshire *at* Edgbaston	1983
226★	W. R. Hammond *and* G. M. Emmett *v* Nottinghamshire *at* Bristol	1946

Seventh Wicket (Qualification 200)

248	W. G. Grace *and* E. L. Thomas *v* Sussex *at* Hove	1896

Eighth Wicket (Qualification 175)

239	W. R. Hammond *and* A. E. Wilson *v* Lancashire *at* Bristol	1938
192	W. L. Neale *and* A. E. Wilson *v* Middlesex *at* Lord's	1938

Ninth Wicket (Qualification 150)

193	W. G. Grace *and* S. A. P. Kitcat *v* Sussex *at* Bristol	1896
159	H. V. Page *and* W. O. Vizard *v* Nottinghamshire *at* Cheltenham	1883
156	H. Wrathall *and* W. S. A. Brown *v* Warwickshire *at* Edgbaston	1898

Tenth Wicket (Qualification 100)

131	W. R. Gouldsworthy *and* J. Bessant *v* Somerset *at* Bristol	1923
112	A. E. Dipper *and* E. G. Dennett *v* Sussex *at* Gloucester	1908
106	H. Wrathall *and* J. H. Board *v* Surrey *at* The Oval	1899
104	W. S. A. Brown *and* F. G. Roberts *v* Sussex *at* Bristol	1903
101	A. E. Wilson *and* T. W. J. Goddard *v* Somerset *at* Bristol	1939

(2) IN LIMITED-OVERS MATCHES

(a) John Player Special League/Refuge Assurance League

1st	186	P. W. Romaines *and* C. W. J. Athey *v* Worcestershire *at* Moreton-in-Marsh	1985
2nd	168★	Sadiq Mohammad *and* Zaheer Abbas *v* Hampshire *at* Bristol	1976
3rd	158★	Zaheer Abbas *and* M. J. Procter *v* Sussex *at* Bristol	1978
	158	P. Bainbridge *and* K. M. Curran *v* Somerset *at* Bristol	1986
4th	107	A. W. Stovold *and* E. J. Cunningham *v* Yorkshire *at* Scarborough	1984
5th	114	K. M. Curran *and* K. P. Tomlins *v* Nottinghamshire *at* Trent Bridge	1986
6th	95	J. C. Foat *and* J. B. Mortimore *v* Middlesex *at* Lord's	1974
7th	101	S. J. Windaybank *and* D. A. Graveney *v* Nottinghamshire *at* Trent Bridge	1981
8th	56★	R. W. Phillips *and* D. A. Allen *v* Yorkshire *at* Gloucester	1969
9th	44	A. S. Brown *and* D. A. Graveney *v* Derbyshire *at* Chesterfield	1973
10th	57	D. A. Graveney *and* J. B. Mortimore *v* Lancashire *at* Tewkesbury	1973

(b) Gillette Cup/NatWest Trophy

1st	164	D. M. Green *and* C. A. Milton *v* Nottinghamshire *at* Trent Bridge	1968
2nd	146	Sadiq Mohammad *and* Zaheer Abbas *v* Leicestershire *at* Leicester	1975
3rd	125	R. B. Nicholls *and* S. E. J. Russell *v* Berkshire *at* Reading	1966
4th	94	Zaheer Abbas *and* A. J. Hignell *v* Leicestershire *at* Leicester	1983
5th	80	D. R. Shepherd *and* J. C. Foat *v* Lancashire *at* old Trafford	1978
6th	97★	A. J. Hignell *and* J. C. Foat *v* Northamptonshire *at* Bristol	1977
7th	107	D. R. Shepherd *and* D. A. Graveney *v* Surrey *at* Bristol	1973
8th	51	D. A. Allen *and* D. R. Smith *v* Lancashire *at* Bristol	1970
	51	D. A. Graveney *and* M. D. Partridge *v* Surrey *at* The Oval	1980
9th	26	D. R. Smith *and* D. A. Allen *v* Surrey *at* The Oval	1964
10th	33	D. R. Smith *and* B. J. Meyer *v* Surrey *at* The Oval	1964

(c) Benson and Hedges Cup

1st	169	A. W. Stovold *and* P. W. Romaines *v* Hampshire *at* Bristol	1984
2nd	161	A. W. Stovold *and* Zaheer Abbas *v* Surrey *at* The Oval	1975
3rd	137★	Zaheer Abbas *and* M. J. Procter *v* Minor Counties 'S' *at* Bristol	1979
4th	106★	Zaheer Abbas *and* D. R. Shepherd *v* Leicestershire *at* Bristol	1976
5th	90	Sadiq Mohammad *and* D. R. Shepherd *v* Somerset *at* Bristol	1973
6th	105	P. Bainbridge *and* J. N. Shepherd *v* Somerset *at* Taunton	1982
7th	40★	A. J. Hignell *and* P. Bainbridge *v* Worcestershire *at* Worcester	1981
8th	58★	D. A. Graveney *and* A. J. Brassington *v* Somerset *at* Taunton	1982
9th	30	A. H. Wilkins *and* B. M. Brain *v* Worcestershire *at* Worcester	1981
10th	19	A. J. Brassington *and* J. H. Childs *v* Somerset *at* Bristol	1979

WICKET-KEEPING RECORDS

(1) SIX OR MORE DISMISSALS IN AN INNINGS

Keeper	Total	Ct	St	Opponents and Venue	Year
H. Smith	6	3	3	Sussex *at* Bristol	1923
A. E. Wilson	6	6	0	Hampshire *at* Portsmouth	1953
B. J. Meyer	6	6	0	Somerset *at* Taunton	1962

(2) NINE OR MORE DISMISSALS IN A MATCH

Keeper	Total	Ct	St	Opponents and Venue	Year
A. E. Wilson	10	10	10	Hampshire *at* Portsmouth	1953

(3) SEVENTY OR MORE DISMISSALS IN A SEASON

Keeper	Total	Ct	St	Season
J. H. Board	75	52	23	2895
B. J. Meyer	75	59	16	1964

(4) 200 DISMISSALS IN A CAREER

Keeper	Total	Ct	St	Season
J. H. Board	1016	699	317	1891–1914
B. J. Meyer	826	707	119	1957–1971
H. Smith	705	441	264	1912–1935
A. E. Wilson	585	416	169	1936–1955
R. C. Russell	402	337	65	1981–1989
A. W. Stovold	312	268	44	1973–1989
J. A. Bush	274	191	83	1870–1890
A. J. Brassington	263	215	48	1974–1988

Catches taken when not keeping wicket are included in the career records.

FIELDING RECORDS

(1) SIX OR MORE CATCHES IN AN INNINGS

Fielder	Total	Opponents and Venue	Year
A. S. Brown	7	Nottinghamshire *at* Trent Bridge	1966
W. R. Hammond	6	Surrey *at* Cheltenham	1928
W. R. Hammond	6	Nottinghamshire *at* Bristol	1933
M. Bissex	6	Sussex *at* Hove	1968

(2) EIGHT OR MORE CATCHES IN A MATCH

Fielder	Total	Opponents and Venue	Year
W. R. Hammond	10	Surrey *at* Cheltenham	1928
W. R. Hammond	8	Worcestershire *at* Cheltenham	1932
C. A. Milton	8	Sussex *at* Hove	1952

(3) FORTY OR MORE CATCHES IN A SEASON

Fielder	Total	Season
W. R. Hammond	62	1928
W. R. Hammond	58	1925
C. A. Milton	58	1956
C. A. Milton	55	1952
C. A. Milton	54	1959
J. F. Crapp	48	1947
C. A. Milton	47	1961
B. H. Lyon	45	1933
W. R. Hammond	44	1932
C. A. Milton	44	1955
C. A. Milton	42	1954
W. R. Hammond	42	1933
B. O. Allen	42	1938
B. O. Allen	41	1947
C. A. Milton	41	1962
A. S. Brown	40	1959

(4) 250 OR MORE CATCHES IN A CAREER

Fielder	Total	Career
C. A. Milton	719	1948–1974
W. R. Hammond	551	1920–1951
A. S. Brown	489	1953–1976
W. G. Grace	373	1870–1899
J. F. Crapp	366	1936–1956
G. L. Jessop	356	1894–1914
J. B. Mortimore	320	1950–1975
T. W. J. Goddard	300	1922–1952
B. O. Allen	290	1932–1951
R. B. Nicholls	286	1951–1975
E. G. Dennett	284	1903–1926
D. R. Smith	282	1956–1970
E. M. Grace	274	1870–1895
C. J. Barnett	274	1927–1948
G. M. Emmett	265	1936–1959

ALL-ROUND CRICKET RECORDS

(1) 100 RUNS AND 10 WICKETS IN THE SAME MATCH

Player	Batting	Bowling	Opponents and Venue	Year
W. G. Grace	150	8-33, 7-46	Yorkshire *at* Bramall Lane	1872
W. G. Grace	179	5-76, 7-82	Sussex *at* Hove	1874
W. G. Grace	167	4-57, 7-44	Yorkshire *at* Bramall Lane	1874
W. G. Grace	127	5-44, 5-77	Yorkshire *at* Clifton	1874
W. G. Grace	89, 35	5-64, 7-92	Middelsex *at* Lord's	1883
W. G. Grace	221★	6-45, 5-75	Middlesex *at* Clifton	1885
C. L. Townsend	139	5-121, 5-83	Warwickshire *at* Edgbaston	1898
C. J. Barnett	168	5-63, 6-40	Lancashire *at* Old Trafford	1938
M. J. Procter	108	7-35, 6-38	Worcestershire *at* Cheltenham	1977
M. J. Procter	73, 35	7-16, 7-60	Worcestershire *at* Cheltenham	1980

(2) 1,000 RUNS AND 100 WICKETS IN A SEASON

Player	Runs ·	Avge	Wkts	Avge	Year
C. L. Townsend	1072	34.32	130	20.60	1898
R. A. Sinfield	1228	31.45	122	23.40	1934
R. A. Sinfield	1001	24.41	129	22.92	1937
J. B. Mortimore	1106	19.96	104	21.44	1964

TEST CAREER RECORDS OF CRICKETERS WHO HAVE PLAYED FIRST-CLASS CRICKET FOR GLOUCESTERSHIRE

Name	Country	Years	M	Runs	Avge	Wkts	Avge
D. A. Allen	England	1959–1966	39	918	25.50	122	30.97
C. W. J. Athey	England	1980–1988	23	919	22.97		
C. J. Barnett	England	1933–1948	20	1098	35.41	0	
J. H. Board	England	1898–1906	6	108	10.80		
C. Cook	England	1947	1	4	2.00	0	
J. Cranston	England	1890	1	31	15.50	0	
J. F. Crapp	England	1948–1949	7	319	29.90		
A. E. Dipper	England	1921	1	51	20.50		
G. M. Emmett	England	1948	1	10	5.00		
J. J. Ferris	Aust/Eng	1886–1892	9	114	8.76	61	12.70
T. W. J. Goddard	England	1930–1939	8	13	6.50	22	26.72
E. M. Grace	England	1880	1	36	18.00		
G. F. Grace	England	1880	1	0	0.00		
W. G. Grace	England	1880–1899	22	1098	32.29	9	26.22
T. W. Graveney	England	1951–1969	79	4882	44.38	1	167.00
W. R. Hammond	England	1927–1947	85	7249	58.45	83	37.80
G. L. Jessop	England	1899–1912	18	569	21.88	10	35.40
D. V. Lawrence	England	1988	1	4	4.00	3	37.00
W. E. Midwinter	Aust/Eng	1877–1887	12	269	13.45	24	25.20
C. A. Milton	England	1958–1959	6	204	25.50	0	
J. B. Mortimore	England	1958–1964	9	243	24.30	13	56.38
C. W. L. Parker	England	1921	1	3	—	2	16.00
M. J. Procter	S Africa	1966–1970	7	226	25.11	41	15.02
R. C. Russell	England	1988–1989	7	408	45.33		
Sadiq Mohammad	Pakistan	1969–1981	41	2579	35.81	0	
R. A. Sinfield	England	1938	1	6	6.00	2	61.50
D. R. Smith	England	1961–1962	5	38	9.50	6	59.83
H. Smith	England	1928	1	7	7.00		
C. L. Townsend	England	1899	2	51	17.00	3	25.00
Zaheer Abbas	Pakistan	1969–1985	78	5062	44.79	3	44.00

Note: The Test career of J. J. Ferris ended prior to his appearances for the county. Part of the Test careers of C. W. J. Athey, T. W. Graveney, W. E. Midwinter, Sadiq Mohammad and Zaheer Abbas took place when those players were not under contract to the county.

CAPTAINS OF GLOUCESTERSHIRE

1870–1898	W. G. Grace
1899	W. G. Grace and W. Troup
1900–1912	G. L. Jessop
1913–1914	C. O. H. Sewell
1919–1921	F. G. Robinson
1922–1923	P. F. C. Williams
1924–1926	D. C. Robinson
1927–1928	W. H. Rowlands
1929–1934	B. H. Lyon
1935–1936	D. A. C. Page
1937–1938	B. O. Allen
1939	W. R. Hammond
1946	W. R. Hammond
1947–1950	B. O. Allen
1951–1952	Sir D. T. L. Bailey
1953–1954	J. F. Crapp
1955–1958	G. M. Emmett
1959–1960	T. W. Graveney
1961–1962	C. T. M. Pugh
1963–1964	J. K. Graveney
1965–1967	J. B. Mortimore
1968	C. A. Milton
1969–1976	J. B. Mortimore
1977–1981	M. J. Procter
1982–1988	D. A. Graveney
1989	C. W. J. Athey

GLOUCESTERSHIRE CRICKETERS TO REPRESENT CAMBRIDGE UNIVERSITY IN FIRST-CLASS MATCHES

Players	Years
B. O. Allen	1932–1933
J. R. Bernard	1958–1960
A. H. Brodhurst	1937–1939
N. H. C. Cooper	1979
W. Fairbanks	1875
A. H. C. Fargus	1900–1901
R. T. Godsell	1903
H. Hale	1887–1890
S. S. Harris	1902–1904
J. A. Healing	1894
W. McG. Hemingway	1895–1896
A. J. Hignell	1975–1978
I. D. Imlay	1906–1907
G. L. Jessop	1896–1899
R. P. Keigwin	1903–1906
R. D. V. Knight	1967–1970
W. Knightley-Smith	1953–1955
R. T. H. Mackenzie	1907–1908
H. Mainprice	1905–1906
B. Meakin	1906–1907
I. N. Mitchell	1949
J. W. W. Nason	1909–1910
G. W. Parker	1934–1935
A. G. Richardson	1897
F. B. Roberts	1903–1904
P. G. P. Roebuck	1983–1985
F. J. Seabrook	1926–1928
D. Surridge	1980
N. O. Taggart	1900
R. C. White	1962–1965
A. R. Windows	1962–1964

GLOUCESTERSHIRE CRICKETERS TO REPRESENT OXFORD UNIVERSITY IN FIRST-CLASS MATCHES

Player	Year
E. T. Benson	1928–1929
J. H. Brain	1884–1887
W. H. Brain	1891–1993
R. H. J. Brooke	1931–1932
L. D. Brownlee	1902–1904
J. W. Burrough	1924–1926
F. H. Bateman-Champain	1897–1900
A. C. M. Croome	1887–1889
J. H. Dixon	1973
E. D. R. Eagar	1938–1939
M. A. Eagar	1956–1959
R. G. P. Ellis	1981–1983
D. M. Green	1959–1961
A. D. Greene	1877–1880
A. H. Heath	1876–1879
L. P. Hedges	1920–1922
J. N. Horlick	1906
W. W. Hoskin	1907
T. W. Lang	1874–1875
B. H. Lyon	1922–1923
M. A. McCanlis	1926–1928
R. F. Miles	1867–1869
W. O. Moberley	1870
D. N. Moore	1930–1931
H. V. Page	1883–1886
E. Peake	1880–1883
J. D. Percival	1922
F. R. Price	1861
D. C. G. Raikes	1931
R. W. Rice	1892–1894
M. G. Salter	1908–1910
E. K. Scott	1938
L. D. Watts	1957–1958
R. K. Whiley	1958
J. P. Winterbottom	1903–1904
C. Wreford-Brown	1887–1888
E. C. Wright	1897–1899

SELECT BIBLIOGRAPHY

H. S. Altham and E. W. Swanton: *A History of Cricket* Vols 1 and 2
Rowland Bowen: *Cricket, a History of its Growth and Development*
Gerald Brodribb: *The Croucher*
Neville Cardus: *Cricket*
Bernard Darwin: *W. G. Grace*
S. Canynge Caple: *The Graces, E. M., W. G. and G. F.*
David Foot: *Cricket's Unholy Trinity*
W. G. Grace: *W. G.: Cricket Reminiscences and Personal Recollections*
W. R. Hammond: *Cricket my Destiny*
Len Hutton: *50 Years in Cricket*
Gerald Howat: *Walter Hammond*
Tom Graveney: *Cricket over 40*
Tony Lewis: *Double Century: a History of M.C.C. and Cricket*
Grahame Parker: *Gloucestershire Road*
M. J. Procter: *Mike Procter and Cricket*
Wisden Cricketer's Almanacks

ACKNOWLEDGEMENTS

The author would like to thank Gloucestershire County Cricket Club for allowing him the freedom of their photographic archives, minute-books and records; thanks also to Bert Avery, whose knowledge of the County's playing history was most valuable.

Special thanks are also due to Bert Avery, who compiled the Statistical Section, and to the following people who supplied photographs: Nottinghamshire County Cricket Club, Gloucestershire County Cricket Club, Patrick Eagar.

David Green
Bristol
1990

INDEX